ENCYCLOPAEDIA OF INDIAN GOVERNMENT: PROGRAMMES AND POLICIES

ENCYCLOPAEDIA
OF
INDIAN GOVERNMENT:
PROGRAMMES AND POLICIES

Vol. 39

Chemicals and Fertilizers

Edited by

Satish Tiwari

ANMOL PUBLICATIONS PVT. LTD.

NEW DELHI - 110 002 (INDIA)

ANMOL PUBLICATIONS PVT. LTD.
4374/4B, Ansari Road, Daryaganj
New Delhi - 110 002

Encyclopaedia of Indian Government: Programmes and Policies

First Edition, 2000
ISBN 81-261-0515-1 (Set)

PRINTED IN INDIA

Published by J.L. Kumar for Anmol Publications Pvt. Ltd., New Delhi - 110 002 and Printed at Mehra Offset Press, Delhi.

Contents

Preface

Encyclopaedia of Indian Government: Programmes and Policies contains authoritative information on about fifty departmental policies and their future developmental programmes.

Organised to be completed in 40 volumes, this gigantic work covers Agriculture; Atomic Energy; Chemicals and Fertilizers; Coal; Commerce; Communication; Culture; Defence; Education; Environment and Forests; External Affairs; Finance; Food & Consumer Affairs; Food Processing Industries; Health and Family Welfare; Home Affairs and Internal Security; Human Resources; Industry; Information and Broadcasting; Labour; Law, Justice and Company Affairs; Non-conventional Energy Sources; Ocean Development; Parliamentary Affairs; Personnel, Public Grievances and Pensions; Petroleum and Natural Gas; Planning and Programme Implementation; Planning and Statistics; Posts and Telegraphs; Power; Rural Development; Science and Technology; Social Justice and Empowerment; Space; States Affairs; Steel; Steel and Mines; Sugar and Edible Oils; Surface Transport; Textiles; Tourism; Urban Development; Water Resources; Women and Child development etc.

Based on the information derived from authoritative sources, this work contains authentic facts and figures. I am deeply beholden to all the scholars whose writings are cited or substantially made use of in the present work. I am also thankful to Anmol Publications Pvt. Ltd. for undertaking publication of this encyclopaedia. I am solely responsible for shortcomings in presentation of matter.

Encyclopaedic in nature, this will prove a dependable reference work for scholars and academics besides those appearing for different competitive examinations.

—**Satish Tiwari**

1

Developments

The production target for 1998-99 has been fixed at 106.82 lakh tonnes of nitrogen and 30.27 lakh tonnes of phosphate. This represents a growth rate of 5.9% in nitrogen and 1.7% in phosphate as compared to the actual production in 1997-98. Production of nitrogenous and phosphatic fertilizers in April-November 1998 was 68.45 lakh tonnes and 19.76 lakh, respectively.

This represented a growth rate of 4.6% vis-a-vis the corresponding period last year. In respect of urea, the production has been 126.60 lakh tonnes by the end of November which is 7. 1 % higher over the corresponding period in 1997-98. Also, the production of DAP registered a growth of 4.1% over the production in the corresponding period of the previous year.

At present, 6 major fertilizer projects involving an estimated capital cost of approximately Rs.4122.02 crore are under implementation in the country. When commissioned, they are likely to add an additional capacity of 9.75 lakh MTPA of urea, 7.90 lakh MTPA of NPK, 23.07 lakh MTPA of DAP and 1 lakh MTPA of NP fertilizers.

No new projects were being sanctioned for quite some time on account of differences in the perception of the demand supply scenario among different Departments. The issue of demand projections in urea has 'been discussed and projections have been revised in consultation with Ministry of Agriculture and Planning Commission. On the basis of this, the projects of PSUs/ Cooperatives have been prioritised. Accordingly, the following projects are being posed to PIB for approval:

— KRIBHCO's Ammonia-Urea Expansion Project at Hazira, Gujarat.

— KRIBHCO's Ammonia-Urea Expansion Project at the existing site of FCI, Gorakhpur.

— RCF's Ammonia-Urea Expansion Project (Third Stream) at Thal, Maharashtra.

The initiatives undertaken to set up joint venture projects in countries with better resource endowments so as to meet the growing demand of fertilizers in the country have made significant progress. The Government has approved the investment of RCF/KRIBHCO to make an equity contribution of US $ 69 million each in a joint venture in Oman for production of 14.52 lakh tonnes of urea and 3.30 lakh tonnes of merchant ammonia per annum. The Joint Venture Company i.e. Oman India Fertilizer Company has been registered in Oman on 18.2.98. All major agreements have been finalised.

The joint venture company of 'Industries Chimiques du Senegal' (ICS) which started production in 1984 has taken up a project for doubling the production of its phosphoric acid plants and development of new rock phosphates mines at a cost of about US $ 215 million. The Government has approved equity contribution of US $ 20 million by IFFCO in ICS Senegal for financing the expansion project. The project is expected to be completed within 30 months from the zero date of 1.7.98. ICS proposes to sell a major portion of the phosphoric acid produced in the expanded plant to India.

In order to involve a strategy for use of Liquefied Natural Gas (LNG) as feedstock, the Government has set up a Core Group on Fertilizer Companies with a view to exploring the feasibility of a delivery system of LNG essentially to meet the demand of fertilizer units and projects. The report of the Core Group is awaited.

The Disinvestment Commission has recommended disinvestment of shares of MFL, FACT, NFL and PPCL. Recommendations of the Commission are under process.

The revival package of HFC and FCI reformulated on the basis of a fresh technical appraisal by an expert group led by ICI from the stand point of the financial institutions were considered by the Government on 1. 10.97. The Government has approved the proposal for the revamp of Namrup units of HFC at an estimated fresh investment of Rs.350 crore.

The project is to be implemented within 30 months of award of Engineering, Procurement and Construction (EPC) contract. The groundwork for launching the project has started. To ensure timely implementation of the scheme, a plan budgetary support of Rs.70 crore has been made in the budget for 1998-99. The decision in respect of the other units HFC and FCI is still to be taken. Proposals in respect of the remaining units of HFC have been reviewed from the angle of unit-wise viability and tie-up of funding arrangements and are presently under inter-ministerial consultation.

The Government of India has continued the supply of urea to farmers at heavily subsidised prices. The farmgate price of urea, currently fixed at Rs.4000 per tonne, continues to be one of the lowest in the region.

Under a scheme administered by Ministry of Agriculture, substantial special concessions are also being provided on decontrolled phosphoric and potassium fertilizers with a view to encouraging the farmers to optimise the use of the three plant nutrients. The revised rates of special concession for Kharif 1998 have been announced recently which recognises the nitrogen content in complex fertilizers while deciding the level of subsidy.' This would give substantial benefits to the manufacturers of complex fertilizers.

The consumption of urea in terms of sales registered 4% growth during Kharif 1998. The trend is expected to be maintained during Rabi 1998-99 during which the area under sowing of wheat and other crops has been substantial on account of unseasonal rains and consequent availability of moisture over more than expected area.

Adequate and timely availability of urea was ensured throughout the country during Kharif 1998. There is no State which complained of nonavailability of urea. During Rabi also, the availability of urea would be adequate in all the States to meet the estimated requirement.

In respect of the decontrolled fertilizers, the requirement had registered a sharp increase following the unforeseen rains during October. All possible support was extended both to the indigenous manufacturers and importers in movement of these fertilizers to the States thus making them available as per their requirement.

Nearly 1.5 million tonnes of DAP was cleared from JNPT and a same quantity from Vizag port by according priority berthing of DAP vessels at both these ports. This helped in meeting the requirements of DAP in the States of Punjab, Haryana, Rajasthan, Madhya Pradesh, Uttar Pradesh and Bihar.

This considerably reduced the complaints in respect of decontrolled fertilizers which would otherwise have been unmanageable. For future, the Government has decided to maintain buffer-stock of decontrolled fertilizers to meet any eventuality arising out of sudden spurt in demand. The Buffer Stocking Scheme shall be operated through Indian Potash Limited (IPL) and necessary preparations for it are under way.

Organistional setup

The main activities of the department of fertilizers include sectional planning, promotion and development of the fertilizer industry, planning and monitoring of production, import and distribution of fertilizers and management of subsidy for indigenous and imported fertilizers.

The work of the department is broadly divided into four divisions dealing with (i) fertilizer projects and planning; (ii) fertilizer import, movement and distribution; (iii) administration, and (iv) finance & accounts. The work of these divisions is handled by three Joint Secretaries. The Joint Secretary in charge of administration division also looks after the work of fertilizer import, movement and distribution. Besides, he is director, grievances and is also part time chief vigilance officer of the department. The Joint Secretary and financial adviser in charge of finance and accounts division is also the financial adviser of the department of chemicals & petrochemicals.

Fertilizer industry coordination committee

The office of fertilizer industry coordination committee (FICC) is an attached office under the department of fertilizers. Headed by an executive director of the rank of Joint Secretary, the office deals mainly with unit-wise fixation and revision of retention prices of fertilizers, fixation of equated freight and payment of subsidy to them.

2

Growth of Fertilizer Industry

At present, there are 63 large size fertilizer units in the country, manufacturing a wide range of nitrogenous and phosphatic/complex fertilizers. Of these, 38 units produce urea whereas 9 units produce ammonium sulphate as a by-product. Besides, there are about 79 small and medium scale units producing single superphosphate. The total installed capacity of fertilizer production in the country which was 104.98 lakh tonnes of nitrogen and 29.51 lakh tonnes of phosphate as on 1.4.98 has risen to 105.20 lakh tonnes of nitrogen and 31.70 lakh tonnes of phosphate as on 30.11.98.

Production

The production of nitrogenous fertilizers during 1997-98 was 100.86 lakh tonnes nitrogen and that of phosphatic fertilizers 29 lakh tonnes of phosphate. The production target for 1998-99 was fixed at 106.82 lakh tonnes nitrogen and 30.27 lakh tonnes of phosphate representing a growth rate of 5.9% in nitrogen and 1.7% in phosphate, as compared to the actual production in 1997-98. As against this, the actual production upto November 1998 was at 68.45 lakh tonnes of nitrogen and 19.76 lak tonnes of phosphate. Taking 'N' &'P' together there was an overall growth of 4.6% over the production of during the corresponding period of last year.

- The production performance of both nitrogenous and phosphatic fertilizers during Kharif 1998 was less than the target due to the following reasons:
- There was a shortfall in production in all the plants of HBJ pipeline including KRIBHCO-Hazira due to curtailment of natural gas from ONGC for the period from 17th to 23rd September 1998 in view of floods in Hazira.
- Power and equipment problems, shortage of raw material and labour problem affected production in many of the plants including two sick companies viz. Fertilizer corporation of India limited and Hindustan Fertilizer Corporation Limited.
- There was a shortage in production of complex fertilizers mainly due to the lower level of imports of Muriate of Potash. The situation is expected to improve in Rabi.

Capacity utilisation

The domestic fertilizer industry has attained levels of capacity utilisation which compare favourably with the best in the world. The capacity utilisation was an all time high in 1997-98 at 101.5% for nitrogen and 101.7% for phosphate. The capacity utilisation is estimated at 99.4% for nitrogen and 94.7% for phosphate during 1998-99.

The capacity utilisation of the fertilizer industry is expected to improve as more and more modern plants based on proven technology and equipment go on stream. The existing plants are being encouraged to improve their capacity utilisation through revamping and modernisation and incorporation of dual fuel/feedstock facilities, wherever feasible.

Strategy of growth

The fertilizer industry has adopted the following strategy to increase fertilizer production:

- Expansion/retrofitting/revamping of existing fertilizer plants;
- Overcoming the constraints in the availability of natural gas by setting up naphtha-based expansion projects and installing dual fuel/feedstock facilities in the existing plants and projects under implementation; and
- Setting up joint venture projects in countries having abundant and cheap raw material resources.

Projects under implementation

Six major fertilizer projects involving an estimated capital cost of Rs.4122.02 crore are under implementation in the country. When commissioned, these are expected to add additional capacities of 9.75 lakh MTPA of urea, 7.90 lakh MTPA of NPK, 23.07 lakh MTPA of DAP and 1.00 lakh MTPA of NP fertilizers. The details of these projects are given below:

- IFFCO are currently implementing a project to set up two additional trains for manufacturing DAP/NPK fertilizers adjacent to their existing plants at Kandla in Gujarat to produce an additional 2.27 lakh MTPA of DAP and 3.70 lakh MTPA of NPK fertilizers at an estimated cost of Rs.212.20 crore. The project is expected to be commissioned, by October 1999.
- Chambal Fertilisers and Chemicals Ltd. (CFCL) are implementing a project for expanding the capacity of their existing plant at Gadepan, Distt. Kota, Rajasthan by an additional capacity of 7.75 lakh MTPA of urea at an estimated capital cost of Rs.1256 crore. This project is expected to be commissioned by 31.12.99.
- Oswal Chemicals & Fertilisers Ltd. are setting up a new DAP/NPK/NP plant at Paradeep in Orissa at an estimated cost of Rs. 1830.00 crore to produce 15

lakh MTPA of DAP, 3.20 lakh. MTPA of NPK and 1.00 lakh MTPA of NP fertilizers. The project is expected to be commissioned in September 1999.

- Duncan Industries Ltd. are implementing a project for expanding the capacity of their plant at Kanpur, Uttar Pradesh, by an additional capacity of 2.00 lakh MTPA of urea at an estimated cost of Rs.636.38 crore. The project is expected to be commissioned in May 2003.
- Godavari Fertilizers & Chemicals Ltd. are implementing a project for expanding the capacity of their plant at Kakinada, Andhra Pradesh by 2.80 lakh MTPA of DAP at an estimated cost of Rs.99.13 crore. The project is expected to be commissioned in December 2001.
- Hind Lever Chemicals Ltd. are implementing a project for expanding the capacity of their plant at Haldia, West Bengal by 3.00 lakh MTPA of DAP and 1.00 lakh MTPA of NPK at an estimated cost of Rs.88.31 crore. The project is expected to be commissioned in March 1999.

Projects under consideration

Project proposals involving a total investment of Rs.6973 crore for creating an additional capacity of 39.04 lakh TPA of urea, have been posed by public sector undertakings/cooperative societies for investment approval of the Government under the prescribed investment approval procedure. These are:—

- Expansion of Panipat plant of NFL in Haryana.
- Expansion of Nangal plant of NFL in Punjab.
- Expansion of Hazira plant of KRIBHCO in Gujarat.
- A new urea plant to be set up by KRIBHCO at the existing site of FCI's Gorakhpur plant in Uttar Pradesh.

- Expansion of Thal plant of RCF in Maharashtra.
- A grass root urea plant to be set up at Nellore by IFFCO in Andhra Pradesh.

Feedstock policy for fertilizers

The feedstock policy for nitrogenous fertilizers had hitherto envisaged establishment of new plants based mainly on natural gas. Realising the constraints in the availability of natural gas which is the preferred feedstock, Department of Fertilizers has set up a Core Group of Fertilizer Companies with a view to exploring the feasibility of importing LNG by forming a consortium of fertilizer companies, along with other interested economic operators, for fertilizer sector in particular and other complementary sectors such as power, domestic fuel etc. The report of the Core Group is awaited.

One of the options being considered envisages the installation of a re-gasification facility at Haldia in West Bengal and the construction of a pipeline connecting the fertilizer plants in the eastern sector with an inter-link to the HBJ pipeline. Existing naphtha based units such as IFFCO-Phulpur, DIL-Kanpur, Nangal, Panipat and Bhatinda units of NFL and new projects like KRIBHCO-Gorakhpur could also be served by this system.

Joint ventures abroad

Due to constraints in the availability of gas, which is the preferred feedstock for the production of nitrogenous fertilizers, and the near total dependence of the country on imported raw materials for production of phosphatic fertilizers, the Government has been encouraging Indian companies to establish joint venture facilities with buy-back arrangements in other countries, which have rich reserves of natural gas and rock phosphate.

The Govt. of India, Indian Farmers Fertiliser Co-operative Ltd. (IFFCO) and Southern Petrochemical Industries Corporation Ltd. (SPIC), are equity partners and are collectively holding 10.64% of the share in the joint venture company in Senegal named 'Industries Chimiques du Senegal' (ICS). The company produces phosphoric acid and finished phosphatic fertilizers in its plants located in Darou and M'Bao in Senegal. It started production in 1984 and after debottlenecking, attained an installed capacity of 3.5 lakh MT of phosphoric acid per annum. During the year 1998, the company produced 3.33 lakh MT of phosphoric acid in terms of P_2O_5, achieving 95% capacity utilisation. The supplies of phosphoric acid to India from this venture in 1998 totalled 2.40 lakh MT.

From 1.1.96, Compagnie Senegalaise Phosphates de Taiba (CSPT), a mining company which supplied rock phosphate to ICS, has been merged with it. ICS is now implementing a project for doubling the production capacity of its phosphoric acid plants and development of new rock phosphates mines at cost of about US $ 250 million. The project is expected to be completed within 30 months from the zero date of 30.9.98. ICS proposes to sell a major portion of the phosphoric acid produced in the expanded plant to India. Government has approved equity contribution of US $ 20 million by IFFCO in ICS Senegal for financing the expansion project.

A joint venture project in Jordan to produce 2.24 lakh MT of phosphoric acid per annum jointly implemented by SPIC and Jordan Phosphate Mines Company Limited is under production since May 1997.

The following overseas projects are under implementation/consideration:

- A Memorandum of Understanding was signed on 30.7.94 between the Government of India/KRIBHCO/

RCF and the Government of Sultanate of Oman/ Oman oil company, expressing the interest of both the parties in sponsoring the design, construction, financing and operation of a world scale fertilizer complex in Oman. The Joint Venture Agreement of the project was signed in April 1997. Other project agreements have also reached the stage of finalisation.

- Based on a Detailed Feasibility Report, which envisages the production of about 14.52 lakh MT of urea and 3.30 lakh MT of merchant ammonia per annum, the Govt. has approved on 1.12.97 the investment proposal of RCF/KRIBHCO to make an equity contribution of US $ 69 million each in the proposed Joint Venture Company (JVC) i.e. Oman India Fertilizer Company which has been registered in Oman on 18.2.98. It is estimated that the joint venture would be commissioned by 2002. The estimated cost of the project is US $ 1106 million.
- A Memorandum of Understanding (MOU) was signed between Govt. of India/IFFCO & KRIBHCO (INDCONS) and Govt. of Iran/Qeshm Free Area Authority (QFAA) on 6.3.94 for exploring the possibility of setting up a fertilizer plant in QFAA. A supplementary MOU was signed on 26.11.96, reflecting the agreed position of the joint venture partners on the price of inputs required for the proposed nitrogenous fertilizer project. The Feasibility Report for the establishment of a 1500 MTPD ammonia and 2200 MTPD urea project at an estimated cost of US $ 470 million has been appraised and adopted by the joint venture partners.

iii) SPIC is setting up a gas-based nitrogenous fertilizer plant at Dubai in United Arab Emirates to produce 4.00 lakh tonnes of urea at an estimated cost of US $ 160 million. The plant and equipment have already been procured and the plant is expected to be commissioned by September 1999.

iv) A joint venture between Office Cherifien Des Phosphates, Morocco and Chambal Fertilizers & Chemicals Ltd. (CFCL) to produce 3.30 lakh tonnes of phosphoric acid at an estimated cost of US $ 228 million is being set up in Morocco. All Govt. clearances have been granted and a JVC under the name "INDO MAROC PHOSPHORE SA" has been formed on 20.11.97. CFCL will hold 50% of the equity of the JVC. The project is expected to go into production in the 2nd quarter of 1999.

Single Superphosphate

Single Superphosphate (SSP) is a straight phosphatic fertilizer. At present, about 79 medium and small scale units, including 5 in the public sector, having a total annual installed capacity of 10.02 lakh MT of phosphate (P_2O_5), are engaged in the production of SSR Along with other phosphatic fertilizers, SSP was also decontrolled w.e.f. 25.8.1992. The estimated production of SSP during 1998-99 is expected about 4.97 lakh MT of phosphate (P_2O_5) nutrient as against 5.07 lakh MT in 1997-98.

Product mix

Among the straight nitrogenous fertilizers, the country is currently producing urea, ammonium sulphate, calcium ammonium nitrate (CAN) and ammonium chloride. The only straight phosphatic fertilizer being produced in the country is SSR The complex fertilizers under production include Di-ammonium phosphate (DAP), and several grades of nitrophosphates and NPK complexes. Urea and DAP are the main fertilizers produced indigenously accounting for 84.5% and 42.8% of the overall capacity of nitrogen and phosphate, respectively.

Bio-fertilizers

Bio-fertilizers are carrier based formulations of live and beneficial micro organism and are a self-generating source of plant nutrients. They are complementary to chemical fertilizers. Besides being cost effective, bio-fertilizers are eco-friendly. To encourage the bio-fertilizers production, Department of Fertilizers has been giving one-time grant-in-aid of Rs.20 lakh (Maximum) to fertilizer PSUs/Cooperatives for setting up a bio-fertilizer plants of capacity of 100 TPA and above.

In the year 1997-98, this Department released a total grant-in-aid of Rs.38.24 lakh to the fertilizer PSUs/ Cooperatives under its administrative control, for setting up bio-fertilizer plants. Out of this grant-in-aid, HFC, MFL availed Rs.24.74 lakh and Rs.13.5 lakh, respectively. The plants at Siliguri, Cuttack, Bhopal and Gwalior of HFC and Udyogarnandal unit of FACT are expected to be commissioned by 1998-99.

3

Plan Performance

Capacity build-up

The installed capacity and production of fertilizers in the country from the end of Seventh Five Year Plan, in the terminal year of the Eighth Plan and in the first and second year of Ninth Plan (1997-98 and 1998-99) are indicated below:

(In lakh Tonnes)

Particulars	At the end of Seventh Five Year Plan (1989-90)	At the end of Eighth Five Year Plan (1996-97)	In the first year of Ninth Plan (1997-98)	In the 2nd year of Ninth Plan (1998-99)
Fertilizers				
1. Capacity				
i) Nitrogen	81.48	97.77	104. 98	105.20
ii) Phosphate	27.50	29.05	29.15	31.70
2. Production				
i) Nitrogen	67.47	85.99	100.86	104.52 (Est.)
ii) Phosphate	17.96	25.56	29.76	30.02 (Est.)

The installed capacity of nitrogen and phosphate in the terminal year (1996-97) of the Eighth Plan was 97.77 lakh NIT and 29.05 lakh MT, respectively. Due to the uncertainty in the wake of decontrol of phosphatic fertilizers, no major phosphatic fertilizer plant was commissioned during the Eighth Plan period. The production of fertilizers during 1998-99 is estimated at 104.52 lakh NIT of nitrogen and 30.02 lakh MT of phosphate. Sector-wise targets and achievements in respect of production and capacity utilisation from 1993-94 onwards are given in Annexures-V & VI.

Plan outlays

An outlay of Rs. 5484 crore was provided for various schemes to be undertaken during the Eighth plan period (1992-97) by the Department of Fertilizers and the public and cooperative sector undertakings under its administrative control. Out of this, Rs. 4464 crore was to be met out of internal and extra budgetary resources and the balance amount of Rs. 1018 crore was to be provided through budgetary support. The actual expenditure during the Eighth Plan was Rs. 4952.98 crore.

For the Ninth Plan (1997-2002), Planning Commission has approved an outlay of Rs. 11,447.37 crore consisting of Rs. 800 crore as Domestic Budgetary Support, Rs. 298.29 crore as External Aid routed through Budget and Rs. 10,349.08 crore to be met out of Internal and Extra Budgetary Resources.

For the year 1997-98, a Plan outlay of Rs. 1728.38 crore was approved by the Planning Commission, with Rs. 1488.60 crore to be met out of internal and extra budgetary resources and the balance amount of Rs. 239.78 crore to be provided through budgetary support. As against this, the actual expenditure for 1997-98 was Rs. 1324.38 crore. For the year 1998-99, a Plan outlay of Rs. 2249.20 crore was approved by the Planning Commission with Rs. 2040.00 crore to be met out of the internal and extra budgetary resources and balance amount of Rs. 209.20 crore to be provided through budgetary support. As against this, the actual expenditure up to November 1998 was Rs. 384.83 crore. For 1999-2000, the Planning.

Commission has approved a plan outlay of Rs. 1828 crore, with Rs. 1663 crore to be met out of internal and extra budgetary resources and the balance amount of Rs. 165 crore to be provided through budgetary support.

Budgetary report

For the year 1998-99, there is a net provision of Rs. 7600.39 crore (Rs. 209.20 crore for Plan and Rs. 7391.19 crore under Non-Plan). In the revised estimates for 1998-99, the net provision is Rs. 9321.22 crore (Rs. 195.46 crore under Plan and Rs. 9125.76 crore under Non-Plan). For the year 1999-2000, there is a net provision of Rs. 9221.17 crore (Rs. 165.00 crore under Plan and Rs. 9056.17 crore under Non-Plan).

Financial performance of public sector undertakings and societies

The Department has nine public sector undertakings and two cooperative societies under its administrative control. One of the undertakings, viz. PDIL, is engaged in consultancy services in design, engineering and implementation of fertilizer projects and production of catalysts. Another undertaking (PPCL) is engaged in mining operations of rock phosphate and pyrites, besides the manufacture of SSP.

While four of the public sector companies (RCF, FACT, MFL and NFL) and the two co-operative societies (IFFCO) and (KRIBHCO) have generally been making profits, two public sector companies (HFC) and (FCI) have been incurring losses right from their inception, mainly due to design and equipment deficiencies and excess manpower.

Madras Fertilizers Ltd., which had consistently been recording profit in the past, recorded a heavy loss during 1993-94 following the decontrol of phosphatic fertilizers. During 11994-95, 1995-96, 1996-97, MFL showed profits.

But during 1997-98, it showed a heavy loss amounting to Rs. 55.35 crore. During 1998-99, the company is likely to make a loss of Rs. 33.63 crore. PPCL, which had been making marginal profits up to 1991-92, has been showing losses since 1992-93 due to decontrol of phosphatic fertilizers.

Capital restructuring of the company was undertaken during 1995-96 and it was hoped that the financial prospects would improve. But no reversal has been shown by the company. PDIL, which is essentially a design and consultancy company, had been making losses in the past, but of late, its profitability has improved with the resurgence in the fertilizer sector. During 1997-98, it showed a profit of Rs. 6.09 crore. Again due to slow down in the flow of new fertilizer projects, the profitability of PDIL has been affected and during 1998-99, the company is likely to make a loss of Rs. 3.07 crore. PPL, which is a comparatively new company, had incurred losses in the earlier years mainly due to raw material constraints, equipment problems and heavy debt servicing burden.

A turn around proposal for PPL was approved w.e.f. 1.4.1994. Thereafter, the company recorded profits till 1995-96. However, it has again been showing a substantial loss. During 1997-98, the company made a loss of Rs. 105.53 crore. During 1998-99, the company is likely to make a loss of Rs. 65 crore. FACT, which has been making profit for the last several years is likely to make a loss of Rs. 50.88 crore during 1998-99. This is due to high interest burden on, account of the new Ammonia Plant project and depressed market for caprolactam coupled with its cheaper import.

4

Public Sector Undertakings and Cooperative Societies

The present status and performance of the 9 Public Sector Undertakings and 2 Multi-State Cooperative Societies under the administrative control of the Department of Fertilizers have been described in the succeeding paragraphs.

Fertilisers and Chemicals Travancore Limited (FACT)

The Fertilisers and Chemicals Travancore Limited (FACT), India's first large scale fertilizer unit, was set up in the private sector in 1943 at Udyogamandal, Cochin. In 1960, FACT became a public sector company. By the end of 1963, Government of India had become its major shareholder.

As on 31..3.1998, the paid-up capital of the company was Rs. 354.77 crore against an authorised capital of Rs. 500 crore.

FACT has grown and diversified into a multi-divisional/ multi -functional organisation with interest in manufacture and marketing of fertilizers and Petro-chemicals, Engineering Consultancy & Design and in fabrication and erection of industrial equipments. FACT recorded a turnover of Rs. 1263.40 crore during 1997-98.

Production

The production performance of the company during 1997-98 and during the current year is as under:

(000 Tonnes)

	1997-98		1998-99 (Est.)	
	Prodn.	% Cap. Utl.	Prodn.	%Cap. Utl.
Nitrogen	293.30	90.1	280.80	86.1
Phosphate	128.50	97.4	138.80	105.2
Caprolactam	40.45	81.0	36.75	73.5

Financial performance

During 1997-98, FACT made a, net profit of Rs.53.94 crore. During the period from April to November 1998, FACT has made a loss of Rs.85.71 crore. During the whole year FACT is likely to incur a net loss of Rs.50.88 crore.

Sales Performance

A total quantity of 12.61 lakh tonnes of fertilizers was sold during 1997-98. During the period from April 1998 to November 1998, the company sold 7.35 lakh tonnes of fertilizers. During the whole year, the company is likely to sell 12. 10 lakh tonnes of fertilizers.

During 1997-98, the company sold 39,550 tonnes of caprolactam. 6187 tonnes of caprolactarn was exported to countries like South Korea, China, Hong Kong and Taiwan. During the period from April 1998 to November 1998, the company sold 24,770 tonnes of caprolactam and during the whole year, the likely sale will be of the order of 38,040 tonnes.

Performance of divisions

The performance of individual units was as follows:

Udyogamandal division

During 1997-98, the Division produced 1,84,556 tonnes of

Ammonium Sulphate and 1,24,026 tonnes of Factomfos 20:20. During the period April-November 1998, the Division produced 96,627 tonnes of Ammonium Phosphate and 1,21,203 tonnes of Ammonium Sulphate. The production target for the year 1998-99 is 1,43,231 tonnes of Ammonium Phosphate and 1,69,034 tonnes of Ammonium Sulphate.

Cochin division

During 1997-98, Cochin Division produced 2,74,200 tonnes of Urea and 5,18,693 tonnes of Complex fertilizers. During April 1998 to November 1998, the division produced 1,12,810 tonnes of Urea and 3,64,500 tonnes of Complex fertilizers NP 20:20. The production target for the whole year is 23,960 tonnes of Urea and 5,32,800 tonnes of NP 20:20.

Petro-chemical division

During 1997-98, the Division produced 40,451 tonnes of caprolactam. During April-November 1998, the Division produced 25,709 tonnes of caprolactam. During the whole year, there is likely to be a production of 36,750 tonnes of caprolactam with a capacity utilisation of 73.5%. Poor off-take of caprolactam in the domestic as well as international markets leading to a high build up of inventory has forced the company to curtail production since September 1998.

Fact engineering & design organisation (FEDO)

FACT Engineering and Design Organisation (FEDO) is engaged in the field of consultancy, design and engineering services for the construction of large fertilizer, petrochemical and chemical projects. FEDO is today executing major jobs for various clients like Indo-Gulf Fertilizers, Oil and Natural Gas Corporation Ltd. and Cochin Refineries Ltd. FEDO has received ISO 9001 re-certification for its activities. During the period from April 1998 to November 1998, FEDO received orders to the value of Rs.324.93 lakh.

Fact engineering works (FEW)

FACT Engineering Works (FEW) has capabilities for manufacture of engineering equipment such as storage tanks, heat exchangers, process columns etc. FEW has also excelled in the field of fabrication and laying of cross country pipelines. FEW is also under audit to receive ISO Certification.

FEW has completed the fabrication and site erection of two large Extraction Tanks for Kerala Chemicals & Proteins Ltd. FEW has also undertaken the development and fabrication work of one set each of Convection Coil/ Radiation Coil for FACT Cochin Division at a total value of Rs.69 lakhs. Till now these coils used to be imported by FACT. During 1998-99, FEW bagged order worth Rs.305 lakhs, upto November 1998.

Research and development (R&D)

The Research and Development Division of the FACT has developed cleaning Powders "SHINE" and "SPARKLE" utilising Phosphogypsum, a waste product. The technology has been commercialised to M/s.Noah's Arc, Bangalore who are taking steps to start manufacture of cleaning powders shortly. R& Centre is co-ordinating a project to produce fib reinforced Polymer Matrix Composite (PM from caprolactam for use as engineering plastic through pultrusion NYRIP process, a process developed by IIT, Madras.

A bio-fertilizer project with a capacity of 150 TPA is being implemented at the R&D premises, with the help of a one time grant of Rs.20 lakh from the Ministry of Agriculture.

National Fertilizers Limited (NFL)

National Fertilizers Limited (NFL) was incorporated on

23.8.1974 for setting up two nitrogenous fertilizer plants, one at Bathinda (Punjab) and another at Panipat (Haryana).On re-organisation of the Fertilizer Corporation of India (FCI), the Nangal Unit (including Nangal Expansion Project) of FCI was assigned to NFL with effect from 1.4.1978.

In June 1984, NFL took up implementation of a gas based ammonia-urea fertilizer project on the HBJ pipeline at Vijaipur in Guna Distt. of Madhya Pradesh, which started commercial production on 1.7.1988. Vijaipur Expansion Project for doubling its existing capacity from 7.26 lakh tonnes of urea to 14.52 lakh tonnes per annum started commercial production w.e.f. 31.3.97. With this, the total installed capacity of NFL has been enhanced to 13.7 lakh tonnes of nitrogen equivalent to 28.05 lakh tonnes of urea and 3.18 lakh tonnes of CAN.

The company also produces industrial products like nitric acid, ammonium nitrate, sodium nitrate/sodium nitrite, sulphur, methanol, liquid nitrogen, liquid oxygen etc. Besides, it is also producing bio-fertilizers at its Indore plant since January 1996. The company commissioned an Argon gas plant at Panipat unit in October 1997, designed to produce 120 NM3/Hr. of argon gas. Methanol Augmentation plant at Nangal was commissioned in October 1998, thereby enhancing the production capacity from 50 TPD to 67 TPD.

The authorised capital of the company as on 31.3.1998 was Rs.500 crore with a paid-up capital of Rs. 490.58 crore. The share holding of the Government of India has reduced to 97.65% by disinvesting the paid up capital amounting to Rs. 11.54 crore in favour of financial institutions, and others.

Production Performance

During 1997-98, NFL produced 15.15 lakh MT of nitrogen

as fertilizers, achieving a capacity utilisation of 110.5%. The company during 1997-98 produced 19,016 tonnes of Methanol at its Nangal unit achieving a capacity utilisation of 115.2%.

During 1998-99 (upto November 1998), the company produced 9.71 lakh tonnes of nitrogen. The urea production upto November 1998 was 20.33 lakh tonnes while CAN production was 1.45 lakh tonnes. The company also produced 13,713 tonnes of Methanol during this period. During the whole year, the company is likely to produce 14.78 lakh tonnes of nitrogen.

Marketing

During 1997-98, the company sold 30.68 lakh tonnes of urea compared to 21.13 lakh tonnes in the previous year.

During Kharif 1998, the company has sold 14.11 lakh tonnes of urea. The urea sales for first two months of Rabi 1998-99 were 7.03 lakh tonnes. The CAN sales for the period April-November 1998 are 1.53 lakh tonnes.

Financial Results

The company during the year 1997-98 earned a gross profit of Rs.496.57 crore. The net profit for the year stood at Rs.189.01 crore. During current year upto November 1998, NFL has made a profit of Rs.46.86 crore (provisional). During the whole year, the company is likely to earn a net profit of Rs.77.44 crore.

During 1997-98, NFL declared a dividend at the rate of 20% of the post tax profit amounting to Rs.37.80 crore.

Pyrites, Phosphates and Chemicals Limited (PPCL)

Pyrites, Phosphates & Chemicals Limited (PPCL) was set up in March 1960 to exploit the pyrites deposits in the country. At present, the company is engaged in the mining of pyrites deposits and production of single superphosphate at Amjhore in Bihar and Saladipura in Rajasthan and mining of rock phosphate from the Mussoorie Phosphorite deposits in Uttar Pradesh. Pyrites is used as a substitute for sulphur in the manufacture of sulphuric acid and is also applied directly for reclamation of alkaline soils. The Company is engaged in trading of imported Fertilizers, also.

Against the authorised share capital of Rs. 100.00 crore, the paid-up share capital of the company was Rs.94.65 crore as on 31.3.98.

Phosphatic Fertilizer Plant at Amjhore (Bihar)

The Amjhore phosphatic fertilizer plant consists of a pyrites based sulphuric acid plant and a Single Super Phosphate (SSP) plant. The SSP plant was commissioned in November 1988 with bought out acid, while the pyrites based sulphuric acid plant was commissioned in November 1989. The installed capacity of the SSP plant is 2,64,000 MT of SSP per annum (equivalent to 42,240 MT of phosphate).

During 1997-98, the Amjhore unit produced 2,05,318 MT of SSP with a capacity utilisation of 78%, During 1998-99 (upto November 1998), the unit produced 60,215 MT of SSP. During the whole year, the unit is likely to produce 1,17,000 MT of SSP with a capacity utilisation of 44.5%.

Phosphatic Fertilizer Project, Saladipura, (Rajasthan)

6.3.5 The Saladipura deposits have reserves of about 120 million MT of medium grade pyrites, equivalent to 25 million MT of sulphur. With a view to exploiting these deposits for the production of sulphuric acid and SSP, PPCL had formulated a proposal for setting up an integrated project at Saladipura, consisting of a 600 MT per day (MTPD) SSP plant and a 240 MTPD pyrites based sulphuric acid plant. In the wake of the decontrol of phosphatic fertilizers and the consequent withdrawal of subsidy support, the viability of the project had to be reviewed because of the higher cost of production in the pyrites route as compared to the conventional sulphur based SSP units. As a cost reduction measure, the scope of the project was drastically reduced to exclude the facilities of production of sulphuric acid from the local pyrites deposits. Accordingly, PPCL took up a project for setting up a 300 MTPD SSP plant based on bought out sulphuric acid. The project was commissioned in November 1996.

During 1997-98, the unit produced 67,018 MT of SSP (equivalent to 10,723 MT of phosphate) with a capacity utilisation of 67.7%.

During 1998-99 (upto November 1998), the unit produced 30,867 MT of SSP. During the whole year, the unit is likely to produce 62,500 MT of SSP with a capacity utilisation of 63.3%.

Dehradun unit

The company produced 1.23 lakh MT of Mussoorie Phos during 1997-98. Consequent on expiry of import substitution scheme w.e.f. 31.8.98, the mining operation has been discontinued w.e.f. 1.9.98. The production during April to August 1998 was 1222 MT of Mussoorie Phos.

Trading activities

During 1997-98, PPCL imported/handled 1.19 lakh MT Urea, MOP etc. During 1998-99, the company had imported/handled 1.08 lakh MT of fertilizers. The sales during 1997-98 was 1.65 lakh MT of fertilizers. The sales during 1998-99 was 1.10 lakh MT of fertilizers.

Financial performance

PPCL incurred a net loss of Rs. 52.98 crore during 1997-98.

The cumulative loss as on 31.3.98 was Rs.87.83 crore. During April-November 1998, the company has made a loss of Rs.33.97 crore. During the whole year, the company is likely to make a loss of Rs.40.16 crore.

Disinvestment Commission (DC), classifying PPCL as non-core PSU, has recommended sale/closure of Dehradun unit and clubbing of Amjhore Unit and Saladipura Unit together for sale to a strategic buyer. In case, sale of Amjhore unit is not possible, it may be made viable by switch over from the pyrites to sulphur route for sulphuric acid production for manufacturing SSP with budgetary support. After completion of switch over, disinvestment of GOI equity can be made. Recommendation of Disinvestment Commission is under examination. Meanwhile, the company has submitted a restructuring proposal to Govt. of India which is under process.

Paradeep Phosphtes Limited (PPL)

Paradeep Phosphates Limited (PPL) was incorporated on 24-12.1981 as a 100% Government of India Enterprise with an authorised capital of Rs.120 crore. A participation agreement between GOI and the Government of Nauru (GON) was signed on 26.5.1982 envisaging 40% equity participation by GON and 60% by GOI. In November 1985, it was decided to increase the participation of GON in the share capital from 40% to 49% with GOI holding balance 51%. PPL has, however, again become a wholly owned GOI Undertaking with effect from June 10, 1993 as the 49% shareholding belonging to GON has been acquired by the Govt. of India.

The authorised capital of the company was increased from RS. 120 crore to Rs.467.65 crore consisting of 35,00,000 equity shares and 11,76,500 non-cumulative Redeemable Preference Shares of Rs.1000/each. The Preference Share Capital was created pursuant to the conversion of outstanding interest on GOI loan of Rs. 117.65 crore as a measure of capital restructuring approved by the Government.

Production performance

The product-wise annual installed capacities of PPL are as under:

Sr.No.	Product	Installed Capacity (Lakh MT per Annum)
I	Di-Ammonium Phosphate [DAP]	7.20
II	Phosphoric Acid	2.25
III	Sulphuric Acid	6.60

During the year 1997-98, the company produced 7,76,105 MT of DAP and 23,590 NIT of NPK with 110% capacity utilisation, which is the record production achieved so far. During the year 1998-99 (upto November 1998), the company produced 4,87, 100 MT of DAP and 3,095 MT of NPK. Production during 1998-99 is likely to be 7,54,195 of DAP/NPK, thus achieving a capacity utilisation of 106%.

During the year 1997-98, the company produced 3,02,440 MT of sulphuric acid with a capacity utilization of 45.8%, which is the record production achieved so far in a year. During the year 1998-99 (upto November 1998), the company produced 1,54,169 NIT of sulphuric acid. It is estimated that during the year as a whole, 2,84,169 MT of sulphuric acid is likely to be produced, thus achieving the capacity utilisation of 43%.

The production of phosphoric acid is continuing with the availability of sulphuric acid and during the year 1997-98, 90,006 MT of phosphoric acid (P_2O_5) was produced, which is 40% of plant capacity utilisation and this is also the record production achieved so far in a year. During the year 1998-99 (upto November 1998), the company produced 41,354 MT of phosphoric acid. It is estimated that during the whole year, 85,354 MT of phosphoric acid will be produced, thus achieving capacity utilisation of 38%.

Sales performance

During the year 1997-98, the company sold 13,13,055 MT of fertilizers. The turnover of the company during the year 1997-98 was Rs. 1168 crore, which is the highest so far achieved in a year.

During the year 1998-99 (upto November 1998), the total volume of sales of fertilizers was 6,90,877 MT. It is estimated that during the whole year, a total quantity of 8,90,877 MT of fertilizer is likely to be sold.

Financial performance

The company made a net loss of Rs.105.53 crore during 1997-98. During the period from April 1998 to November 1998, the company has made a loss of Rs.67.70 crore. During the whole year, the company is likely to make a loss of Rs.65 crore. The company has submitted a capital restructuring proposal for consideration of the Government.

Revamping of Sulphuric Acid plant

Due to persistent technical problems, the performance of sulphuric acid plant has been poor since commissioning. To improve the performance of the sulphuric acid plant, the revamping of one stream of sulphuric acid plant has been taken up which is scheduled to be completed by May 1999. The second stream of SAP is planned to be revamped in 1999-2000.

Indian Farmers Fertiliser Cooperative Limited (IFFCO)

Indian Farmers Fertiliser Co-operative Limited (IFFCO) is a multi-state co-operative society engaged in production and distribution of chemical fertilizers. Registered on

3.11.1967, the Society commissioned its first two plants at Kalol and Kandla in Gujarat in 1975 for production of Urea and NPK/DAP, respectively. It expanded its production facilities in 1981 by commissioning two additional streams of phosphatic fertilizers at Kandla and a new urea plant at Phulpur. A gas-based plant was commissioned in 1988 at Aonla, Uttar Pradesh. During the period from December 1996 to December 1997, the installed production capacity of urea was doubled by expanding the plant capacities at Aonla, Kalol and Phulpur from 16.2 lakh tonnes to 32.2 lakh tonnes. In addition, IFFCO has also set up one dry ice plant at Kalol. At present IFFCO's installed capacity in terms of nutrients is 16 lakh tonnes of nitrogen and 3.09 lakh tonnes of phosphate per annum.

The authorised share capital of the Society as on 31.3.98 stood at Rs. 1000 crore with a paid-up capital at Rs.373.41 crore, including Rs.289.61 crore Government equity.

Production performance

During the year 1997-98, IFFCO produced 14.97 lakh tonnes of nitrogen and 4.78 lakh tonnes of phosphate. The capacity utilisation in terms of nitrogen was 113.3% and in terms of phosphate it was 154.6%.

In year 1998-99 (upto November 1998), IFFCO produced over 12.02 lakh tonnes of nitrogen. During the same period, Kandla plant produced 3.18 lakh tonnes of phosphate. During the whole year, the Society is likely to produce 17.67 lakh tonnes of nitrogen and 4.44 lakh tonnes of phosphate.

Marketing

IFFCO sells its fertilizers exclusively through a network of about 34,421 cooperative societies spread over 17 States. During the year 1997-98, IFFCO sold 40.49 lakh tonnes of fertilizers and achieved a sales turnover of Rs.3413.00 crore. The Society has sold 28.02 lakh tonnes of fertilizers during April-November 1998.

FFCO has 167 Farmers Service Centres which provide all necessary inputs and know-how to the farmers under one roof. IFFCO has also been attempting to bring in overall socio-economic development of villages through its village adoption programme. Some of the extension services of IFFCO are tribal and dry land area programmes, farmers integration programme, farm forestry, establishing farmers community centres in remote and backward areas, organising soil tests. The Society has reoriented its agricultural services to lay more emphasis on balanced use of fertilizers for sustainable agriculture.

Financial performance

IFFCO made a profit of Rs.474.53 crore before tax during 1997-98. After paying a tax Rs.35.68 crore, the net profit for the year 1997-98 stood at Rs.438.85 crore. The net worth of the Society as on 31.3.98 was Rs. 1817.00 crore. The Society declared 16% dividend during the year 1997-98.

The Society's net cash profit during period April-November 1998 was estimated Rs.254.74 crore which includes prior period subsidy of Rs.41.39 crore. The Society is likely make a profit of Rs.289.27 crore.

Investment outside IFFCO

IFFCO has invested Rs.97 crore in the equity of Krishak Bharati Cooperative Limited (KRIBHCO), Rs.7.97 crore in Godavari Fertilizers and Chemicals Limited (GFCL) and Rs. 7.80 crore as equity shares in ICS, Senegal, a joint venture with Govt. of India and SPIC. The ICS joint venture has planned expansion of its present capacity by another 3.13 lakh tonnes of phosphoric acid per annum at a cost of US $ 275 million. The Society has also invested Rs. 3.24 crore in Indian Potash Limited, Rs. 10 lakh in Maharashtra State Cooperative Bank Ltd. and Rs. I lakh each in Indian Tourism Cooperative Ltd. and National Films and Fine Arts Cooperative Ltd.

Projects abroad

IFFCO and KRIBHCO in association with Qeshm Free Area Authority (QFAA) are jointly exploring the possibility of setting up a fertilizer plant in Qeshm Island of Iran. The Feasibility Report for the establishment of 1500 MTPD ammonia and 2200 MTPD urea project at an estimated cost of US $ 470 million has been appraised and adopted by the joint venture partners. Bids for engineering procurement and construction of the plant, were invited along with financial packages. Only one valid bid was received. The project authorities are evaluating the implications of opening the single bid.

Krishak Bharati Cooperative Limited (KRIBHCO)

KRIBHCO was incorporated as a multistate Cooperative Society on 17.4.1980 to implement the ammonia-urea fertilizer project at Hazira, based on natural gas from Bombay High/South Bassein. The Society commissioned its ammonia-urea plant in 1985.

The Hazira complex has two streams of 1350 MTPD ammonia capacity each and 4 streams of I 100 MTPD urea capacity each. The annual installed capacity of urea plants is 14.52 lakh MT (6.68 lakh MT in terms of nitrogen). The steam generation facility consists of 3 boilers and a 30 MW capacity captive power plant. In addition, the annual installed capacity of Bio-fertilizers plant in operation at Hazira has been increased from 100 MT to 250 MT. As on 31.3.1998, the authorised capital of the Society was Rs.500 crore with a paid-up share capital Rs.463.61 crore, including Rs.328 crore of Government of India.

Production performance

During 1997-98, KRIBHCO produced 17.72 lakh MT of urea (8.15 lakh MT of nitrogen) achieving a capacity utilisation of 122%. The Society also produced 168 MT of bio-fertilizers during the year.

During the year 1998-99 (upto November 1998), the Society has produced 10.3 lakh tonnes of urea (4.7 lakh tonnes in terms of nitrogen) and 147 MT of bio-fertilizers. During the whole year the Society is likely to produce 6.93 lakh tonnes of nitrogen.

Marketing

During the year 1997-98, the Society sold 17.09 lakh tonnes of own urea. Besides own urea, the Society has sold 0.46 lakh tonnes of NFCL urea in the State of Andhra Pradesh and 0.62 lakh tonnes of surplus ammonia during 1997-98. It has also sold 165 MT of bio-fertilizers.

In the year 1998-99 (upto November 1998), the Society has sold 9.85 lakh tonnes of own urea and 0.35 lakh tonnes of surplus ammonia. Besides this, 0. 12 lakh tonnes of NFCL urea was also sold upto November 1998.

The Society has also sold 136 MT of bio-fertilizers upto November 1998.

The Society organised a variety of extension activities such as Crop Seminars, Farmers Meetings, Field Demonstration on various Crops etc. In addition, soil and water samples were collected, tested and recommendations made available to the farmer. Under the Command Area Development Programmes, various programmes were organised for overall socio-economic development. KRIBHCO also provides services to the farmers through Krishak Bharati Sewa Kendras (KBSK).

Financial results

During the year 1997-98, the Society made a net profit before tax of Rs.447.96 crore and a net profit after tax of Rs.299.61 crore.

During the year 1998-99 (upto November 1998), the Society made a profit before tax c Rs.283.43 crore (provisional) and a net profit aft(tax of Rs. 194.45 crore (provisional). During the whole year, the Society is likely to make a profit of Rs.385.62 crore (before tax) and Rs.265.45 crore (after tax).

The Society declared a dividend @ 18 for the year 1997-98 and accordingly Rs.59. crore was paid to Government of India as dividend

Expansion and diversification plans

Government has approved investment of US $ 69 million by KRIBHCO and RCF to set up a urea plant in Oman in collaboration with Oman Oil Company to produce 14.52 lakh tonnes of urea and 3.30 lakh tonnes of Merchant Ammonia per annum. All major agreements have been finalised. Arranging banks which have been mandated to finalise the project have completed the due diligence process. Discussions are being held with the arranging banks to finalise the financing package.

IFFCO and KRIBHCO in association with Qeshm Free Area Authority (QFAA) are jointly exploring the possibility of setting up a fertilizer plant in Qeshm. Island of Iran. The Feasibility Report for the establishment of 1500 MTPD ammonia and 2200 MTPD urea project at an estimated cost of US $ 470 million has been appraised and adopted by the joint venture partners. Bids for engineering procurement and construction of the plant were invited along with financial packages. Only one valid bid was received. The project authorities are evaluating the implications of opening the single bid.

Projects in India

The following project proposals of KRIBHCO are being posed before the Public Investment Board (PIB): —

- A third ammonia-urea stream at Hazira, Gujarat to produce an additional 7.26 lakh TPA of urea; and
- A new ammonia-urea plant at the existing site of FCI at Gorakhpur to produce 7.26 lakh TPA of urea.

The first stage clearance has been accorded for preparation of Detailed Feasibility Report (DFR) for setting up a 615 MW combined cycle power project at Pipavav (Gujarat).

Rashtriya Chemicals and Fertilizers Limited (RCF)

RCF was incorporated as a separate company on 6.3.1978 consequent to reorganisation of the erstwhile Fertilizer Corporation of India Limited. At the time of its formation, RCF had only one operating unit at Trombay and two major projects under implementation, viz. Trombay-IV and Trombay-V Expansion. The gas-based Thal Vaishet fertilizer complex established by RCF at Thal Raigad District commenced commercial production on 1.6.1985.

As on 31.3.1998, the company had an authorised share capital of Rs.800 crore with a paid-up capital of Rs.551.69 crore. Consequent on disinvestment effected in 1991-92, 1993-94 and 1994-95, Government of India shares stand reduced to 92.5% of the paid up capital.

Production performance

The annual Installed capacity of all the units of RCF is 10 lakh MT of nitrogen and 1.20 lakh MT of phosphate. The production of the company during 1997-98 was 8.92 lakh MT of nitrogen and 1.01 lakh MT of phosphate. During the year, the Thal unit produced 14.02 lakh MT of Urea. During the period April-November 1998, the company has produced 5.64 lakh MT of nitrogen and 0.64 lakh MT of phosphate. During the whole year, the company is likely to produce 9.32 lakh MT of nitrogen and 1.07 lakh MT of phosphate.

Besides fertilizers, the company produces a number of industrial products such as Methanol, Concentrated Nitric Acid, Methylamines, Ammonium Nitrite and Dimethyl Formamide

Sales performance

The sale of fertilize.-S during the year 1997-98 was of the order of 8.57 lakh MT of nitrogen and 1.21 lakh tonnes of phosphate. During the period April-November 1998, the company sold 6.06 lakh MT of nitrogen and 0.67 lakh MT of phosphate.

Operating results

During the year 1997-98, the company made a net profit of Rs. 189.37 crore, out of which Rs.38.62 crore was distributed as dividend at the rate of 7% of the paid-up capital. During the period April to November 1998, the company has made a net profit of Rs. 113.39 crore. During the whole year, the company is likely to make a profit of Rs.250.00 crore.

Modernisation/expansion schemes

The company has taken up the following modernisation programmes:

- Revamp of two streams of Ammonia Plant at Thal (Retrofit Phase-II).
- Erection of Formic Acid Plant at Thal during 1998-99.
- Atmospheric Ammonia Storage Tank at Trombay.
- Mechanisation of Bagging Plant.

The company has submitted a proposal to set up an ammonia-urea plant with a capacity to produce 7.26 lakh

TPA of urea. The proposal is being placed before the Public Investment Board (PIB).

Projects abroad

Government has approved investment of US $ 69 million by KRIBHCO and RCF to set up a urea plant in Oman in collaboration with Oman Oil Company to produce 14.52 lakh tonnes of urea and 3.30 lakh tonnes of Merchant Ammonia per annum. All major agreements have been finalised. Arranging banks which have been mandated to finalise the project completed during diligence process. Discussions are being held with the arranging banks to finalise the financing package.

Madras Fertilizers limited (MFL)

Madras Fertilizers Limited (MFL) was incorporated in December 1966 as a joint venture between GOI and AMOCO India Incorporation of USA (AMOCO) with GOI holding 51% of the equity share capital.

In accordance with the participation agreement between GOI, AMOCO and the National Iranian Oil Company (NIOC), NIOC acquired 50% of the shareholding of AMOCO in MFL on 22.11.1972. The shareholding pattern upto 21.7.1985 was as follows:

GOI	51.0%
AMOCO	24.5%
NIOC	24.5%

On 22.7.1985, the shares of AMOCO were purchased by GOI and NIOC in their respective proportions. The shareholding pattern upto May 11, 1997 was as under:

On May 12, 1997, MFL brought out its maiden Public Issue of 2,86,30,000 shares of face value of Rs. 10/- at a premium of Rs.5 per share. Of these, 2,58,09,700 shares were, subscribed. After the public issue, the shareholding pattern is as follows:

	Rs. Crore	% age
GOI	95.85	58.74
NIOC	41.52	25.44
Public	25.81	15.82
Total	163.18	100.00

As on 31.3.1998, the authorised: share capital of the company was Rs. 175 crore and the paid-up capital was Rs. 161.77 crore.

Production performance

The company had taken up a project for revamp of its plants at an estimated cost of Rs.601.43 crore. The project was commissioned in March 1998. With the commissioning of the project, the installed capacity has substantially been increased. The annual installed capacity before and after revamp are as follows:

Annual Capacity (MT)

	Pre-Revamp	Post-Revamp
Terms of product		
Ammonia	247, 500	346,500
Urea	292, 050	486,750
NPK	540, 000	840, 000
In Terms of Nutrients		
Nitrogen	176, 000	254, 280
Phosphate	112, 000	142, 800

During 1997-98, the company produced 106.4 thousand tonnes of nitrogen and 83.3 thousand tonnes of phosphate with a capacity utilisation of 52.7% and 69.1%, respectively. During the period from April to November 1998, the company produced 137.5 thousand tonnes of nitrogen and 81.7 thousand tonnes of phosphate. During the whole year, the company is likely to produce 224.3 thousand tonnes of nitrogen and 121.9 thousand tonnes of phosphate with a capacity utilisation of 88.3% and 85.2%, respectively.

During 1997-98, the company produced 325 tonnes of Bio-fertilizers. During 1998-99, the company is likely to produce 345 tonnes of Bio-fertilizers.

Sales performance

The sales performance of the company during 1997-98 and during the current year is as under:

	Actuals 1997-1998	Actuals April-Nov. 1998	Estimates 1998-1999
Urea	52,758	1,37,608	2, 70, 000
NPK	4, 05, 855	5, 09, 458	7, 82, 737
Potash	1,23,896	16,971	41, 971
DAP	73,089	18,563	18, 695
Total Sales	6,55,598	6,82,600	11, 13, 403

Financial performance

During 1997-98, the company made a net loss of Rs.55.35 crore. During the period from April to November 1998, the company has reported a loss of Rs.49.66 crore. During the whole year, the company is likely to make a loss of Rs.33.63 crore.

Hindustan Fertilizer Corporation Limited (HFC)

HFC was incorporated on 14.3.1978 consequent upon the re-organisation of the erstwhile Fertilizer Corporation of India Ltd. (FCI). HFC owns production units at Namrup-Assam, Barauni-Bihar and Durgapur-West Bengal, besides the Haldia Project in West Bengal.

As on 31.3.98, the company had an authorised share capital of Rs. 1200 crore and a paid up capital of Rs.729.11 crore.

Production performance

The total annual installed capacity of the 5 manufacturing units of HFC at Barauni, Durgapur & Namrup (I, II & III) was 6.53 lakh MT of nitrogen, which has been de-rated to 4.24 lakh MT w.e.f. 1. 11. 1994. The total production of the company during 1997-98 was 1. 11 lakh MT of nitrogen at an average capacity utilisation of 26.1 %. During the period from April to November 1998, the company produced 35,700 tonnes of nitrogen. During the whole year, the company is likely to produce 67,500 tonnes of nitrogen at an average capacity utilisation of 15.9%. The performance of Namrup-I, Namrup- II and Barauni unit has not been satisfactory, mainly due to ageing of the plants and equipment/ design deficiencies. The production in Namrup-II was suspended since 1. 11. 1994 due to shortage and unsteady supply of natural gas. Similarly, Durgapur plant has remained under shutdown since 24th June 1997 due to heavy fire on top of primary reformer caused by rupturing of dog tail.

Financial performance

During 1997-98, the company made a net loss of Rs. 647.83 crore. During 1998-99, the company has made a net loss of Rs.452.19 crore and during the whole year, the estimated loss would be Rs.725.33 crore.

Reference to bifr

In terms of Section 3(l) of the Sick Industrial Companies (Special Provisions) Act, 1985, the case of the company was referred to the Board for Industrial and Financial Reconstructions (BIFR), which declared it a sick company on 12.11.1992. After evaluation of various alternatives, a revival package for HFC was formulated which envisaged the limited revamp of Durgapur, Barauni and Namrup units. However, the revival package could not be implemented for want of funds. The revival package of HFC reformulated on the basis of a fresh technical appraisal by an expert group led by ICICI from the stand point of the financial institutions were considered by the Government on 1. 10.97.

The Government has approved the proposal for the revamp of Namrup units at an estimated fresh investment of Rs.350 crore. The project is to be implemented within 30 months of award of Engineering, Procurement and Construction (EPC) contract. The groundwork for launching the project has started.

To ensure timely implementation of the scheme, a plan budgetary support of Rs.70 crore has been made in the current year. The revival package in respect of the remaining units of HFC have been reviewed from the angle of unit-wise viability and tie-up of funding arrangements and are presently under Inter-Ministerial consultation.

Haldia project

Though the Haldia Fertilizer Project was mechanically completed in November 1979, due to a variety of equipment related problems, the suspension of commissioning activities had to be ordered in October 1986. Thereafter a number of options for its rehabilitation were explored by the Government but none of them were found to be economically viable.

Government has, therefore, decided to hive it off. HFC is planning to engage SBI Capital Market as the Consultant so as to initiate actions in respect of various processes involved in hiving off the unit.

Projects and Development India Limited (PDIL)

Projects & Development India Limited (PDIL), an erstwhile e division of the Fertilizer, Corporation of India Ltd.(FCI), was registered as separate company in March 1978. The company has its registered office at Sindri, Bihar.

Against the authorised share capital of Rs.60 crore, the paid up equity of the company stood at Rs.53.52 crore as on 31.3.98.

PDIL has three divisions namely, Engineering and Consultancy, Division, Catalyst Division, and Research and Development Division.

Operating results

The company made a net profit of Rs.6.09 crore during 1997-98. During the period April to November 1998, the company has made a net loss of Rs.3.49 crore. During the whole year, the company is likely to make a loss of Rs.3.07 crore.

Engineering and consultancy division

The Engineering and Consultancy Division is engaged in the design, engineering, procurement, inspection store management and supervision during construction and commissioning of fertilizer and chemical plants. The Consultancy Division also handles market research, project planning, non-destructive testing services, technical and inspection services. During 1997-98, PDIL has commissioned the following major fertilizer projects:

- Ammonia/Urea Plant of IFFCO Phulpur
- Ammonia/Urea Plant of NFCL, Kakinada
- Revamping of Ammonia Plant IFFCO, Kalol

The following major projects/assignments in the fertilizer sector are under execution:

- Engineering Consultancy Services for
- Ammonia Plant revamp of Deepak Fertilizer and Petrochemicals Limited, Taloja.
- Providing of consultancy services for mixed fuel firing in primary reformer for IFFCO Aonla, IGFCCL-Jagdishpur and CFCL-Gadepan.
- Thai Retrofit-II project of RCF.
- New Ammonia Synthesis loop of fertilizer plant of Neyveli Lignite Corporation onLSTK basis.
- Augmentation of New Naphtha handling & storage facilities at NFL-Vijaipur.
- Methanol Revamp Project at NFL-Nangal.

During 1997-98, the company has secured consultancy for revamping of HFC's Namrup plants and Ammonia-I Synthesis Loop Revamp of RCF, Trombay.

As a measure to expand its sphere of activities, PDIL has been making sustained efforts to diversify and secure jobs in other sectors, especially in the gas and oil sector. As a major break through during 1997-98, PDIL was awarded the job of consultancy services as a prime contractor for Product Pipeline Hook up from IOCL Gujarat Refinery at Vadodara to BPCL-Koyall Project Terminal and Engineering service for laying/hooking up of product pipeline from, jetties of Kandla Port Trust to BPCL terminal Kandla. Besides, PDIL in association with Flu Daniel, USA and Mitsubishi Heavy Industries Japan has prepared a Detailed Report i Feasibility of LNG Import Terminal at Cochin for M/s.Gas Authority of India Ltd.

PDIL has also been entrusted a prestigious project by the Defence Research and Development Laboratory (DRDL) of the Defence Research and Development Organisatic (DRDO) to render engineering consultancy services for its SFD-DRDL project for improve quality rocket propellant fuel.

The following are some of the major jot in oil and gas sector under execution:

- Consultancy service for coastal oil installation, BPCL, Paradeep.
- Consultancy service for LPG bottling plant, IOCL Kandla & IOCL Delhi.
- Consultancy service for LPG Tank Trust loading at Karnal Bottling Plant.
- Mounded storage tanks for LPG, IOCL, Gujarat Refinery.
- Mounded LPG storage facility at Mahul Refinery BPCL, Mumbai.
- LPG Import facilities Phase-I IOCL, Haldia

Catalyst division including fabrication shop

After three decades of continuous efforts through in-house R&D, PDIL is now in a position to supply a wide range of catalysts required for the production of ammonia. The production of three main catalysts i.e. HT shift conversion, LT shift conversion and nickel based catalysts including Zinc Oxide and Sodium Nitrate during 1997-98 was 1003 MT as compared to 1000 MT during 1996-97. During 1998-99, the company is likely to produce 808 MT of catalysts, excluding Sodium Nitrate.

Research and development division

The Research & Development Division undertakes research projects including sponsored and client oriented schemes in the field of fertilizer and allied technology. The company receives an annual grant-in-aid of Rs.4.0 crore from the Government for R&D activities. The division has made considerable progress in the development of a range of new catalysts. PDIL is striving to improve and commercialise a number of products developed by the R&D Division. These include low pressure methanol synthesis catalyst, new supported multicomponent HT shift catalyst, FCC catalyst and Improved Styrene catalyst.

ISO certification

During 1997-98, PDIL has been awarded ISO-9001 certificate for Project Management and Engineering Consultancy including Design Engineering, Procurement, Construction, Commissioning, Third party Design review, Inspection, Life Expectancy, Assessment of plants and other related services. The certificate is valid up to 18.5.2001 which will further be renewed after thorough auditing.

Bifer status

PDIL was declared a sick company by BIFR on 17.12.92 under Sick Industrial Companie. Revival package for the company has been sanctioned by the BIFR which has been approved by the Government. The required actions for implementation of different provisions of the revival package have been completed. Under the approved package, 395 employees have been given voluntary retirement.

Fertilizer corporation of India Limited (FCI)

Incorporated on 1st January 196 1, FCI was reorganised with effect from 1.4.1978. It has four fertilizer manufacturing units, one each at Sindri (Bihar), Gorakhpur (Uttar Pradesh), Ramagundam (Andhra Pradesh) and Talcher (Orissa), with a total annual capacity of 5.87 lakh MT of nitrogen per annum. Besides, it has a mining unit known as the Jodhpur Mining Organisation, which is engaged in the mining and selling of gypsum. The authorised share capital of the company as on 30th November 1998 was Rs.800 crore with the paid up capital of Rs.723.74 crore.

Production performance

During 1997-98, the company produced 188.5 thousand MT of nitrogen with an average capacity utilisation of 32.1%. During 1998-99 (upto November 1998), the company produced 102.4 thousand MT of nitrogen. The estimated production during 1998-99 is likely to be 166.2 thousand MT of nitrogen with a capacity utilisation of 28.3%.

Sindri

The Sindri Unit produced 95.9 thousand MT of nitrogen during 1997-98 with a capacity utilisation of 63.2%. During 1998-99 (upto November 1998), the unit produced 65.3 thousand MT of nitrogen. The estimated production during 1998-99 is likely to be 107.5 thousand MT of nitrogen with a capacity utilisation of 70.8%. The production during the period April 1998 to November 1998 was affected mainly due to interruption in supply of power from DVC.

Gorakhpur

The Gorakhpur Unit has been closed since June 1990 following an accident. A new fertilizer plant is proposed to be established by KRIBHCO using existing infrastructure. Action is in hand for transfer of land and part of assets of Gorakhpur plant from FCI to KRIBHCO.

Ramagundam

During 1997-98, the Ramagundam unit produced 46.6 thousand MT of nitrogen with a capacity utilisation of 30.7%. During 1998-99 (upto November 1998), the unit produced 16.8 thousand MT of nitrogen, The estimated production during 1998-99 is likely to be 25.9 thousand MT of nitrogen with a capacity utilisation of 17.1%. The production during the period from April 1998 to November 1998 was affected mainly due to work-to-rule agitation from 8.6.98 to 30.7.98 resorted to by officers' association and due to equipment problems in Steam Generation Plant.

Talcher

During 1997-98, the Talcher unit produced 46 thousand MT of nitrogen with a capacity utilisation of 30.3%. During 1998-99 (upto November 1998), the unit produced 20.3 thousand MT of nitrogen. The estimated production during the year 1998-99 is likely to be 32.8 thousand NIT of nitrogen with a capacity utilisation of 21.6%.

The production during the period April 1998 to November 1998 was affected mainly due to shutdown of the plant from 2.4.1998 to 6.5.1998 for repair of L.P.Turbine Rotor of Raw Gas Compressor by BHEL. The plant operation was also affected due to disruption in supply of power from GRIDCO.

Sales performance

FCI sold 4.02 lakh tonnes of fertilizers during 1997-98. During 1998-99 (upto November 1998), the company sold 2.26 lakh tonnes of fertilizers.

Financial results

During 1997-98, the company incurred a net loss of Rs.724.93 crore (after prior period adjustment). During 1998-99 (upto November 1998), the company incurred a net loss of Rs.573.63 crore (provisional). During 1998-99, the company is likely to make a loss of Rs.837.74 crore.

Reference to bifr

FCI was declared a sick company on 6.11.92 by BIFR under the Sick Industrial Companies (Special Provisions) Act, 1985. After evaluation of various alternatives, a revival package for FCI was formulated envisaging the limited revamp of Sindri, Ramagundam and Talcher units. However, the revival package could not be implemented for want of funds. The package was reformulated taking into account the consideration of unit-wise viability. The decision on the revival package was deferred. The proposals have been reviewed from the angle of unit-wise viability and tie-up of funding arrangements. The revised proposals are under Inter-Ministerial consultations.

The revamp of Gorakhpur unit has not been found to be techno-economically viable. KRIBHCO is processing a proposal for setting up a new ammonia-urea plant at the existing site at Gorakhpur using the existing infrastructure of FCI.

5

Subsidy on Fertilizers

The sale price of controlled fertilizers are fixed by the Government of India (Department of Agriculture & Cooperation) under the Fertilizer (Control) Order, 1985 is i sued under the Essential Commodities Act, 1955. At present, only urea, which is the main nitrogenous fertilizer constituting about 60% of the total fertilizer consumption in the country, is under statutory price control.

With effect from 29.1.99, the farmgate price of urea has been fixed at Rs.4000 per tonne excluding local levies. Notwithstanding this increase, the farmgate price of urea is amongst the lowest in the region and is heavily subsidised.

Payment of subsidy in respect of controlled fertilizers is regulated through the mechanism of Retention Price-cum- Subsidy Scheme (RPS). RPS enables the manufacturers of controlled fertilizers to recover their normative cost of production along with a reasonable return on networth.

The cost of production of various fertilizer units differ from unit to unit and even from month to month, depending upon the health and vintage of the plant, the feedstock used, the levels of capacity utilisation, energy consumption, distance from the source of feedstock/raw materials, cost of inputs etc. At present, urea, being the only controlled fertilizer, is covered under RPS.

The RPS provides for fixation of retention price of each controlled fertilizer after taking into account the normative capacity utilisation prescribed by the Government and a combination of norms and actuals in respect of various cost elements and expenses. Pre-tax return on networth corresponding to post-tax return of 12% is given as a part of the retention price after covering various elements of cost.

The retention prices of controlled fertilizers are normally fixed once in three years after scrutinising the cost data of the units for three years for which audited accounts are available. During the currency of the pricing period, escalations/reductions are provided to reflect variations in the prices of major inputs. Escalations are also allowed in respect of certain other items of cost (viz. salaries and wages, chemicals and consumables, repairs and maintenance, overheads etc.) where there is a significant variation during the currency of the pricing period due to unavoidable factors.

In addition to the retention price subsidy, equated freight subsidy is paid to the manufacturers of controlled fertilizers to cover the cost of transportation from the production points to the consumption centres. Since the consumer prices of both indigenous and imported fertilizers are fixed uniformly, subsidy is also paid on imported fertilizers in order to bridge the difference between the cost of imports and the statutorily fixed consumer price.

The subsidy paid on indigenously produced and imported fertilizers from the year 1985-86 onwards is indicated below:

Year	Subsidy on Indigenous Fertilizers	Subsidy on Imported Fertilizers	Total Subsidy
1985-86	1600.00	323.71	1923.71
1986-87	1700.00	197.12	1897.12
1987-88	2050.00	113.95	2163.95
1988-89	3000.00	200.70	3200.70
1990-91	3771.00	771.10	4542.10
1991-92	3729.73	659.33	4389.06
1992-93	4800.00	996.11	5796.11
1993-94	3800.00	598.97	4398.97
1994-95	4075.00	1166.00	5241.00
1995-96	4300.00	1935.00	62350.00
1996-97	4743.00	1163.08	5906.08
1997-98	6600.00	721.96	7321.96
1998-99(BE)	6000.00	983.00	6983.00
1998-99(BE)	7360.00	238.00	6983.00
1999-2000(BE)	8000.00	750.00	8750.00

The steady increase in fertilizers subsidies over the years has largely been the result of increasing production/ consumption and increases in the inputs of indigenous fertilizers and prices of imported fertilizers from time to time. The cost of various inputs/utilities, such as coal, gas, naphtha, rock phosphate, sulphur, ammonia, phosphoric acid, electricity, etc. as also the cost of transportation went up significantly during the eighties. The gas-based fertilizer units commissioned during this period also involved higher capital investment per tonne of installed capacity, necessitating constant upward revisions in the retention prices. The selling prices of fertilizers to the farmers, however, remained almost at the same level between July 1981 and July 1991. The Government effected an increase of 30% in the issue prices of fertilizers in August, 1991 after a gap of a decade. The selling price of urea, which was reduced by

10% in August 1992, was revised upwards by 20% in June 1994 followed by another increase by 10% with effect' from 21.2.97. However, even this price hike did not materially alter the position in terms of the absolute, there has been a decline in amount of annual subsidy bill, because of the steady growth in production to meet the growing demand and rise in the costs of inputs. However, due to a sharp fall in the international price of urea there has been a decline in subsidy for imported urea from 1996-97 onwards.

Consequent upon the decontrol of phosphatic and potassic fertilizers w.e.f. 25.8.92, the prices of these fertilizers registered a sharp increase vis-a-vis the price of urea. However, in order to cushion the impact of increase in prices of these fertilizers, the Ministry of Agriculture introduced a scheme of Concession on sale of decontrolled fertilizers. In a major policy initiative taken by the Government on 5.7.96, the scale and coverage of the special concession was substantially increased to give impetus to the stagnating demand for these fertilizers and to ameliorate the nutrient imbalance in the soil which is essential for sustaining the desired growth in agricultural productivity.

Again in 1997-98, along with the increase in urea price effected on 21.2.97, it was decided to increase w.e.f. 1.4.97, the concession on indigenous DAP from Rs.3000 to Rs.3750 per tonne and on imported DAP from Rs. 1500 to Rs.2250 per tonne, on MOP from Rs.1500 to Rs.2000 per tonne, on SSP from Rs.500 to Rs.600 per tonne and proportionately for indigenous complex fertilizers. These measures were calculated to induce the farmers to optimise the use of the three plant nutrients.

The rates of concession for Rabi 1997-98 effective from 1.10.97 were reduced by Rs.250 per tonne in respect of DAP and proportionately in respect of indigenous complex fertilizers. Notwithstanding this, the consumption of phosphate and potash registered an increase from 28.44 lakh tonnes and 8.84 lakh tonnes in 1992-93 to 39.71 lakh tonnes and 13.71 lakh tonnes, respectively in 1997-98. For Kharif 1998, based on cost evaluation by the Bureau of Industrial Costs and Prices (BICP), the level of concession has been fixed at Rs.4400 PMT for indigenous DAP, Rs.3400 PMT for imported DAP, Rs.3000 PMT for MOP and Rs.600 PMT for SSP.

The level of concession has been proportionately fixed for various complex fertilizers taking into account the NPK content in these fertilizers. During 1997-98, an expenditure of Rs.2596 crore was incurred under the scheme. During 1998-99, as against the B.E. of Rs.3000 crore, a R.E. of Rs.3800 crore has been proposed. For 1999-2000, a budget provision of Rs.4500 crore has been proposed.

Given the importance of fertilizer pricing and subsidisation in the overall policy environment impinging on the growth and development of the fertilizer industry, the need for streamlining these policies has been felt for a long time.

A High Powered Fertilizer Pricing Policy Review Committed was constituted to review the existing system of subsidization of urea, suggest an alternative broad-based, scientific 'and transparent methodology, and recommend measures for greater cohesiveness in the policies applicable to different segments of the industry. The report of the Committee was submitted on 3rd April 1998. Inter-ministerial consultation has been initiated on the recommendations of the Committee. Dialogue with the industry has also started regarding reassessment of installed capacity of urea manufacturing units and formulation of a Modified Retention Price Scheme (MRPS).

6

Fertilizer Availability, Imports and Movements

Availability of fertilizers

The availability of urea, which is the only fertilizer under price and movement control of Government, remained satisfactory throughout the season in Kharif 1998. Kharif 1998 season had field opening stock of 24 LMTs on 1.4.1998 compared to 12.3 LMTs during the previous Kharif. The opening stock coupled with increased indigenous production helped in progressively ensuring higher availability to the States throughout the season. The cumulative availability of urea at the end of the season was nearly 120 LMTs against the assessed requirement of 105 LMTs for the season . However, the expected growth in consumption (10%) did not materialize. The sales during the season were 4% higher over the sales of urea during previous Kharif.

The monsoon was satisfactory on the whole in the country except in the States of Madhya Pradesh and West Bengal which had less than the normal rainfall. But the erraticity of rainfall had effect on the sales of urea during Kharif which kept low at 98.43 LMTs . As a result, the consumption during Kharif would be lower than the estimated 105 LMTs. State-wise position of sales varied widely if compared to Kharif'97. They were high in the States of Andhra Pradesh (16%), Uttar Pradesh (12%), Bihar (5%), Tamil Nadu (3%), Karnataka (2%) and Punjab (2%) while there was negative growth in West Bengal (4%), Maharashtra (3%), Rajasthan (3%), Gujarat (2%), Haryana and Madhya Pradesh (I%) each. In Orissa, the sales were at the same level as in previous Kharif.

Rabi 1998-99 has opened with the inventory of 20.77 LMTs in the States which is almost at the same level as in Rabi 1997-98. During the first three months, despatches of 55.32 LMTs have been made. As a result, cumulative availability of 76.09 LMTs of urea has been achieved by 31st December 1998. The off-take of urea during the ongoing Rabi season is expected to be higher as the area under wheat cultivation has increased partly on account of unforeseen rains during October-November 1998 (which improved the moisture in the soil) and partly due to receding of water from the flood affected districts in Eastern U.P. and Bihar. No problems are envisaged in meeting the assessed requirement of 111 LMTs of urea for the season as the cumulative availability together from the indigenous production, imports and opening stocks is estimated to be nearly 126 LMTs.

Decontrolled fertilizers

The availability of decontrolled phosphatic and potassic fertilizers are dependent on market forces operating within the framework of the Concession Scheme. The Scheme is administered by the Department of Agriculture & Cooperation (DAC). Due to non-announcement of rates of concession which were linked to the study by the Bureau of Industrial Costs & Prices (BICP), the contracting of imports of both DAP & MOP was affected. 2.54 LMTs of DAP and 1. 15 LMTs MOP imports were brought during April-May 1998 against imports of 4.59 LMTs and 3.41 LMTs reportedly during April-May 1997.

In case of MOP, the international suppliers had reportedly cartelised in the hope of extracting sizeable increase over the prices of MOP of 1997-98. Since the BICP Report was to take time, Department of Agriculture & Cooperation (DAC) was given assessment of MOP prices which could pre-emptively be considered.

A breakthrough in contracting of MOP from Jordan and Israèl became possible in June 1999. In the remaining period of Kharif 1998, 7.04 LMTs of MOP imports were brought by the importers.

As a result, the cumulative availability of 7.43 LMTs MOP was achieved in Kharif. This was lower if compared to Kharif 1997. The lower level of availability resulted in shortages which were experienced in major MOP consuming States of Andhra Pradesh, Karnataka, Tamil Nadu and Kerala besides others.

As regards DAP, 9.6 LMTs of imports were made in Kharif 1998 compared to 12.88 LMTs in Kharif 1997. However, due to buoyancy in indigenous production (19.65 LMTs), the cumulative availability of 33 LMTs became possible in field which was lower if compared with availability during Kharif 1997 (36 LMTs). However, no shortages were reported by any of the States.

The table below gives the cumulative availability and sales of DAP and MOP during Kharif 1998:

(in Lakh tonnes)

Product	Cumulative Availability	Cumulative Sales
DAP	33.00 (35.92)	27.98 (28.78)
MOP	7.43 (12.73)	6.67 (10.80)

Unlike in the past when concessions announced under the Concession Scheme were reviewed for each season, the Government in Department of Agriculture & Cooperation announced long-term policy under the Scheme on 28.8.98 in which concessions would remain anchored. The rates of concessions were enhanced over that of Rabi 1997-98.

It was notified that these rates of concessions would remain in force till 31.3.2000. At the same time, it was announced that the Maximum Retail Prices (MRPs) would be determined by the market forces. The new policy in which MRPs were freed, spurred contracting of additional imports for Rabi 1998-99. Within a month of the announcement of the policy, nearly 5 LMTs of DAP imports were additionally contracted.

However, before the policy could be made effective from 1. 10.98, it was rolled back and the Government decided that MRPs would continue at the same level as that of Kharif'98 and that rates of concessions would be announced separately. Consequent to change in policy, cancellation was made of the contracts amounting to 1.30 lakh MTs as the industry was apprehensive of locking up of funds under the continuing uncertainty about the rates of concessions since Kharif 1998.

Despite this, however, 8.20 lakh MTs of DAP had landed in the country upto the end of December 1998 compared to 1.7 lakh MTs during the entire season in the previous Rabi. Since large arrivals were scheduled between October-November 1998, it led to bunching of vessels. Nearly 5 lakh MTs were destined for 2 ports, namely Vishakhapatnam and JNPT which led to congestion and, consequent, delay i evacuation from these ports.

The difficulties in handling at Vizag port were compounded by the cyclone which hit the coast during

November 1998. Due to all these reasons, DAP could not be pre-positioned in the States. The demand for DAP is highly seasonal.

So the Government intervened and extended support by granting priority (a) in berthing of DAP vessels at the ports and (b) in movement of DAP by rail. The priority in movement by rail was accorded also from the plants.

The accelerated evacuation of DAP from plants and ports together helped in redressing the localised shortages as DAP couldn't be pre positioned in view of the foregoing reasons in the States of Punjab, Haryana, Rajasthan, Madhya Pradesh and Uttar Pradesh.

The shortages were also felt because preponement of sowing resulted in peak demand during October-November and due to increase in area sown under wheat.

In respect of other decontrolled fertilizers including MOP, there have been no shortages. During Rabi, 17 lakh MTs of imports are estimated to be delivered which are adequate to meet the projected requirement.

Temporary disruption was caused in movement of MOP to West Bengal by the cyclonic disturbances at East Coast but this was made good by accelerated despatches of MOP subsequently.

The following table summarizes the season-wise position in respect of the availability and sales of the major fertilizers i.e. Urea, DAP and MOP in 1997-98 and 1998-99 (upto 31.12.98):

(in Lakh MT)

Crop Season	Assessment	Cumulative Availability	Cumulative Sales	%age of Availability to assessed demand
Kharif 1997				
Urea	107.79	115.74	94.96	107%
DAP	**	35.92	27.78	-
MOP	**	12.73	10.79	-
Rabi 1997-98				
Urea	109.18	126.07	102.09	115%
DAP	**	29.50	24.22	-
MOP	**	12.52	11.54	-
Kharif 1998				
Urea	104.18	119.88	98.76	114%
DAP	**	30.33	27.97	-
MOP	**	7.43	6.67	-
Rabi 1998-99				
Urea	110.74	76.04	55.18	69%
DAP	**	25.15	21.33	-
MOP	**	11.05	8.07	-

Movement of fertilizers

Under the Allocation of Business Rules, the Department of Fertilizers is entrusted the primary responsibility of ensuring the movement and distribution of controlled fertilizers from various plants/ports in accordance with the State-wise allocations made by the Department of Agriculture & Cooperation (DAC) under the Essential Commodities Act, 1955 (ECA). The distribution of imported urea is made keeping in view the requirements both in time and space of each of the States.

The major share in transportation of fertilizers is of the Railways. During 1997-98, Railways had moved about 74% of the fertilizers produced and imported in the country. In 1998-99, the demand of railway wagons for the transportation of fertilizers was met in full. During April-November 1998, 179.80 LMTs of fertilizers was moved by the Railways as against 178.90 LMTs in the corresponding period of 1997-98.

Judicious management of the demand supply balance has helped to reduce the average lead of fertilizer movement by rail. As compared to the average lead of 854 KMs. for the full year in 1997-98, average rail lead of 812 KMs. was attained during April- October 1998. This is the lowest since 1989-90 as may be seen from the following table:

(in KM)

Year	Average lead
1989-90	975
1990-91	940
1991-92	935
1992-93	908
1993-94	933
1994-95	922
1995-96	920
1996-97	881
1997-98	854
1998-99	812

Import of fertilizers

Imports of urea on Government account are made to bridge the gap between the indigenous availability and requirement through designated canalising agencies like MMTC Ltd., State Trading Corporation (STC) and Indian Potash Ltd. (IPL). The other major fertilizers like DAP and MOP are freely importable on private trade account.

Due to temporary shut down of plants of CIS producers, the AG suppliers had quoted artificially high prices for urea imports during February-March'98 for deliveries during April to June'98. In view of this, purchases of urea were deferred from June to July'98 as the overall availability of urea was adequate in the country.

With the resumption of production by IS countries and consequent increase of supplies, the canalising agencies could make purchases at prices ranging from US

$ 86 to US $ 90.50 PMT (FOB) which were considerably lower than those quoted earlier in the range of US $ 109-113 PMT FOB.

The deliveries of imported urea at low prices has resulted in considerable savings of subsidy on urea imports as compared to the previous year as can be discerned from the table below:

(Rs. Crore)

Year	Total Cost and Freight Value	Subsidy on Imported Fertilizers
1989-90	1538.77	771.10
1990-91	1335.82	659.33
1991-92	1934.19	1299.60
1992-93	2216.00	996.11
1993-94	1030.43	598.97
1994-95	1603.62	1166.00
1995-96	2840.14	1935.00
1996-97	1701.75	1163.08
1997-98	1296.57	721.96
1998-99	259.77	138.20

The urea imports during 1997-98 were, handled at 7 ports in the country on both the east and west coasts to bridge the gap between availability and requirement in the deficit States. The performance of the agencies appointed by the Department at the ports to handle urea vessels improved over the previous year and this resulted in faster turn-around of the ships carrying urea consignments to the country's ports.

Fertilizer education projects

Most of the fertilizer companies are carrying out agricultural extension work with emphasis on education of farmers in the scientific application of fertilizers out of their own resources. However, Krishak Bharati Cooperative Ltd. (KRIBHCO), Indian Farmers Fertiliser Cooperative Ltd. (IFFCO) and Indian Potash Ltd. (IPL) are also implementing projects with foreign assistance details of which are given below:

Rainfed farming projects (RFP)

KRIBHCO is implementing Rainfed Farming Projects in Western and Eastern India. These projects aim at improving the livelihood of the poor families in the target areas through farming systems development and research., institution building and beneficiary participation for ensuring sustainability and replicability. Both these projects are being implemented in technical and financial collaboration with the Department for International Development (DFID) of the British Government. The Western India project, which was launched originally for 5 years on 1. 1.93, has been extended upto March 1999. Out of the total project cost of Rs.19.05 crore, DFID would fund Rs. 17.5 2 crore and Rs. 1. 5 3 crore will be funded by KRIBHCO. The project is being implemented in the districts of Panch Mahal (Gujarat), Jhabua (Madhya Pradesh) and Banswara (Rajasthan). This project is to be continued by 1.499 in the shape of RFP Phase-II for which the project grant agreement is under discussions. The Eastern India project is for a period of 5 years beginning from 1.4.1995 which has been extended till March 2003. The total project cost is Rs. 38.66 core, out of which Rs.36.41 crore would be funded by DFID and implemented in 12 districts West Bengal, Orissa and Bihar in a phased manner.

Indian Farm forestry Development Cooperative Project (IFFDC)

The project is being implemented by IFFCO since 1.4.1995 in six districts of Uttar Pradesh, Madhya Pradesh and Rajasthan with the help of grants received from Indian Canada Environment Facility (ICEF) from April 1, 1995. The duration of the Project is five years. The main objective of this Project is to improve the productivity of degraded lands for the benefit of rural poor by the application of farm forestry systems through village level cooperative societies and also to reclaim wastelands and marginal agricultural lands. The total projects cost will be Rs. 35 crore out of which Rs.31.5 crore is being contributed by ICEF and Rs. 3.5 crore by IFFCO.

Environment Improvement in Rainfed Areas Project (EIRAP)

Indian Potash Limited (IPL) has been implementing the Project since 1.12.95 in Chhindwara District of Madhya Pradesh and Amravati District of Maharastra. The aim of the project is to conserve, develop and manage natural resources for sustainable improvement in environmental quality through people's participation. The estimated cost on 31.12. 1999 is Rs. 16.70 crore, of which Rs. 14.60 crore is to be funded by ICEF and Rs. 2.10 crore by IPL.

7

Programmes for Minorities

Representation of SCs/STs/OBCs & PHPs in the department

Due care has been exercised during the year under review to implement Government orders regarding recruitment and promotion of candidates belonging to the SCs, STs, OBCs and Physically Handicapped in various group of services in the Department. The representation of these categories in the Department as on 1. 11. 1998 was as under:

Group	Total No. of Posts	SCs	STs	OBCs	PHPs
A	35	6	Nil	Nil	Nil
B	95	14	5	Nil	1
C	113	28	3	2	2
D	59	23	Nil	6	1
Total	302	71	8	8	4

Representation of SCs/STs/OBCs and PHPs in public sector undertakings

The Presidential directives on reservation for the candidates belonging to the Scheduled Castes and Scheduled Tribes which have been issued from time to time by the Department of Public Enterprises, have been implemented in all the PSUs/Cooperatives under the administrative control of the Department.

The Presidential directive regarding reservation for Other Backward Classes (OBCs) in appointments in Public Enterprises has been made applicable w.e.f. 8.9.1993. IFFCO and KRIBHCO, the multi-state Cooperative Societies have adopted the guidelines for OBCs w.e.f. 1.4.1995 and 1. 10. 1995, respectively.

Implementation of these directives was monitored through the Quarterly Review Meetings. 127 SCs, 63 STs, 183 OBCs and 11 Ex-servicemen were recruited, out of a total requirement of 706 persons made during 1998 by the Public Sector Undertakings/Cooperative Societies under the administrative control of this Department.

Besides providing employment, PSUs/Cooperatives have also been advised to prepare and implement special programmes for education of tribals in the scientific use of fertilizers, building up of dealer/retailer network in the tribal areas, and making available fertilizers in small packs in the tribal areas.

Welfare of minorities

The Public Sector Undertakings under the Department have been advised to provide pre-examination coaching to the minority community candidates, wherever feasible, and to take steps to increase the awareness of candidate belonging to the communities about employment opportunities. They have also been advised to include a representative of the minorities in the recruitment/ selection boards to ensure that the minorities get an adequate share in the services and benefit from development schemes.

Reservation in fertilizer dealerships

In 1978, instructions were issued by the Department to all the public sector undertakings under its administrative control to reserve at least 25 percent of dealership of fertilizers for the members of SCs/STs. To ensure availability of a sufficient number of suitable SCs/STs candidates, the following concessions are generally given by the undertakings:

— exemption/relaxation from security deposits;

— preference in supply of fast moving materials;

— higher rate of dealership margin as compared to that allowed to general dealers; and

— free training in handling of fertilizers.

As on 30.6.1998, the share of fertilizer dealership awarded to members belonging to SCs/STs has gone upto 1732 as against of the number of 1605 as on 30.6.1997 reflecting an increase of 7.9%.

The PSUs have also been advised to reserve 10% of fertilizer dealership for ex-servicemen.

8

Information Technology Support to Fertilizer Sector

Integrated Fertilizer MIS [IFMIS] -Background

The Department of Fertilizers (DOF) in collaboration with National Informatics Centre (NIC) has introduced computer-based methods for decision support. The database covers the areas of Production, Imports and Distribution of Fertilizers. An Integrated Fertilizer Management Information system (IFMIS) is under implementation in the Department of Fertilizers. The Integrated Fertilizer Management Information system (IFMIS) with major objective to evolve an evaluation system which would ensure a uniform system of planning and control mechanism with signalling system to highlight deviations from the desired performance indicators by plants and organisations is being executed by NIC.

The project covers Requirement Specifications, Analysis & Design of Database, Application Design, Coding, Testing, Documentation and Implementation. The software development and implementation is in final stage. An amount of Rs. 1.70 crore has been made available to NIC by Department of Fertilizers for setting up of computer and communication infrastructure including application software and training under this project.

Further, with a budget provision of Rs.24 lakhs for the year 1998-99, the computer and communication infrastructure has been maintained/strengthened.

Computer and Communication Infrastructure

DOF has established with the assistance and support of NIC state-of-the-art Information Technology tool viz. Local Area Network (LAN) with Internet capability. This includes operationalisation of LAN at Shastri Bhavan (extended to Krishi Bhavan) with Frequency Time Division Multiple Access Very Small Aperture Terminal (FTDMA VSAT) at Department of Fertilizers.

Radio Frequency Link (RF Link) connectivity has been provided at FICC Office, Sewa Bhavan which is being made use of through Ethernet LAN. Other sites of the Department i.e. Janpath Bhavan and Super Bazar Building have been, provided the dial-up connectivity. Presently, more than 80 interactive terminals and 45 PCs are in use in the Department. Further, intelligent PCs are being provided in a phased manner to work in client server environment for various officials. E-mail services and INTERNET access have been operationalised.

Training

A series of In-house training programmes on UNIX Based Office Productivity Tools were conducted for the Department, of Fertilizers to cover more than 200 officials.

Further, 140 officials have also been trained on File Monitoring System. In addition, Need based Hands-on training on usage of Windows-95, MS-Office and E-mail/ Internet were provided to the concerned officers to make use of 45 client systems installed in the Department. Two training programmes on "Computer Based Office Productivity Tools" conducted during January 18-25, 1999 and February 15-19, 1999 respectively.

Information facilitation counter

The WEB database created in the Department for Public Information and Facilitation Centre (PIFC) is the first step to establish INTERNET in the Government for fertilizer sector as a whole in the country. The setting up of NICNET based Public Information & Facilitation Centre in the Ministry will bring in the complete transparency of government information in the area of fertilizer sector for common man through NICNET which has got its nodes all over the country.

Web site

Fertilizer home page has been created for the Department of Fertilizers and this will be placed at the web site of NIC to enable access for Internet users.

Fertilizer Network - FERTNET

FERTNET, a Close-User-Group on NICNET is meant to serve as a decision support system facilitates information exchange, dissemination and analysis among planners, manufacturers/suppliers, R&D organisations, promoters and grass root level consumers. The existing computer based system/databases/nodes on fertilizer sector would strengthen the proposed IFMIS on FERTNET. FERTNET has been extended to some of the companies by installing FTDMA VSATs at IFFCO, NFL, MFL and GNFC and with Dial-up connectivity to FCI and HFCL. NICNET connectivity to other companies (public/ co-operative/ private) of fertilizer sector will strengthen FERTNET in future.

Information technology strategy

The Expert Group for Computerisation of the Information on Personnel and Citizen Services in its report had recommended, inter-alia, that each Ministry/Department to have a Five Year Plan for Information Technology (IT) with a provision of 2 to 3% of the

Department's budget. Further, Planning Commission has also issued guideline, on the recommendation of the PM's National Task Force on Information Technology & Software Development (IT&SD).

In addition, the recom-mendations of the National Conference on Informatics for Sustainable Agricultural Development (ISDA-95), organised by NIC in collaboration with the Department of Fertilizers, (Ministry of Chemicals and Fertilizers) in May, 1995, were as follows:

IFMIS to be implemented by extending NICNET facilities to other areas/institutions/ non -governmental organisations including private sector fertilizer manufacturers.

IT based Integrated Nutrient Management for Sustainable Agricultural Development to be taken up on higher priority.

The strong fertilizer database on macro/micro level to be built in view of changing agro-scenario environment.

A constant vigil is to be kept on impact of fertilizers on agricultural production by establishing necessary linkages with the National network of Information on Agriculture.

The IT Plan proposal for the Fertilizer Sector has been formulated on the basis of these directives/ recommendations .

Thus, an uniform approach for sectoral IT development will facilitate to promote : (i) Corporate INTRANET & EXTRANET over NICNET, by having state-of-the-art computer communications equipment such as VSAT, for corporate office/production units/ zonal marketing/main regional offices, and connectivity through nearest NICNET centre for regional/area offices, (ii) On-Line Transaction Processing (OUP) through GUI based S/W in client-server environment, specifically, Web-Enabled Application System, (iji) Executive Information System, Model based system and Office automation system, (iv) information sharing for mutual assistance, (v) Training for effective IT, and (vi) Public Information and Facilitation.

9

Performance of Industries

The Pharmaceutical Industry in India today is one of the largest and most advanced among the developing countries. Indian Pharmaceutical Industry manufactures bulk drugs belonging to several major therapeutic groups requiring various manufacturing processes and has developed excellent facilities for production of all dosage forms like tablets, capsules, liquids, orals and injectables etc. This achievement is strengthened by an assurance with regard to quality of the products.

Over the last several years, policy inputs have been directed towards promoting the growth of the industry and in helping it to achieve a broad base in terms of the range of products and technologies needed to produce them from as basic a stage as possible. The results have been very encouraging. As on date, there are about 250 large units and about 8000 small scale units in operation which form the core of the industry (including 5 Central Public Sector Units).

These units produce the complete range of formulations i.e. medicines ready for consumption by patients and about 350 bulk drugs i.e. chemicals having therapeutic value and used for production of formulations. Today, India is in a position to meet 70% of the country's requirement of bulk drugs and almost all the demands for formulations.

The setting up of Pencillin factory at Pimpri, Pune in the early 1950's and the construction of Indian Drugs & Pharmaceutical Ltd. (IDPL) plants at Rishikesh and Hyderabad in 1960's are important milestones in the history of the pharmaceutical industry in the country and public sector investment in the pharmaceutical industry in the initial stages played the role of a catalyst in the development of the industry over the last three decades.

Production

The following table shows the value of production of bulk drugs and formulations from 1989-90 to 1997-98.

(Rs. in Crores)

Year	Bulk drugs	Formulations
1989-90	640.0	3420.00
1990-91	730.00	3840.00
1991-92	900.00	4800.00
1992-93	1150.00	6000.00
1993-94	1320.00	6900.00
1994-95	1518.00	7935.00
1995-96	1822.00	9125.00
1996-97	2186.00	10494.00
1997-98	2623.00	12068.00

Above data shows that the Drugs and Pharmaceuticals sector has continued to maintain steady growth in terms of production.

During 1998-99 several proposals for foreign collaboration for joint ventures, research and developments, establishing new undertakings/expansion of existing units (manufacture of new articles in the existing units) have been received.

Following delicensing of the pharmaceutical industry, a number of IEMs for manufacture of various bulk drugs/drug intermediates/ formulations were received.

The major items covered in IEM include various bulk drugs, intravenous fluids, formulations etc. During the period ending October, 98, 67 IEMs were filed by pharmaceutical companies for various bulk drugs formulations and intermediates.

These IEMs would generate employment to approximately 10178 people and there would be an investment of approximately Rs. 352 crores on these projects. During the same period, foreign investment proposals worth approximately Rs. 443.32 crores were approved.

Exports

From a meagre Rs. 46 crores worth of pharmaceutical exports in 1980-81, the exports have risen to over Rs. 4978.00 crores during 1997-98. The details of the exports (excluding Castor Oil) Bulk Drugs.

During April 1997- March 1998, total exports (excluding Castor Oil) amounted to Rs. 4978.00 crores which was 21.70% higher than the performance during 1996-97.

The export of formulation was of the order of Rs. 2805 crores which is an increase of 11.78% over the achievement during the previous year. In the case of bulk drugs the exports were of the order of Rs.2173.00 crores—an increase of about 37.44% over the last year.

Imports

In accordance with the information available from DGHS imports of bulk drugs and formulations for the last five years have been as under:

(Rs. in Crores)

Year Formulations	Finished drugs	Bulk	Total
1	2	3	4
1988-89	157.29	242.87	400.00
1989-90	314.20	350.50	664.770
1990-91	371.40	413.40	784.80
1991-92	508.70	722.60	1231.10
1992-93	553.70	856.60	1410.30
1	2	3	4
1993-94	771.80	1029.60	1801.40
1994-95	924.00	1260.70	2184.70
1995-96	1239.00	1098.00	2337.00
1996-97	2509.20	1581.00	4090.30
1997-98	2805.00	21773.00	4978.00

During the first 5 months of 1998-99 also, the export performance has been encouraging:

April '98/ '98	Exports April '97/ Aug '97	Exports Change (1/2)	Percentage A u g
Bulk Drugs	1056.00	691.40	
Finished Formulations	1341.50	1092.50	
Total	2397.50	1793.90	(+)34.4

(*Source: CHEMEXCIL*)

There have been no reports of shortage in recent years. As already indicated, the country is almost self-sufficient in case of formulations required by the consumers. It may also be mentioned that Industrial licensing has been done away with. The manufacturers are free to produce any drug duly approved by the Drug Control Authority except for a few items reserved for Public Sector Units.

Additionally almost all drugs are allowed to be imported under Open General Licence. In view of these steps no shortage of medicines is likely to occur. Imports can take place from any part of the world-there being no general restrictions.

Value of imports (Rs. in crores)

Year Formulations	Finished drugs	Bulk	Total
1993-94	612.74	138.33	751.07
1994-95	811.43	173.02	985.45
1995-96	1630.00	270.00	1900.00
1996-97	1705.00	345.00	2050.00
1997-98	1827.00	430.00	2257.00

(Source: DGHS)

Requirement of pharmaceuticals during ninth plan

The Working Group on Drugs and Pharmaceutual for the Ninth Five Year plan period (1997-98 to 2001-2002) has worked out future growth rate as follows:

a) Growth rate for domestic consumption of formulations as 15%

b) Growth rate for exports of formulations as 10%

c) Growth rate for exports of bulk drugs as 20%

d) Growth rate for bulk drug production as 20%

e) Imports of bulk drugs (CIF value) be restricted to 12% of the total value of bulk drug requirement

f) Growth for the total bulk drug requirement for exports and form formulation activity (for both domestic consumption and exports) as 16%

g) The ratio of value of consumption of bulk drugs for production of formulations to the value of formulations produced as 1:4.

It may be stated that no country can become entirely self-sufficient in case of pharmaceuticals. Therefore, imports are expected to continue even with the advanced level of technological inputs.

Import of a drug would be dependent upon a variety of factors like incidence of disease for which it is used, feasibility of its production in the country or, if already being produced, status of its current indigenous production, availability of alternate/ equivalent drugs, international price vis-a-vis price of indigenous produce, tariff rates, import policy etc.

Research and development

A new programme for promoting R&D in Drugs and Pharmaceuticals Sector has been initiated by the Department of Science and Technology (DST). A two tier structure has been set up by DST to manage the programme viz. an Apex Executive Committee at the Secretariat level, chaired by Secretary, DST and an Expert Committee at the operational level. To be globally viable in R&D, high level expertise and adequate human resources as also modern facilities in specified areas of drug developments are required.

It was therefore, decided that the DST programme, besides new drugs development projects, should also support creation of facilities that were essential for new drugs development. Accordingly, facilities that were needed urgently and that would need to be created namely (a) DHA gyrase screening facility; (b) Quantity

Structure-Activity-Relationship (QSAR) facility; (c) Immunomodulators modelling and screening and (d) Pharmacological testing were identified.

Under the said programme 21 proposals have so far been cleared. There is a proposal to set up an R&D Cell in the Department of Chemicals and Petrochemicals. A budgetary provision of Rs. 20 lakhs has been made for the year 1998-99.

National pharmaceutical pricing authority (NPPA)

As per the Resolution, the National Pharmaceutical Pricing Authority (NPPA) was established on 29.08.1998 and is now fully functional. With a view to enforcing the provisions of the Drugs (prices control) Order (DPCO) and to perform the functions assigned, upto 15.11.1998 the following actions/steps have been taken by NPPA since its inception:

(i) Revised/fixed the prices of 12 bulk drugs and 635 formulation packs.

(ii) NPPA vide its Order published in the Gazette of India; Extraordinary dated 27th January 1998, has asked the manufacturers of all the scheduled formulation pack sizes to work out the prices of different pack sizes of tablets and capsules of the same strength or composition packed in different strips or blisters on pro-rata basis of the latest ceiling price fixed. This was done to ensure that (i) the manufacturers do not change their pack sizes in a bid to remain out of price control and (ii) manufacturers are not forced to approach the government/NPPA frequently for price approvals for different pack sizes.

(iii) Compiled the data on production and imports of bulk drugs for the year 1997-98.

(iv) Analysed price movement between 1994 and April, 1998.

(v) Fixed the prices of three commonly used IV Fluids by exercising the powers available under para 10 (b) of DPCO 1995. These prices are lower by about 40% than the prices charged earlier by the companies from the consumers.

(vi) To keep a check on the prices of drugs, besides advising the state government to enforce the prices of scheduled formulations, NPPA held a meeting at New Delhi with the State Drug Controllers of Karnataka, Andhra Pradesh, Gujarat, Delhi, Tamilnadu and Maharashtra. Another meeting was held in October '90 at Mohali, Chandigarh with the State Drug Controllers of Haryana, Punjab, Himachal Pradesh, Jammu & Kashmir, Rajasthan and Union Territory of Chandigarh.

Field visits to Calcutta, Lucknow, Chandigarh and Jaipur were undertaken during the year in connection with monitoring and enforcement of DPCO, 1995 and meetings were held with the Principal Secretaries of Health, Uttar Pradesh, Himachal Pradesh and Special Secretary (Health) Rajasthan.

(vii) NPPA advised the States and Union Territories to nominate/set up nodal officers/monitoring cells to enforce/ monitor the prices and availability of medicines. Accordingly, so far, in the states of Rajasthan, UP, Karnataka, Andhra Pradesh, Gujarat, Madhya Pradesh and Sikkim nodal officers/cells have already been nominated/ set up.

(viii) An expert committee has been set up in NPPA to review the norms of conversion cost (CC), packing charges (PC) and process loss (PL).

(ix) Overcharging cases were pursued vigorously by NPPA and as a result, to begin with, the concerned companies agreed to deposit an amount of Rs. 2.55 crores in the court/ government.

Rifampicin policy

Rifampicin is an important anti-TB drug. India is a major consumer of this drug. Its manufacturing technology is difficult and guarded. Till 1991-92, this drug was manufactured in India exclusively from imported 3-FRSV and later from imported Rifamycin-S (Rifa-S) a stage previous to 3-FRSV. From 1991-92, M/s. Gujarat Themis Biosyn Ltd (GTBL), Vapi commenced production of Rifa-S from the basic stage of fermentation.

M/s. Lupin Chemicals Ltd. followed suit in 1992-93 at their plant in Tarapur, Maharashtra. Towards the end of 1996-97 M/s. Ciba-CKD has commenced production of Rifampicin from basic stage. At present GTBL is converting Rifa-S into 3 FRSV and thereafter produces Rifampicin whereas Lupin is converting Rifa-S into Rifampicin directly.

Since the indigenously produced Rifampicin and Rifampicin intermediates were not sufficient to meet the requirements, it becomes necessary to frame Rifampicin Policy every year to regulate the import and to protect indigenous manufacturers after taking into account the demand and supply in the previous year, the estimated production as well as the country's demand for the current year.

After taking into account the demand and supply of Rifampicin intermediates, a Policy was taken on 13-8-96 intimating that no import will be allowed for Rifa-S against indigenous lifting. All the consumers are permitted to lift their requirement from the indigenous producers. This policy continues presently.

Pen. G policy

Pencillins are Betalacturn antibiotics, produced by the growth of various Pencillin species of moulds. Potassium Pencillin G First Crystals (Pen.G) are indigenously produced by fermentation process and then converted to injectable grade pencillins, namely, Sodium Pencillin G IP Procine Pencillin G IP and Benzathine Pencillin G IP.

Since the indigenously produced Pencillin G (Pen.G) was not sufficient to meet the country's requirement it became necessary to frame a Pen. G policy every year to regulate the import and also for allocation of indigenous material, after taking into account the demand and supply in the previous year, the estimated production as well as the country's demand for the current year.

Till November, 1986, manufacture of Pencillin was reserved for public sector in accordance with the provisions of the Drug Policy, 1979, alongwith two private sector units at that time were also engaged in its production in the country.

However, in 1988 it was decided to d-resesrve the item considering the fact that fresh investments on a large scale would be required to meet future demands of Pen-G for the manufacture of semisynthetic Pencillins. Presently, the following units are engaged in the manufacture of Pen. G :-

- M/s. Indian Drugs and Pharmaceuticals Ltd. (A Public Sector Undertaking)
- M/s. Hindustan Max- GB Limited
- M/s. Alembic Chemicals Works Company Limited
- M/s. J.K. Pharmachem Limited
- M/s. SPIC Pharmaceuticals Limited
- M/s. Torrent Gujarat Biotech Limited

All pencillins are included in the Negative List Imports under the existing Export- Import Policy. In order to support the indigenous basic stage manufacturers of Pencillin G and to keep the imports to the barest minimum, a policy for regulating imports has been in operation for quite some time and this is referred to as the Pen. G Policy which is framed for every financial year.

Keeping in view the demand and supply of Pen. G. a policy decision was taken on 13.8.96 that the allocation of Pen. G has totally been done away with. The convertors can lift Pen. G as per their requirement from any of the indigenous manufacturers. This policy continues to operate presently.

Export promotion cell

An Export Promotion Cell in the Pharmaceutical Division has been created with the objective of boosting pharmaceutical exports and to act as a nodal centre for all queries/issues regarding pharma exports.

The Cell also undertakes promotional activities for acceleration of pharma exports and consider suggestions for modifications in EXIM policy from the Industry. In order to give adequate attention to day-to-day problems faced by the exporters, the cell interacts with various Ministries/Departments and Indian Missions abroad.

The cell collects statistical data on export and import of pharmaceuticals in the country and provides commercially useful information for developing and increasing drugs and pharmaceutical exports.

The cell has also been entrusted with the organisation of seminars and workshops on standards, quality control requirements etc. of important countries so as to prepare the domestic companies for exporting their products.

Drugs prices equalisation accounts (DPEA)

The Department has referred 72 important assessment cases involving an amount of Rs. 220 crores to the Drug Prices Liabilities Review Committee (DPLRC). The Committee has already furnished its recommendations in 24 cases involving liability of Rs. 90 crores to the Department.

The Department is taking further action on the recommendations of the DPLRC to recover the amount. However, some companies have again gone to the Court. The Committee has put into motion the process of hearing in all other cases by issuing notices to them.

The Committee is giving adequate opportunity to the parties to present their point of view and after hearing, it is giving its recommendations in individual cases to the Department. Till date, an amount of Rs. 22.50 crores has been deposited into the Drug Prices Equalisation Account by the Pharmaceutical companies. The tenure of the DPLRC has been extended upto June, 1999.

Chemicals, Pesticides and Allied Industries

A large number of chemicals are manufactured in the country and the country is mostly self-sufficient in meeting the demands. The industry has maintained a steady growth.

The chemical industry is highly heterogenous encompassing many sectors like organic, inorganic chemicals, dyestuffs, paints, pesticides, speciality chemicals, etc. Some of the prominent individual chemical industry sectors are caustic soda, soda ash, carbon black, phenol, acetic acid, methanol and azo dyes. Industrial licensing has been done away with for all products except a small list of hazardous chemicals as a part of liberalisation of industrial policy.

Entrepreneurs are now free to set up chemical industries by following the Industrial Entrepreneurs' Memorandum (IEM) route. The liberalisation policy of the Government 'is committed to the globalisation of the economy in which all inputs including those from the chemical sector are to be made available to consumer at international prices.

In order to achieve this objective, a gradual process of reducing customs duties on chemical products has been initiated and the earlier policy of ensuring that indigenisation be achieved in as many sectors as possible is no longer imperative. Tariff levels have been reduced substantially after the announcement of the liberalisation policy. Majority of the chemical items can now be freely imported or exported through simplified procedures.

The main thrust in the chemical sector is modernisation so as to improve the efficiency by lowering operating costs. This is all the more so as rapid technological obsolescence is one of the prominent features of the chemical industry. With the liberalised policy of the Government, it is expected that closely held technologies in certain specific areas of Hydrogen Peroxide, Citric Acid, Titanium Dioxide, MDI and TDI would now be available.

Some of the significant factors that have helped in the growth and development of chemical sector in India are (1) technically trained manpower, (2) priority to invest in the inputs for the agricultural sector resulting in investment in the basic chemicals required for the manufacture of fertilizers and pesticides, (3) importance of textiles and leather industry which has encouraged production of chemicals required for dyestuffs, finishing of fabric and production of high quality leather, (4) abundance of salt along the long coast line, facilitating manufacture of caustic soda and soda ash.

Safety, health and environment protection are the key concerns for the chemicals industry. Alongwith modernisation to improve the operating efficiency of the plants and energy conservation, safety in operations, health of the workers engaged in the processing industry as well as environment concerns are the prime need of the hour.

Management of toxic chemicals is also receiving increasing attention. In the manufacture of caustic soda, more and more units are shifting to the membrane cell technology from the conventional mercury diaphragm technology. Over 55% of the total installed capacity in caustic soda manufacture is now based on the membrane cell technology which is a much cleaner technology.

The pesticide industry has developed substantially, contributing significantly towards India's agriculture and health. In agro chemical sector, high volume low priced pesticides are being substituted by low volume high priced pesticides.

Besides, use of natural pesticides, use of bio-pesticides is gradually picking up in the country. To utilise the idle capacity available with the pesticides units, the country has entered the competitive field of export of pesticides.

The country has started producing some new pesticides, but the manufacturers are continuing to import their intermediates in the absence of technology for producing them.

Efforts are being made to acquire the right technology to manufacture intermediates for pesticides. The growth in dyestuff industry has also been noteworthy. Dyes and dye intermediates offer immense possibilities for exports from India in view of their international quality and competitive prices.

Production performance of some of the important chemicals including pesticides and dyestuffs are given below:

Item	Installed capacity (In '000 tonnes)	Production '000 tonees 1995-96	1996-97	1997-98 (Provisional)
Soda Ash	1904.6	1522.1	1563.5	1545.8
Caustic Soda	1878.5	1243.1	1246.5	1303.6
CCarbon Black	286.2	223.6	248.4	250.0
Calcium Carbide	150.0	85.3	90.6	85.0
Phenol	66.6	63.7	57.4	69.3
Methanol	386.0	350.2	373.1	394.0
Tech. Pesticides	109.2	96.5	94.4	82.5
Dyestuffs	55.2	31.2	377.4	40.6

Export of chemicals

There has been a steady growth in the exports of chemicals during the last three years. Export achievements of chemicals for the last three years are mentioned hereunder.

(Rs. in crores)

	1995-96	1996-97	1997-98
1. Dyes & Dye Intermediates	1545.8	1944.8	2228.0
2. Basic Organic & Inorganic chemicals including Agro-chemicals	2025.6	2081.5	2195.0

Chemical weapons convention

India is one of the original State Parties to the Convention on the Prohibition of the Development, Production, Stockpiling and Use of Chemical Weapons and on their Destruction (Chemical Weapons

Convention) which concluded in 1993. The convention has entered into force on 29th April, 1997. The convention is being implemented by the Organisation for the Prohibition of Chemical Weapons (OPCW) established in the Hague.

As National Implementation measures and in order to fulfill its obligations under the Convention, each State Party has to designate or establish a National Authority to serve as the National focal point for effective liaison with the organisation and other State Parties. In India the National Authority has already been established. The Chemical Weapons Convention is a multilateral, non-discriminatory, universal, disarmament treaty which prohibits development, acquisition, retention, stockpiling, transfer and use of chemical weapons.

The Treaty does not discriminate between the chemical weapons possessor states and the non-possessor states. The Treaty requires each State Party to destroy within a specified time frame the chemical weapons and chemical weapons production facilities it possesses, as well as any chemical weapons it may have abandoned on another State's Territory.

State parties are not to use riot control agents as method of warfare, not to engage in military preparations for use of chemical weapons and not to assist or encourage others to engage in any of the prescribed activities. The Convention will be verified through a combination of reporting requirements, routine on site inspection of declared sites and short notice challenge inspections.

The verification provisions of the Convention will affect the civilian chemical industry through certain restrictions and obligations regarding the production, processing, consumption and trade of chemicals that are considered relevant to the objectives of the Convention.

In the past few years, there has been a very healthy growth of chemical industry in India and there have been substantial exports of pharmaceuticals, dyes and pesticides.

The Indian chemical industry is highly developed encompassing many sectors like organic and inorganic chemicals, plastics, fibres, fertilizers, dyestuffs, paints, speciality chemicals, drugs and pharmaceuticals etc. As a result of innovative low cost technologies evolved by the chemical industry, India is increasingly becoming internationally competitive in this sector.

It has to be, therefore, ensured that the momentum of growth of the chemical industry and particularly its exports do not receive a setback on account of any non-fulfilment of the obligations under the Chemical Weapons Convention.

The Chemical Weapons Convention stipulates verification procedures including surprise (Challenge) verification which could adversely affect the trade and exports of chemicals in India if we lack in the implementation. It is, therefore, essential that all requirements with reference to various obligations are fulfilled in time.

The Convention stipulates submission of annual declarations not later than 90 days after the beginning of each following calendar year. Substantial changes in declarations are also required to be reported during the year. The annual declarations for the year 1997 have already been made by the country to fulfil its obligations.

The Department of Chemicals and Petrochemicals has taken a number of measures to ensure that the Indian Industry is sensitised with the requirements of the Chemical Weapons Convention so that they are fully prepared to fulfil their obligations. The Department is making all efforts to ensure that the growth of the chemical industry is not adversely affected while fulfilling the obligations of the Convention. Seminars, Workshops, meetings and discussions are organised for this purpose. Trial inspections are also carried out on the industrial units which are engaged in the production and manufacturing of chemicals relating to the Convention.

Petrochemicals industry

Indian Petrochemicals industry has made rapid strides in terms of production and consumption. Production of major petrochemicals (excluding fibre intermediates) increased from 2605 KTs in 96-97 to 3562 KTs in 97-98 registering an increase of 37% vis-a-vis 13% in the previous year. Consumption of major petrochemicals also increased from 3292 KTs in 96-97 to 3834 KTs in 97-98 registering an increase of 16%. Viewed in the backdrop of general economic slowdown and adverse impact of crisis in South East/East Asian countries on domestic petrochemical sector, above growth figures assume added significance. The country is poised towards increasing self reliance and reduction in import dependency in this sector. In the Table given below are production and consumption of major petrochemicals :-

(Figures in KT)

Category	1996-97		1997-98		1998-99 (Est.)
	Prodn.	Consp.	Prodn.	Consp.	Prodn.
Syn. Fibres	979	1026	1246	1237	1350
Polymers	1351	1952	2016	2256	2200
Syn. Rubber	52	97	62	106	65
Synthetic Detergents	223	217	238	235	240
Total	2605	3292	3562	3834	3855

To remain competitive, in the wake of lowering of tariff barriers, the petrochemical industry is adopting state of the art technologies and are producing quality petrochemical products of the international standards. The exports of about 225 KT of petrochemical products in the year 1997-98 bear testimony to the quality standards of domestic petrochemicals industry.

With the initiation of liberalisation process, the economy is growing at a rapid pace, therefore, demand of petrochemicals are expected to grow significantly in the future. To meet the growing demand massive investments are underway.

Two gas based crackers of IPCL & GAIL, each with installed capacity of 3 lakh tons of ethylene, is expected to be commissioned in 199899, which will result in significant increase in production of polymers. To meet the fast growing demand of petrochemicals, the Government has sanctioned several mega petrochemical complexes, details of which are given below.

Olefinic complexes

Auraiya gas cracker complex

This project with a capacity of 3 lakh TPA of Ethylene and downstream products is being implemented by the Gas Authority of India (GAIL) at Auraiya in U.P. The cracker is expected to be commissioned in 1998-99.

Gandhar cracker complex

This project with a capacity of 3 lakh TPA of Ethylene and downstream products is being implemented by IPCL at Gandhar, Gujarat. The cracker is expected to be commissioned in 1998-99.

Haldia petrochemicals complex

This project will be implemented by Haldia Petrochemicals Ltd. in joint sector with West Bengal

Industrial Development Corporation (WBIDC) to manufacture 4.2 lakh TPA of Ethylene and other downstream products, The cracker is expected to be commissioned in 1999-2000.

Nocil cracker project

NOCIL has been permitted to expand its capacity of the existing cracker from 63,000 TPA to 3 lakh TPA of ethylene at Thane-Belapur Road, Maharashtra and also several downstream products.

Assam gas cracker project

Assam Industrial Development Corporation (AIDC) has been granted letter of intent for a cracker complex to be set up in Assam having a capacity of 3 lakh TPA of ethylene. The project is being implemented by M/s Reliance Assam Petrochemicals Ltd., (RAPL) a joint venture of M/s Reliance Industries Ltd., (RIL) and AIDC.

The project is proposed to be located at Tengaghat in Dibrugarh District of Assam. Keeping in view the inherent difficulties such as prolonged rainy season resulting in less effective working time, difficult geographical terrain, higher cost of transportation etc., the central Government has approved onetime capital subsidy of Rs. 377 crores for the Assam Cracker project. In addition, a provision of supply of gas at Rs. 600 per thousand standard cubic meter for a period of 15 years has been made.

Punjab cracker project

The Punjab State Industrial Investment and Development Corpn. Ltd. (PSIIDC) has been given letter of intent for setting up a Naphtha cracker project at Payal, Punjab with a capacity of 3 lakh TPA of ethylene.

Mangalore cracker project

The Karnataka State Industrial Investment and

Development Corpn. Ltd. (KSIIDC) has been given letter of intent for setting up a Naphtha cracker project at Mangalore, Karnataka with a capacity of 3 lakh TPA of ethylene.

Jamnagar cracker project

RIL has been issued a letter of intent for setting up a Naphtha cracker having capacity of 8 lakh TPA of ethylene at Jamnagar in Gujarat.

MPSIDC

The Madhya Pradesh State Industrial Development Corporation (MPSIDC) have been issued a letter of intent for setting up a Naphtha cracker project with a capacity of 3 lakh TPA of ethylene.

TIDCO

The Tamil Nadu Industrial Development Corporation have been issued a letter of intent for setting up a Naphtha cracker project with a capacity of 3.5 lakh TPA of ethylene at Cuddalore in Tamil Nadu.

KSIDC

The Kerala State Industrial Development Corporation have been issued a letter of intent for setting up a Naphtha cracker project with a capacity of 5 lakh TPA of ethylene in Kasargod in Kerala.

The Petrochemical Sector is greatly constrained in attaining higher growth rates due to inadequate infrastructure. Improvement in port facilities for handling and storage of feedstocks, intermediates etc. will give desired impetus to this sector.

High rate of import duties on capital goods and high rates of local levies are also inhibiting growth of petrochemical sector in the country.

Aromatic complxes

	Project (000 tpa)	P-Xylene capcity
i)	Assam Industrial Dev. Corp. Ltd., Assam	152
ii)	ATV Petrochemicals Ltd., Mathura, U.P.	100
iii)	Bongaigaon Refinery & Petrochemicals Ltd., Bongaigaon, Assam. (after expansion)	102
iv)	Chemplast Sanmar Aromatics Ltd., Tamil Nadu	250
v)	Grasim Industries Ltd., Mangalore, Karnataka	250
vi)	J.K. Aromatics, Dahej, Bharuch, Gujarat	140
vii)	Indian Oil Corp. Ltd., Panipet, Haryana	300
viii)	Modern Petrochemical, Vagra, Bharuch, Gujarat	200
ix)	Mardia Chemicals Ltd., Dahej, Bharuch, Gujarat	78
x)	Reliance Industries Ltd., Jamnagar Gujarat	1400
xi)	SPIC, Manali, Tamil Nadu	200
xii)	NAPCO, Manali, Tamil Nadu	170

The Jute Packaging Materials (compulsory use in packaging commodities) Act, 1987, envisages compulsory packing of entire production of foodgrains and sugar and 20% urea in jute bags.

The above Act is stifling growth of plastic woven sacks industry. With the increase in consumption of plastics in the country, plastic waste generation is bound to increase in the coming years. This Department is actively cooperating with other agencies and trying to device strategy for management of plastic waste.

10

Bhopal Gas Leak Disaster

Bhopal Gas Leak Disaster

Following the leakage of the lethal gas known as Methyl Iso-Cyanate (MIC) stored in the storage tanks of Union Carbide factory at Bhopal, causing death and injury to a large number of people of the Bhopal city, various relief and rehabilitation measures were undertaken by the state and the central Government.

Action plan for the rehabilitation of Bhopal gas victims

The Central government had provided financial assistance to the extent of Rs. 102 crores over a period of 4 years from 1985 for rehabilitation work. Subsequently, an Action Plan with an outlay of Rs. 163.10 crores was approved by the Central Government for medical, economic, social and environmental rehabilitation of the victims.

The major component of the Action plan was the medical rehabilitation which, inter-alia, included addition of 785 bed-capacity by constructing 5 new hospitals. On the expiry of the Action plan on 31.3.95. and at the request of the state Government, the period of the Action plan was extended in stages upto 31.3.97 and the outlay was enhanced to Rs. 188.50 crores to enable completion of the works programmes. A review of the implementation of the Action Plan was undertaken in July, 97 which revealed that many of the rehabilitation schemes were still incomplete. In order to ensure that all the schemes under the Action Plan are physically completed, it was decided, in consultation with the Government of Madhya Pradesh, to further extend the period of the Action plan upto 30.9.98. and also to increase the outlay by Rs. 69.50 crores.

With this revised outlay, the total funds earmaked for the Action plan amounts to Rs. 258 crores. It has been decided that for subsequent maintenance and recurring expenditure in respect of all the schemes under the Action Plan, the State Government would make appropriate provision in their Annual plan. The Central Government stands committed to meet its share of 75% of the outlay.

Speciality Hospital at Bhopal

The Supreme Court, vide its Order 3.10.1991, directed that the Union Carbide Corporation (UCC) should fund the construction, equipping and functioning of a hospital for the Bhopal Gas victims for a period of eight years. The company agreed to do so if they were allowed to raise funds by sale of Union carbide India Limited (UCIL)'s shares held by them which were attached by the trial court in the criminal case against the company.

Acceding to the request, the Supreme Court directed the sale of shares and released Rs. 65 crores from the proceeds thereof to the company for the purpose. The Government of India made available Rs. 57 crores which were recovered as capital gains tax on the sale of company shares (Rs. 53.5 crores) and the dividend (Rs. 3.5 crores) on the shares under attachment.

The State Government made available 52.34 acres of land (free of cost) and subseqently made available additional 28.45 acres of private land. The Supreme Court, in April 1996, released a further amount of Rs. 187 crores plus interest, from the attached amount, for setting up of additional facilities viz: Cardio Thoracic Surgery Unit, Research-Cum-Teaching Centre and setting up of upto 10 Mini Units.

The Hospital will have 300 beds. As per the directions of the Supreme Court, a new Trust, named the 'Bhopal Memorial Hospital Trust' has been set up under the chairmanship of retd. Chief Justice Mr. A.M. Ahmadi in August' 98 to oversee the construction, equipping and management of the speciality hospital.

The Trust held its first meeting on 12th August, 1998. The funds of the Bhopal Hospital Trust, London, stand transferred to the new Trust as per directions of the Supreme Court.

Adjudication of Compensation claims

The process of adjudication of claims for payment of compensation to the victims of the disaster commenced in February '92. The actual disbursement of the money could be started only in October '92 when the compensation amount which had been deposited by the Union Carbide India Ltd with the Reserve Bank of India under the orders of the supreme court was transferred to the Welfare Commissioner adjudicating the claims.

To give an opportunity to those persons who may not have filed their claims even during the five years period that was allowed for filing of claim applications, a notification under section 4(l) of the Bhopal Gas Leak Disaster (Registration and Processing of claims) Scheme, 1985 was issued on 2nd December, 1996.

The total number of claims including those filed in response to notification dated 2.12.96 is 10,26,767. It is expected that all the claims filed will disposed of by the year 2000. The position of adjudication of compensation claims as on 31.12.98 is as follows:

Category Registered	Cases	Decided Awarded	No. of Pending Cases Cases	No. of amount Awarded	Total amount ed (Rs. in crores)	Total Disbursed (Rs. in crores)
Injury	1001723	714047	383172	287675	1013.36	920.61
Loss of livestock	658	536	210	122	0.09	0.06
Loss of property, means of livelihood, business etc.	4901	4,467	388	434	0.09	0.05
Death	22149	16854	12083	5295	78.15	75.57

11

Public Sector Performance

Drugs and Pharmaceuticals

There are five Central Public Sector Undertakings and six Joint Sector Undertakings in the Pharmaceutical Industry Sector under the administrative control of the Department of Chemicals and Petrochemicals. Besides this, there are two wholly owned subsidiaries and a registered Society. The brief profile of these organisations is in the subsequent paragraphs.

Indian drugs and pharmaceuticals ltd. (IDPL)

Indian Drugs and Pharmaceuticals Limited (IDPL) was incorporated on 5th April, 1961 with the primary objective of creating self sufficiency in essential life saving drugs and medicines. The company has presently three manufacturing plants: one each at Rishikesh in Uttar Pradesh, Hyderabad in Andhra Pradesh and Gurgaon in Haryana.

IDPL has two wholly owned subsidiaries, namely, IDPL (Tamil Nadu) Ltd. Chennai in Tamil Nadu and Bihar Drugs and Organic Chemicals Ltd. at Muzaffarpur, Bihar. In addition, IDPL has three Joint Sector undertakings, promoted in collaboration with the respective State Pharmaceuticals Ltd. (RDPL), Uttar Pradesh Drugs and Pharmaceuticals Ltd. (UPDPL), Orissa Drugs and Chemicals Ltd. (ODCL) Bhubaneshwar.

IDPL was formally declared sick by the Board for Industrial and Financial Reconstruction (BIFR) on the 12th August, 1992. On sustained efforts, a revival package for the company was formulated and the package was approved by BIFR on the 10th February, 1994. The revival period was ten years beginning from 1994-95.

The cost of the scheme was Rs. 155.10 crores over a period of 4 years beginning from 1993-94 excluding the value of the sacrifices of the Government of India in terms of capital restructuring from 1.4.1993. Additional financial assistance of Rs. 119.24 crore was envisaged in the scheme from the promoters in three years from 199394 to 1995-96. As against this, the Government had actually released a sum of Rs. 140.31 crores.

IDPL could not achieve the targetted levels of production, sales and profitability in the year 1994-95, the first year of the revival operations. Consequently, the company suggested the modifications in the package. The modifications, inter alia, envisaged additional financial assistance of Rs. 98 crores from the Government.

The Government, therefore, decided to approach the BIFR for a techno economic analysis of the modifications proposed before any commitment about additional financial assistance was given. The BIFR, on the basis of the performance reports of IDPL upto September, 1995 and the stand of the government with regard to the modifications proposed, passed orders under section 17(3) of the SICA, 1985 appointing the IDBI Mumbai as the operating agency for a techno economic viability study for long term rehabilitation measures for IDPL.

The report of the Operating Agency indicated that it would not be possible to prepare a viable and acceptable rehabilitation plan for IDPL. The Government had, thereafter been considering various options with regard to the future of IDPL.

IDPL was advised to submit revised rehabilitation proposal as a whole and unitwise with a cut-off date as on 30.9.98 and 31.12.98 respectively. As per the latest Rehabilitation proposal submitted by IDPL computed as on 30.9.98, the total cost is Rs. 2034.12 crore including Rs. 48.01 crore towards capital expenditure, direct cash financial assistance of Rs. 646.96 crore with the component of sacrifices being Rs. 696.97 crore and write off of Rs. 674.68 crore. A view of the Government is yet to be taken.

The operations of IDPL are closed except marginal production in some of the units. The wage and salaries of the employees and workers of the company are being paid from the non-plan Assistance released from time to time by the Government.

Hindustan antibiotics Ltd. (HAL)

Hindustan Antibiotics Ltd. (HAL), Pimpri, Pune was incorporated on the 30th March, 1954. This was the first public sector company in drugs and pharmaceuticals. HAL has its plant located at Pimpri. There are three joint sector units promoted by HAL in collaboration with the respective state Governments.

These are Karnataka Antibiotics & Pharmaceuticals Ltd. (KAPL), Bangalore in Karnataka, Maharashtra Antibiotics & Pharmaceuticals Ltd. (MAPL) at Nagpur in Maharashtra and Manipur State Drugs & Pharmaceuticals Ltd. (MSDPL) at IMPHAL in Manipur.

The main products of HAL are bulk drug Penicillin-G, various salts of Penicillin and Streptomycin. The company produces a wide range of pharmaceutical formulations including agro-vet products. HAL has been incurring losses since 1993-94. The company was referred to the BIFR in January, 1994. The BIFR declared the company as formally sick on 31.3.1997. The BIFR has appointed the Industrial Development Bank of India (IDBI), Mumbai as the Operating Agency for a techno economic viability study and report. The BIFR also simultaneously directed the existing management/ promoters to submit their long term revival proposals.

The rehabilitation proposal prepared by HAL was submitted to the Operating Agency in June 1997. The Operating Agency has submitted its report to the Government. A view of the Government in regard to funding and sacrifices is yet to be taken.

Bengal chemicals and pharmaceuticals ltd. (BCPL)

This was a sick company in the private sector in the name and style of Bengal Chemicals and Pharmaceuticals Works. The management of the company was taken over by the Central Government with effect from 15th Dec., 1977. It was nationalised from the 15th Dec., 1980. A new public sector company in the name and style of Bengal Chemicals & Pharmaceuticals Ltd. (BCPL) was incorporated on 17th March, 1981.

The company has four manufacturing units one each at Maniktala and Panihati at Calcutta (West Bengal) one at Mumbai (Maharashtra) and the fourth one at Kanpur (UP). The company manufactures and markets a wide range of industrial chemicals Sulphuric Acid, Ferric Alum, a large number of drugs and pharmaceuticals besides Cosmetics and Home products. In the home products, the well known products are Cantharidine Hair Oil and Lamp Brand Phenol.

The company was formally declared sick by the Board for Industrial and Financial Reconstruction (BIFR) on the 14th January, 1993. A revival package on the basis of the report of the Industrial Reconstruction Bank of India (IRBI), (now Industrial Investment Bank of India (11131), Calcutta), an Operating Agency appointed by the BIFR and the support extended by the Government of the India, was approved by the BIFR on the 4th April, 1995.

The revival period was for ten years beginning from 1994-95. The company could achieve a consistent growth of about 20% in the years 1994-95 to 1996-97. The net losses per annum have also come down significantly. The Company could finalise the sale of surplus land of 8 acres to the Coast Guard Organisation of the Ministry of Defence and raised Rs. 15.68 crore in 1995-96.

As per the sanctioned scheme, the outstanding old dues of IRBI (now 11131) and United Bank of India have been paid out of the sale proceeds of the surplus land. The company is on the path of recovery and progressing according to the BIFR sanctioned revival plan. BCPL has, in its efforts to augment its non-operations income and thereby improve its overall financial position taken up a plan for development of its surplus land at Prabhadevi, Mumbai.

Bengal immunity ltd., (BIL)

This was a sick company in the private sector in the name and style of Bengal Immunity Company Ltd. The management of the company was taken over by the Central Government with effect from 18th May, 1978. It was nationalised from 1st October, 1984. A new public sector company in the name and style of Bengal Immunity Ltd. was incorporated on 1st October, 1984.

The company has two manufacturing units, one each at Baranagar at Calcutta (West Bengal) and at Dehradun (UP). The main products of the company are Sera, Vaccines and Toxoids with its own knowhow and indigenous raw materials.

The company was formally declared sick by the Board for Industrial and Financial Reconstruction (BIFR) on the 9th March 1993. The BIFR on the basis of the report of the Industrial Reconstruction Bank of India (IRBI) (now the Industrial Investment Bank of India), Calcutta, the Operating Agency appointed by the BIFR and the support extended by the Government of India, approved a revival package for this sick company on 3rd January 1995. The revival period is 10 years beginning from 1994-95.

The performance of BIL during the first three years of the revival period i.e. 1994-95 to 1996-97 had been below the targets envisaged. The concerned Bench (Bench 11) of the BIFR took a review of the progress in the implementation of the sanctioned revival package in a meeting held on 11.1.1996 at Calcutta.

The BIFR directed the BIL management to prepare a perspective plan for the next five years. The BIFR also directed that BIL should get a manpower study conducted by a professional Consultant/Organisation with a view to laying down work norms and to determine option of utilisation of manpower. BIL entrusted the manpower-cum-productivity norms study to the West Bengal Productivity Council (formerly Calcutta Productivity Council).

The revised projections prepared by the company are being examined in consultation with the Operating Agency. Pending a decision on the future of BIL, non-plan assistance is being released from time to time for payment of wages/salaries of the employees and workers.

Smith stanistreet pharmaceuticalslimited (SSPL)

It was a sick company in the private sector in the name and style of Smith Stanistreet Company Limited. The management of the company was taken over by the Central Government with effect from 4th May, 1972. It was nationalised on 1st October, 1977 and a new public sector company in the name and style of Smith Stanistreet Pharmaceuticals Ltd.. (SSPL) was incorporated on 19th July, 1978.

The company has its manufacturing and th registered Office at 18, Convent Road, Calcutta (West Bengal). SSPL manufactures pharmaceutical formulations namely, Tablets, Capsules, Parenterals, Liquid orals etc.

The company was formally declared sick by the Board for Industrial and Financial Reconstruction (BIFR) on 21st December, 1992. The BIFR, on the basis of the report of the Industrial Reconstruction Bank of India (IRBI) (now the Industrial Investment Bank of India (11131), Calcutta, the Operating Agency appointed by it and the support extended by the Government of India approved a revival package on 31st August, 1994. The revival package is for ten years beginning from 1994-95.

The performance of the company in the first three years of the revival period had been far below the targets for a variety of reasons including shortage of key manpower. The Bench I Special of the BIFR reviewed the implementation of the scheme in a hearing held on 3.7.1996. The BIFR noted that the performance in 199495 and 1995-96 was far behind the targets.

The BIFR, however, taking the efforts being made by the management and the promoters took the view that the progress could be watched for some more time. The BIFR decided that the projections for the years 1996-97 to 2003-2004 would need reworking and passed directions to the Operating Agency (11131), Calcutta to rework the projections.

The BIFR also directed the SSPL mangement and promoters to furnish revised projections to the Rating Agency. The company has prepared the revised projections and forwarded the same to the Operating Agency (11131), Calcutta. The comments of the Operating Agency have been received. The report of the Operating Agency (11131) indicates that the company would need extraordinary levels of support and sacrifices from the

Government and others for revival. However, another PSLI, BCPL was also advised to prepare a Revival Package for SSPL. A view is yet to be formulated by giving due consideration to the reports.

Joint sector undertakings

Rajasthan drugs and pharmaceuticals limited (RDPL)

This is a joint sector undertaking promoted by Indian Drugs & Pharmaceuticals Limited (IDPL) and the Rajasthan Industrial Investment Corporation (RIICO). IDPL holds 51 % of the equity shares and the rest is with RIICO.

The company was incorporated in 1978 and the commercial production was commissioned in April, 1981. The company has its manufacturing unit and the registered office located at V.K.I. Industrial Area, Jaipur (Rajasthan). This is a formulation unit engaged in the production of Tablets, Capsules, Liquid Orals and Injectables.

Uttar Pradesh drugs and pharmaceuticals limited (UPDPL)

This is a joint sector undertaking promoted by Indian Drugs & Pharmaceuticals Ltd.. (IDPL) and the Pradeshiya Industrial Investment Corporation of Uttar Pradesh (PICUP). IDPL holds 51 % of the equity shares and the rest is with PICUP.

The company was incorporated in 1978 and the commercial production was established in October, 1979. The company has its manufacturing unit and the registered office located at Lucknow (Uttar Pradesh). The main products and pharmaceutical formulations are in the form of Tablets, Capsules, Powders, Liquid Orals and Injectables.

The Board for Industrial and Financial Reconstruction (BIFR) formally declared the company as sick on the 30th December, 1992. After prolonged and sustained efforts, a revival package for the company has been sanctioned by the BIFR on 22nd August, 1995. The revival period is ten years beginning from 1995-96. However, before the revival package could be put into operation, the two bankers, namely, the Bank of Baroda and the Indian Bank and one of the promoters, namely, PICUP went in appeals against the sanctioned scheme to the Appellate Authority of Industrial & Financial Reconstruction (AAIFR).

The Appellate Authority through its order dated 14.10.1996 has set aside the sanctioned scheme and remanded the case back to the BIFR. The Operating Agency, IDBI, Mumbai has been directed to sort out the issues relating to the viability of UPDPL and failing a resolution of the issues, to look for change of management.

The case of UPDPL is still before the BIFR. In the last hearing held on 27.8.1997, the BIFR passed directions that one time settlement of the dues of banks should be negotiated by PICUP, one of the two promoters of UPDPL. The Operating Agency was directed to update and prepare a revised package and the promoters directed to make all efforts to bring in the requiste equity support.

Orissa drugs and chemicals limitted (ODCL)

This is a joint sector undertaking promoted by Indian Drugs & Pharmaceuticals Ltd. (IDPL) and the Industrial Promotion and Investment Corporation of Orissa (IPICOL). IDPL holds 51 % of the equity shares and the rest is with IPICOL. The company was incorporated in 1979 and commissioned fully for production from September, 1983.

The company has its manufacturing unit and its registered office in Mancheshwar Industrial Area, Bhubaneshwar in the state of Orissa. The company is engaged in the manufacture of pharmaceutical formulations in the form of Tablets, Capsules, Powders, Ointments etc. ODCL was formally declared sick by the Board for Industrial and Financial Reconstruction (BIFR) on the 26th October, 1992.

On the basis of the report of the Operating Agency, appointed by the BIFR and the support extended by the promoters, the BIFR approved a revival package for ODCL on the 18th August. 1994. The revival operations had begun from year 1994-95. The BIFR in a review held in the month of March, 1997, concluded that the previous sanctioned scheme dated 18-.8.1994 has failed. The BIFR has re-appointed IDBI, Mumbai as the Operating Agency for preparation of a revised scheme and also take action for change of management.

Karnataka antibiotics and pharmaceuticals ltd. (KAPL)

This is a Joint Sector Undertaking promoted by Hindustan Antibiotics Ltd. (HAL) in collaboration with Karnataka State Industrial and Investment Development Corporation (KSIIDC). HAL holds 51% of the equity shares and the rest is with KSIIDC.

The company was incorporated on the 13th March, 1981 and the commercial production established from August, 1984. The manufacturing units and the registered office of the company is located at Bangalore (Karnataka). The main products are pharmaceutical formulations like Tablets, Capsules, Injectables, etc. KAPL has from the very first year of its operations been earning profits.

Maharashtra antibiotics and pharmaceuticals ltd. (MAPL)

This is a joint sector undertaking promoted by Hindustan Antibiotics Ltd. (HAL) and State Industries Corporation of Maharashtra (SICOM). HAL holds 51% of the equity shares and the rest is with SICOM. The company was incorporated in November, 1979 and the commercial production established in May, 1981.

The registered off ice and the factory of the company is located at Nagpur (Maharashtra). This is also a pharmaceutical formulation unit manufacturing Tablets, Capsules, Liquid Orals, Ointments, injectable etc. The company had incurred a net loss in 1995-96 and consequently the net worth of the company became negative.

On a reference by the Board of Directors of the company, the BIFR has formally declared MAPL as sick on 14.1.1997. IDBI, Mumbai was appointed as the Operating Agency for a techno-economic viability study. The Operating Agency made a techno-economic analysis and found that the revival of MAPL would require restructuring of the previous loans and fresh financial assistance of about Rs. 1.26 crore from the two existing promoters.

Since the two promoters did not come forward with the requisite support, the Operating Agency reported the matter to the BIFIR for further directions. The BIFR in a hearing held on 25.6.97 passed directions, inter-alia-to the Operating Agency to proceed for issue of an advertisement for change of management. The BIFR also directed that proposals, if any, of the existing promoters, should be furnished and such proposals would be given preference.

Manipur state drugs and pharmaceuticals ltd. (MSDPL)

This is a joint sector undertaking promoted by Hindustan Antibiotics Ltd. (HAL) and in collaboration wit Manipur Industrial Development Corporation (MANIDCO). HAL holds 51% of the equity shares and the rest is with MANIDCO.

The company was incorporated on the 18th July, 1989. The project with are estimated original outlay of Rs. 2.50 crore is yet to be fully commissioned. A part of the production facilities, has been commissioned. The manufacturing unit and the registered office is at IMPHAL (MANIPUR)

Wholly owned subsidiaries

IDPL (Tamil Nadu) limited, Chennai

In terms of the approved revival package the Surgical and Formulation Unit of IDPL at Chennai has been converted into a wholly owned subsidiary in the name and style of IDPL (Tamil Nadu) Limited, Chennai with effect from the 1st April, 1994. IDPL holds the entire equity capital of this unit. The past long-term liabilities amounting to Rs. 59 crore as on 31.3.1994 have been taken over by IDPL.

Bihar drugs and oranic chemicals ltd. Muzaffarpur

In terms of the revival package approved by the Board for Industrial & Financial Reconstruction (BIFR) the Organic Chemicals and drug manufacturing unit of IDPL at Muzaffarpur (Bihar) has been converted into a wholly owned subsidiary in the name and style of Bihar Drugs & Organic Chemicals Ltd. Muzaffarpur with effect from 1st April, 1984. IDPL holds the entire equity capital of this unit. The past long term liabilities amounting to Rs. 36 crore as on 31.3.1994 have been taken over by IDPL.

Performance in 1996-97

Rs./crores

Name of PSU	Production	Sales	Net **Profit/(Loss)**
IDPL	42.79	42.82	(151.24)
HAL	116.82	134.71	(332.25)
BCPL	36.48	30.61	15.75
BIL	8.24	8.78	(9.91)
SSPL	7.16	7.70	(4.93)

Performance in 1997-98

Rs./crores

Name of PSU	Production	Sales	Net Profit/(Loss)
1	2	3	4
IDPL	3.29	N.A.	(157.39)
1	2	3	4
HAL	109.62	108.42	(23.50)
BCPL	43.63	35.50	(3.37)
BIL	13.40	11.72	(8.81)
SSPL	4.377	5.43	(5.07)

Performance in 1998-99

Rs./crores

Name of PSU	Production	Sales	Net **Profit/(Loss)**
IDPL	2.75	N.A.	N.A.
HAL	52.72	45.16	(9.62)
BCPL	25.53	23.55	(0.50)
BIL	2.71	3.23	(7.68)
SSPL	0.81	N.A.	N.A.

Petrochemicals industry

Indian petrochemicals corporation limited (IPCL)

The formation of Indian Petrochemicals Corporation Limited (IPCL) as a public sector company was a culmination of the thought process of the Government on the industry. The Corporation was incorporated on 22nd March, 1969 as a Company under the Companies Act, 1956 with its registered office at PO: Petrochemicals, District Vadodara 391 346.

Capital structure

The Capital structure of the Corporation as on 3 March, 1998 was as under:—

	(Rupees in crore)
A) Share Capital	
Authorised	400.00
Issued and Subscribed	248.22
Government	148.80
Others	99.42
Add: Shares forfeited (amount) originally paid up	0.83
B) Loans	
Secured	1651.06
Unsecured	2686.48

Location of the units

The company has three mega petrochemical complexes based at Vadodara and Gandhar, District Bharuch in Gujarat and Nagothane, District Raigad in Maharashtra.

Production-operation profile

The company during 1997-98, achieved an all time high production from its petrochemical complexes situated at Vadodara, Nagothane and Gandhar. The operational performance of these units during 1997-98 was as under:

Vadodara complex

The production of major saleable products at Vadodara Complex for 1997-98 stood 4.18 lakh metric tonnes compared to 3.5 lakh metric tonnes last year and registered 18 percent growth which was noteworthy despite ageing plants. The polypropylene copolymer (PPCP), linear alkyl benzene (LAB) and benzene plants of Vadodara Complex operated much above the nameplate capacity whereas low density polyethylene (LDPE), polybutadiene rubber (PBR-1), acrylic fibre (AF) and acrylates plants operated at close to nameplate capacity.

The products like acrylonitrile (ACN), ethylene, butadiene, monoethylene glycol (MEG), ethylene oxide (EO) recorded ever highest production and exceeded the targets set for the year. The overall capacity utilisation of the Complex including the recently commissioned polypropylene (PP) and polybutadiene rubber (PBR-II), plants was around 87 percent. The newly commissioned PP plant achieved over 120 percent of the MOU target signed with the Government of India.

Nagothane complex

The Company's gas cracker complex at Nagothane in Maharashtra achieved an all time high and record production by producing over 3.71 lakh metric tonnes of saleable products during 1997-98 compared to 3.44 lakh metric tonnes production achieved in the previous year and registered a growth of 8 percent.

The gas cracker plant produced over 3.31 lakh metric tonnes of ethylene and exceeded the nameplate capacity of 3.00 lakh metric tonnes. All down stream plants operated well above nameplate capacity, with overall capacity utilization touching 101 percent.

Gandhar complex

In the first year of operation, the production at Gandhar Complex touched a figure of 1.76 lakh metric tonnes. The polyvinyl chloride (PVC) and caustic chlorine plants which were commissioned towards the end of the previous financial year have now stabilized. The polyvinyl chloride and caustic soda plants operated at 95 percent and 82 percent of its capacity during the second half of fiscal 1997-98 and successfully overcame the low capacity utilization registered in the first half of fiscal 1997-98.

The combined production of all the three complexes taken together stood at 9.65 lakh metric tonnes as against 7.69 lakh metric tonnes achieved in the corresponding previous year and registered a growth of 36 percent. The contribution of polymers, fibre and fibre intermediates and chemicals in the said production from all three Complexes, during the year was 69 per cent, 11 per cent and 20 per cent respectively.

All the three production Complexes during the year, gainfully utilized the infrastructure created at Dahej and Pirpau. At both places, significant quantities of Ethylene, Propylene and Naphtha were imported and this helped in running the plants at high capacities and saving on account of competitive feed stock costs from imports. The savings on account of import of naphtha was substantial, over and above improvement in production on account of superior quality of imported naphtha.

Production trend of major products

The production trend for major products during the last 3 years were as under:

(Figures in metric tonnes)

Product Group	Installed capacity	Production in 1997-98	1996-97	1995-96
Polymers	752500	664506	491180	488102
Fibre and Fibre Intemediates	114000	103910	97169	102078
Chemicals	270000	165698	94780	115107
Total	1136500	934114	683129	705287

Sales and marketing performance

The financial year 1997-98 proved to be another eventful year in the annals of Company's marketing strategies pursuant to achievement of new landmark in sales. During the year under review, the sales volume kept pace with the sterling production performance despite down trend in the petrochemicals business world over and turmoil in Southeast Asian countries.

A record 10 lakh metric tonnes of products from the Company's three mega Complexes reached customers spread across the country as against 8.15 lakh metric tonnes sold in the corresponding previous year and registered a growth of 23%.

The gross sales during the year under review was Rs. 3,692 crore as against Rs. 3,430 crore achieved in the previous year. The contribution of polymer, chemical and fibre and fibre intermediate products in the entire volume of sales was 62%, 27% and 10% respectively and the balance was accounted for by traded goods and residuary products.

The polymer prices were depressed throughout the year, particularly, during the last four-five months of the year. The substantial price difference amongst various polymer products as well as price volatility, resulted in inter polymer shifts in consumption.

PVC market witnessed tremendous over supply and severe price erosion. Consequently, marketing activities were focussed to preserve the Company's share of LDPE and increase its share in the growing LLDPE markets. One such activity was the development of special formulation for an experimental LLDPE grade, ready to use LDPE/ LLDPE blends and introduction of nine other new grades.

The Product Application Development Centre in association with R&D Centre, developed grades for thermoforming of polypropylene. To combat the severe price competition in the wire and cable compound business, a new cost effective wire and cable sheathing compound formulation was successfully developed for field evaluation. A few grades of LDPE, PPCP and HDPE were also approved for international use in automobile sector.

The Chemical Business Group registered significant increase in volumes. The Group, during the year, successfully launched two new products viz. caustic soda and poly-iso-butylene. The marketing of caustic soda and its by-products posed an entirely new challenge to the marketing team as the volumes were large, market competitive and customers totally new.

Despite all hurdles, the Group successfully sold out volumes and through its sales policies, even influenced the marketing of caustic soda in the country. The fibre & fibre Intermediate Group also performed consistently well despite stiff competition.

In the sphere of value addition, the Group worked towards conversion of DMT/MEG to PSF and further conversion to PV yarn. The Company despite global competition during the year, achieved an export turnover of Rs. 149 crore as against Rs. 107 crore achieved in the corresponding previous year and registered 39% growth in export earning.

Finance

During the year, steps were initiated for raising funds for implementation of second phase of Gandhar projects by tapping the External Commercial Borrowing (ECB) route. However, pursuant to deregulation of the interest rates by the Reserve Bank of India, avenues for raising funds from domestic market being attractive, reduction in Bank rates, improved liquidity conditions in the Capital Market, options were kept open to raise funds in the domestic market to ensure that the project fund requirements are adequately met. During the year, the Company made a successful placement of secured redeemable non-convertible bonds aggregating Rs. 300 crore.

The Rupee-300 crore bond issue was overwhelmingly subscribed and was the country's first ever issue on the line of price discovery through book building route normally practiced- in the international market. The commercial paper programme worth Rs. 300 crore backed by P1+ rating floated during the year to meet the working capital requirements of the Company was well received by the participating Banks/ Institutions.

Despite tight money market conditions, the public deposit scheme of the Company, during the year, could attract an all time high deposit of Rs. 441 crore as against the deposit of Rs. 197 crore in the corresponding previous year. There were no overdue deposits during the year under review.

Refinancing of EURO Loan

During the year, the EURO loan facility of US Dollars 75 million, earlier syndicated by Citibank at the rate of LIBOR plus 0.98 percent per annum as secured loan was refinanced at LIBOR plus 0.61 percent as unsecured loan, resulting in considerable reduction in the cost of funding and savings to the Corporation.

Foreign exchange Earnings and outgo

(Rupees in crore)

Foreign exchange earnings	200
Foreign exchange outgo	615

Inventory management

Effective and efficient management of inventory and receivables ensured that year-end stocks of finished goods were just around 29 sales days and restricted receivables to 46 sales days which in terms of value was Rs. 697 crore.

Memorandum of understanding

The Company's performance in the evaluation of Memorandum of Understanding signed with the Government for the year 1997-98 was commendable in terms of physical performance achieved in production, sales and project implementation.

Working results and financial higlights

During the year under review, the Company achieved an aggregate net income of Rs. 3095 crore representing an increase of 8% over the previous year. The gross income of the Company increased from Rs. 3,430 crore to Rs. 3,692 crore as compared to 1996-97.

The highlights of the financial results for the corporate financial year ended 31st March, 1998 are as under :

(Rs. /Crore)

	1997-98	1996-97
Net Sales	2,983	2,785
Other Income	112	778
Gross Profit	510	741
Depreciation	237	148
Profit before Tax	2772	593
Net Profit after Taxation	244	510
Appropriations		

Dividend	99	99
Dividend percentage	40%	40%
Corporate tax on dividend	10	10
General reserve and surplus	25	60
Earnings per share (Rs.)	9.82	20.56
Book valuepershare (RS.)	121.61	118.58

The Company by recording a turnover of Rs. 3,692 crore, has met all the physical and financial targets in the areas of production, sales and project completion. Despite higher production and sales, the bottomline suffered on account of poor product prices which were further worsened by currency turmoil in the Far East.

The profits of the Company were also adversely affected by abnormal escalation in input prices primarily of petroleum products, power, transportation and higher interest cost, while the market situation did not allow for matching increase in output prices to neutralise the adverse impact.

The South East Asian economic crisis that began in July, 1997 started showing its full impact in November, 1997 and the worst sufferer of the crisis was Polypropylene where the drop in price was substantial. Prices of PVC also dropped dramatically on account of over supply in the domestic market.

Dividend

The Directors in consideration of commendable production/sales performance, recommended 40% dividend for the financial year ended 31st March, 1998, despite depressed profits.

Progress of major projects, expansion/diversification plans

IPCL's strategy is to concentrate on its polymer business and cement its dominance in the industry by achieving economies of scale, continued backward integration, increase the distribution network throughout India, develop and market new applications of products and simultaneously develop new products and emphasize on volume driven growth. There has been tremendous growth in the Petrochemicals Industry both internationally and in India.

The demand supply gap for polyethylene and polyvinyl chloride over post 2000 period continue to be favourable for setting up additional facilities. The Company being a major player and market leader in polymer products, it is imperative that further investments are made in this sector to continue to retain the market leadership and capture the opportunity of demand growth taking place in this sector. Keeping this in view, the projects conceived by the Corporation in all the three complexes during the 9th plan period are as under: —

Vadoara

Setting up of a 3 lakh metric tonnes per annum capacity Naphtha Cracker plant; a downstream unit for Polyethylene to meet the demand-supply gap; High Rubber Graft facility of 20,000 metric tonnes per annum; and plant for manufacture of Butene and Isobutylene.

Nagothane

Increasing the capacity of ethylene to 5.50 lakh metric tonnes per annum by sourcing additional feed stock from Oil and Natural Gas Corporation Limited's Usar gas separation complex; 10,000 metric tonnes per annum alpha olefin and derivatives plant; and increasing the capacity of linear low density polyethylene (LLDPE) plant from 80,000 to 1,40,000 metric tonnes per annum.

Gandhar

Increasing the ethylene plant capacity from existing 32000

to 4 lakh metric tonnes per annum; setting up of 1.5 lakh metric tonnes per annum capacity PVC plant; 1 lakh metric tonnes per annum capacity ABS plant to effectively use the additional ethylene; and acrylonitrile (ACN) plant with a capacity of 1 lakh metric tonnes per annum and single buoy mooring to facilitate import and export trade.

The various expansions in each of these complexes would need additional utilities, which is proposed to be met by increasing capacity in the respective offsite projects. Once the above mentioned projects are completed, the company will not only be the market leader and the largest ethylene manufacturer in the country but would also make it capable of competing internationally with major competitors.

The total capital expenditure of various expansions and the spill over expenditure of Eighth Five Year Plan would work out to Rs. 7651 crore of which estimated expenditure during the Ninth Five Year Plan period would be Rs. 6000 crore.

The Company believes that these expansion projects will enhance the efficiency of operation through improved economics of scale, increased integration and process. In addition, the expansion and enhancement projects will allow the Company to take advantage of the availability of more cost effective feed stock including ethane/propane for its cracker at the Nagothane/Gandhar Complexes and imported naphtha for Vadodara Complex.

Joint ventures

GE Plastics India Limited

During the year under review, GE Plastics India Limited, a joint venture company set up by the corporation, achieved a turnover of Rs. 200 crore as against Rs. 143

crore achieved in the corresponding previous year. The Company's revenue during the year stood at Rs. 200 crore and registered 40 percent growth as compared to previous year.

Despite growth in revenue, the Company suffered a net loss of Rs. 14.66 crore due to inflation in raw material cost and erosion in prices because of aggressive pricing by South-East Asian players. The Company despite these difficulties has set a realistic target for 1998-99 and is hopeful of registering profit by better performance.

The Company had formed a manufacturing and sourcing alliance for plastics with Polychem Limited and Rajasthan Polymers & Resins Limited. These two companies will manufacture its cycolac brand of acrylonitrile butadiene styrene. The alliance demonstrates the Company's commitment to develop and drive the growth of engineering plastics in India through improving its capability and building sustained partnership with the local industry.

Through the strategic alliance, the company is strongly positioned to meet the needs of the growing market of ABS in India—where the major applications of cycolac (ABS) include appliances, housing, car, interiors, two wheelers, telephone computers etc. The alliance sets the stage for a long term co-operation being planned to set up additional grass root manufacturing facilities for ABS, Styrene, Acrylonitrile (ACN) and High Rubber Graft.

Gujarat Chemical Port Terminal Company Limited (GCPTCL)

The liquid chemical port envisaged by another Joint Venture - Gujarat Chemical Port Terminal Company Limited (GCPTCL) is fast coming up at Dahej in the Gulf of Khambhat in Gujarat. The Construction work on the 2.4 Km. long jetty has already commenced and onshore store works are also in progress. The port is expected to become operations by last quarter of 1999 and would give flexibility of operation to the Corporation in augmenting feed stock requirements and also facilitate easy handling of export consignment.

The Company's contribution towards equity in the Joint Venture Company would be freezed at around Rs. 46 crore or 30% of the total equity and continues to be the largest equity holder in the joint venture.

Indian Petrovin Limited

The joint venture partners- IPCL and Vinmar Petrochemicals Limited have been engaged in the selection of technology for the manufacture of Methyl Methacrylate (MMA) /Polymethyl Methacrylate (PMMA). During the course of discussions with various prospective process licensers, one of the leading companies having technical know-how for MMA/ PMMA- Rohm Gmbh Chernische Fabric of the Federal Republic of Germany (ROHM) belonging to the HULS Group-expressed their interest in the supply of technology to the joint venture company as part of their strategy to commence direct investment in India.

Rohm's technology for both MMA and PMMA including related end product development being amongst the best, they have been inducted as third partner in the joint venture. Pursuant to this arrangement, the Company has entered into a fresh Memorandum of Understanding with ROHM and VINMAR for equity participation. After securing necessary Government approval, the project is expected to start during 1998.

Other joint venture

In pursuance of the approval accorded by the shareholders, the Company is in the process of taking necessary steps for seeking approval of the appropriate authorities for setting up an acrylic fibre plant of 50,000 MTA capacity in association with Malwa Cotton Spinning Mills Limited and strategic alliance for conversion of acrylic fibre into yarn with GSL India Limited.

Contribution in the areas of environment, safety and energy conservation

In pursuit of continuing commitment, highest priority was accorded to safety and environment control programmes at all levels. Safety and environment management are integrated into the business process through carefully devised strategies and systems.

In addition to adhering to local and national Government regulations, to protect the environment, the Company has established its own guiding principles and a complimentary set of specific guidelines, tailor made for its business.

Self regulation in the management of safety, health and environment is accorded the highest priority. Through careful process audits, reduction in the usage of fresh water and emissions in the manufacturing operations have been achieved. Effluent treatment plants and emission control devices are maintained in regular operating conditions and all statutory regulations are complied with.

The specific energy index during the year under review, in all the three production Complexes of the Corporation, in its totality, stood at 4.90 MMKCal per metric tonne as against 5.40 MMKCal per metric tonne of production registered in the previous year. The reducing trend in the energy index is due to the Company's commitment to energy conservation and adoption of energy efficient technologies and processes in its plants at all locations.

The Nagothane Complex of the Corporation was awarded the first prize by the Union Ministry of Power for its achievement in Energy Conservation. The Complex has its own 85 MW captive power generation facility to cater to the energy requirements of various plants.

Higher capacity utilisation of various production plants, minimization of wastes, maintenance of quality standards of products and overall widespread energy consciousness were the main criteria enabling the Company to receive the coveted award.

During the year, the Company also received a Certificate of Honour by the Gujarat State Safety Council and Gujarat State Factory Inspectorate for conducting safe operation of the plants. The honour was conferred on the Company for conducting more than 3 million manhours of accident free operation at Vaclodara Complex.

Besides the certificate, the Company was also conferred the Rotating Trophy and Citation for its low disabling-injury index. This recognition is over and above the prestigious Certificate of Honour, Metric Certificates, Shields, etc. received by the company from organisations like National Safety Council, USA and the British Safety Council, UK.

Employment position as on 31.3.1998

The manpower strength of the Company in all its production complex/units based at Vadodara, Nagothane, Gandhar and Thane as on 31st March, 1998 was 13,319 inclusive of supervisory/non-supervisory employees and Company trainees. The employment position in respect of Scheduled Caste/Scheduled Tribes and Other Backward Classes as on 31st March, 1998 was as under:

Scheduled Caste	–	1844
Scheduled Tribe	–	618
Other Backward Classes	–	108

The age-wise employment in different age groups as on 31st March, 1998 was as under:

Age Group	Numbers
Upto 34 years	4718
Between 35 & 49 years	6847
50 years & above	1754

Date of annual general meeting

The date of 28th and 29th Annual General Meetings for the year 1996-97 and 1997-98 were 26th September, 1997 and 29th September, 1998 respectively.

Research and development

The Research and Development Centre of the Corporation Continued to support the Company's business. Linkages with national and international scientific and academic institutions were further strengthened. The science base of Research & Development Centre continues to be consolidated through collaborative interactions with international laboratories.

During the year, Company's Research & Development Centre made considerable progress in developing catalyst and process for AO technology. This has led to the international majors approaching the Corporation, offering help to develop technology together. The Company ultimately plans to set up a 50,000 tonnes per annurn AO Plant at Nagothane after increasing ethylene capacity.

The company was granted a US patent for developing a catalyst for dehydrogenation of normal paraffin. The dehydrogenation catalyst developed by a team of the Company's scientists and engineers is a critical item in the dehydrogenation process to manufacture linear alkyl benzene.

The catalyst has been developed by the Company's Research Centre at Vaclodara and is manufactured at the Company's Catalysts and Absorbents Division based at Thane. In order to successfully commercialize Dehydrogenation Catalyst, a project of 20 metric tonnes per annum capacity is being set up at CATAD Unit at an estimated cost of Rs. 6 crore and is likely to be commissioned shortly.

Petrofils cooperative limited (PCL)

1. Petrofils Cooperative Limited (PCL) was registered in 1974 as a joint venture of Government of India and Weavers Cooperatives. PCL is governed under the Multi- state Cooperative Societies Act, 1984. The principal objective is to provide the benefits of modern technology of Polyester Filament Yarn (PFY) to the weavers in the co-operative sector, a weaker section of the society. PCL has 1446 Weavers Cooperative Societies from all over the country as its members.
2. The authorised capital of PCL is Rs. 50 crore of which the paid-up capital is asunder:

		Rs./Lakh	%
(a)	Government of India	1716	83
(b)	National Cooperative Development Corpn.	100	5
(c)	Cooperatives	259	12
	Total	2075	100

3. PCL produces Polyester filament yarn, Nylon-6 chips and Spandex yarn in its four plants located at Vadodara and Naldhari in Gujarat. PCIL sells Methanol being its by-product.

3.1 Polyester Plant, Vadodara.

PCIL having switched over to job-conversion since November, 1996, has been producing above rated capacity through this plant. The capacity utilisation for the year 1997-98 has been 112%.

3.2 Nylon plant, Naldhari

This plant has achieved a capacity utilisation of 92% in PFY manufacturing during the year 199798 which is higher by 65% as compared to previous year. The plant has also produced 7478 MT of Nylon-6 chips under job-conversion at 62% capacity during the year. The second VK tube was charged in January, 1997 to improve plant performance.

3.3 Polyester Plant, Naldhari

The capacity utilisation of this plant has been 90% during 1997-98. The chips plant after hookup of Direct-Melt-Spinning (DMS) facility during previous year has produced 13456 MT of Polyester chips at a capacity utilisation of 67%.

3.4 Spandex Plant, Naldhari

After commissioning the plant in June, 1996, PCL produced 30 MT of Spandex Yarn during 1996-97. Thereafter with the inability to import raw material for want of working capital, the production reduced to 4 MT in

1997-98. PCL has now signed an Agreement with DUPONT, USA for utilising Spandex Plant on conversion basis.

4. The production performance for the years 1996-97 and 1997-98 and Targets for the year 1998-99 are given below:

Name of Unit/ Plant	Capacity	98-99 Target	98-98 Actual	96-97 Actual
Vadodara	7000	7680	7870	6668
Naldhari				
Nylon	6000	6800	5511	3348
Polyester	8000	8400	77174	664
Spandex	300	177	4	30
Total-PFY	21000	22880	20555	10680
Capacity Utilisation (%)		109%	98%	51%
Grand Total	21300	23057	20559	10710

5. The sales turnover of PCIL has increased from Rs. 144 crore in 1996-97 to Rs. 161 crore (provisional) in 1997-98. The net loss has been reduced from Rs. 98 crore in 1996-97 to Rs. 74 crore (provisional) for 1997-98.

6. PCIL is presently passing through a severe cash crunch resulting in reduction in the capacity utilisation as well as shifting of operations to the conversion basis for the other parties. The working capital Bankers and the Financial Institutions are insisting upon the induction of long-term interest free funds for the revival and revitalisation of PCL's operations in absence of which, the continuing cooperation of these agencies is becoming more and more difficult and PCL remains in arrears for certain

vital statutory dues as well as electricity bills and delayed payments of wages to the workers making even holding on operation difficult and its continuity uncertain.

7. PCIL is in the process of shortly submitting a Rehabilitation Package mainly with an objective of assessing techno-economic viability of each of the plants on stand-alone basis. An external consulting agency has been engaged for necessary assistance.

Chemicals and pesticides undertakings

Hindustan organic chemicals limited

HOC was set-up by the Government in 1960 with the objective of attaining self-reliance in basic organic chemical needs. In fact this was the first endeavour to indigenise manufacture of basic chemicals and to reduce country's dependence on imports of vital organic chemicals.

HOC which started as a small chemical manufacturing unit, has today acquired the status of a multi-unit company with three fast growing plants. The Company's present turnover is about Rs. 480 crores. HOC's networth as on 31/03/1998 was Rs. 375.58 crores. This is 5.58 times its equity base.

It was expected that indigenous manufacturer of these chemical intermediates will give impetus to downstream industry resulting in setting up of chemical units and achieving self-sufficiency for the country in this area.

This objective of setting up HOC has been achieved since at present more than 500 units based on HOC's products have been set up all over the country which have not only succeeded in meeting the goal of self-sufficiency but have also entered the international market earning precious foreign exchange by exporting chemicals, dyes and drugs.

Main manufacturing units of HOC:

— The main Organic Chemical Complex at Rasayani in Raigad District (Maharashtra)

— The Phenol Complex at Kochi (Kerala)

— The Polytetrafluoroethylene (PTFE) Complex (Subsidiary) at Rudraram, Hyderabad (Andhra Pradesh)

Hoc provides basic organic chemicals essential for vital industries

The products manufactured by HOC are Phenol, Acetone, Nitrobenzene, Aniline, Nitrotoluene, Chlorobenzenes and Nitrochlorobenzenes. The raw materials used by HOC are Benzene, Toluene, LPG, Methanol, Naphtha and Sulphur, majority of which come from petroleum refineries.

HOC provides the basic organic chemicals essential for vital industries, pesticides, drugs and pharmaceuticals, dyes and dye intermediates, resins and laminates, rubber chemicals, paints, textile auxiliaries and explosives, touching virtually every facet of everyday life. It also produces the versatile engineering plastic Polytetrafluoroethylene (PTFE) through its subsidiary.

Capital structure

Upto March 1992 HOC was a 100% Government of India enterprise. 20% shares were disinvested by the Government of India during April 1992 to October 1994 in favour of Mutual Funds and UTI. The Company also made a public issue of equity to the extent of Rs. 18 Crores (face value) in November 1994 thus raising its Paid up Capital from Rs. 49.35 crores to Rs. 67.27 crores. Consequently the share holding of the Government of India now stands reduced at 58.61 %.

Hoc's performance during the last five years

During the last five years i.e. from 1993-94 HOC

registered significant improvement in various fields. This is evident from the facts set out in the following tables:

Capacity utilisation

The company has maintained a steady growth in its capacity utilisation. Data for the last five years in the table below bears this out.

	1993-94	1994-95	1995-96	1996-97	1997-98
Installed Capacity (MT)	307696	336196	336110	336110*	377735
Production (MT) Capacity	249490	272523	304977	300182	353325
Utilisation (%)	81	81	91	89	93

While increasing installed capacity, HOC has, during the last five years also registered significant increase in capacity utilisation. In 1997-98, HOC's capacity utilisation was of the order of 93%.

Sales turnover

The company has maintained a steady growth in its Sales Turnover. Data for the last five years is as follows:

	1993-94	1994-95	1995-96	1996-97	1997-98
Value of Production (Rs. Crores)	265.14	307.38	389.47	350.52	418.16
Sales Volume (MT)	136656	146587	160478	173360	190476
Sales Turnover (Rs. Crores)	314.47	359.2	460.98	429.14	476.34

Volume of sales (in MT) and Sales Turnover (in Rs Crores) have also maintained an upward trend. During the financial year 1997-98, the Volume of Sales were of the order of 190476 MT compared to 136656 MT in 1993-94 and the Sales Turnover was at Rs. 476.34 compared to Rs. 314.47 crores in 1993-94.

Financial performance

Net Profit recorded during last five years: During the last five years financial performance of HOC in terms of Operating Profit, Gross Profit & Net profit was as follows:

(Rs. Crore)

	1993-94	1994-95	1995-96	1996-97	1997-98
Operating profit	37.83	48.64	83.10	36.35	48.13
Gross Profit before interest	29.99	38.89	69.70	18.97	23.73
Net Profit	21.36	27.89	54.30	9.28	-5.09
Payment to Exchequer	64.62	97.78	116.78	106.25	109.60

It is evident from the above table that the operating profit before interest and depreciation increased from Rs. 36.35 crores in 1996-97 to Rs. 48.13 crores in 199798 thereby registering an increase of 35%.

Exports

The following table indicates the growth in exports during the last three years.

	1995-96	1996-97	1997-98
Exports (Rs. Crores)	9.61	7.04	20.22

For the first time Phenol was exported in ISO tanks with substantially improved realisation from Cochin Port.

Compared to export earnings of Rs. 7.04 crores in 199697, its exports earnings during 1997-98 were of the order of Rs. 20.22 crores, thereby registering an increase of 187 percent.

New Initiatives taken by HOC

Responsible care

The International focus in chemical industry through "responsible care" movement is well recognised. The company, as one of the signatories of this concept is committed to maintain clean environment, safe operations, industrial health of its people and well being of the community around the area the company operates. In recognition of the contribution in this area, the company received the safety award from the National Safety Council and an award for maintaining clean operation by the Pollution Control Board.

ISO Certification

Cochin unit has already been accredited with ISO 9002 certification for its products Phenol and Acetone. The certification has been given by Bureau Vertias Quality International, UK. The unit is planning to implement environment management system to meet the requirement of ISO 14001. Significant progress has been made and efforts are on to implement the same during 1998-99. Rasayani unit has also received ISO 9002 certification.

MOU (target v/s performances)

HOC is a MOU signing company. Ever since the company started signing MOUs with Government of India (1991-92 onwards) the company has been achieving commendable performances there by surpassing the targets. In the year 1997-98, based on the audited performance, HOC has been accorded "Very Good" rating.

Performance highlights during 1997-98

The performance during 1997-98 was the best achieved so far in HOC with highest level of production, sales volumes and sales turnover. Production increased from 300182 MT in-1996-97 to 353325 MT in 1997-98 (17% increase), Sales volume from 173360 MT in 1996-97 to 190476 MT in 1997-98 (10% increase), Sales turnover from Rs. 429.14 crores in 1996-97 to Rs. 476.34 crores in 1997-98 (11 % increase).

Capacity utilisation increased from 89% to 93%, energy efficiency improved by 14%, improvement in consumption norms of both Cochin and Rasayani Units, reduction in inventory levels, improved debtors to sales ratio, increase in average realisation per tonne of sale and enhancement of capacity of phenol unit by 15%, savings in power costs due to efficient running of cogen plant. Phenol plant achieved a capacity utilisation of 110%. All these factors contributed to improvement in operating profit. In recognition of this, HOC received 'Productivity Award' from the National Productivity Council.

Projects completed/commissioned growth through joint venture

Company has incorporated a joint venture company under the name "HOC-Chematur" to set up the 20,000 TPA MIDI project at a total cost of about Rs. 400 crores undertechnology and financial tie up with M/s Chernatur Engg. A.B, Sweden. Shareholders have approved the incorporation of the new joint venture company with HOC's equity participation upto Rs. 48 crores. HOC and M/s Chernatur will jointly hold 51% of the equity of the joint venture in the ratio of 3:2.

The balance of 49% will be offered to the public. This project constitutes a major step towards backward integration and value addition and the process is based on Du Pont USA technology. M/s BOB Capital Markets Ltd. has appraised the project and has been appointed as the lead managers for the project. The syndication of term loan tie up is in progress. The project work has already commenced. The basic engineering package has been received from Chematur Engg. AB, Sweden, the technology supplier M/s IBI Chernatur (Engineering & Consultancy) Ltd., Mumbai has been appointed as Indian Consultant to carry out the detailed engineering, procurement assistance, construction supervision and commissioning of plant as well as off-site.

They have commenced the job and site preparation has already commenced. Procurement and civil construction will commence soon. The project will commence production by November, 2001.

Expansion and diversification

Hydrogen peroxide concentration unit: The Hydrogen Peroxide Plant with a capacity of 5225 TPA (100% concentration basis) set up at Cochin Unit with the technical collaboration of Krup-UHDE Germany was commissioned in 1997 well ahead of schedule. In order to meet the requirements of various end-users, a concentration unit has been set up at a cost of Rs. 10 crores to produce Hydrogen Peroxide of various strengths and grades.

Phenol plant capacity expansion: As a preliminary step additional process air compressor is being installed to optimise the process air requirement of the unit. With this addition the phenol plant can produce 15% more than the rated capacity. This process air supply system optimisation will be completed by May, 1999.

Polyurethane systems house: The commercial production of Polyurethane Systems house project foam section has started during the, year 1998. The Application Division Center and the full scale lab facilities for quality assurance of the product are already in operation. HOC has entered this market in competition with international companies like ICI, DAV, Elastogram etc. besides local competition from companies like Manali Petrochemicals Ltd. In spite of this, the company is able to penetrate the market to the targetted level.

Systems in the area of automotive, furniture construction, etc. have been introduced. Sales turnover to the extent of approx Rs. 400 lakhs was achieved as a part of market seeding. HOC is also introducing PU Foam system for packaging. The commercial production of the special chemicals is expected to start shortly. Market seeding work in this area has also been initiated and results are encouraging.

Recognitions and Awards.

HOC has won the following recognitions and awards during 1997-98

(i) HOC has been conferred the "Export House" status

(ii) HOC has been conferred "Mini Ratna" status by the Government of India.

(iii) The Kochi Unit of HOC received the National Safety Council Award for the eighth successive year for its safety performance

(iv) The Kochi Unit received Productivity Award among large industries in Kerala

(v) National Energy Conservation Award for the Company for its excellent energy management

Corporate ninth five year plan

The economic reforms policy changes brought about in July, 1991 have made tremendous impact in the Corporate scene. HOC found itself competing with the world giants but with handicaps in terms of scale of operation, technology, etc. During the 9th Five Year Plan, an attempt has been made to work through the organisational strength and exploit the opportunities.

HOC's mission is to retain leadership and improve corporate excellence by acquiring leadership role in the chemical field in the global context. To maintain continuous growth in turnover the company has identified 10% annual rate of growth as one of its objectives.

Based on the growth strategy company has plans to implement schemes focussing on expanding in core business and adding value to main products. The capital outlay of the Company for the 9th Five Year Plan is Rs. 229 crores, which includes HOC's equity participation in the Joint Venture.

HOC's research and development activities

Improvement in Yields by changing process parameters in phenol plant, improvement in process operations for Dichlorobenzene, Application Development in Polyurethanes are a few significant contributions by R&D team.

This area will continue to receive highest priority. In close interaction with Indian Institute of Chemical Technology, Hyderabad and National Chemical Laboratory, Pune new strategies are being evolved for enhancing value addition as well as improvement in yields & quality of existing product range.

Hindustan fluorocarbons ltd. (HFL) (Subsidiary of HOC)

Consequent on erosion of net worth and other factors, HFL became a sick company and was referred to BIFR in 1994. The BIFR's Order of December, 96 involving merger of HFL could not be implemented by HOC in the absence of two additional income tax concessions, which decision as approved by HOC Board was conveyed to BIFR. Further directions from BIFR are awaited.

HFL's performance during 1997-98 are as follows:

Operations

During the year under report, the company has achieved production of 260 Mts as against 392 Mts in previous year. The production of CFM-22 is lower at 960 Mts as against 1212 Mts during the previous year. The company has targetted and implemented cost reduction programme, process optimisation and achieved better plant efficiencies during the current year.

Using inhouse facilities, the company has developed free flowing compounded resin which has been accepted even in the international markets. "Free Flow" properties are almost mandatory for the export market. The quality of the company's product is maintained at high levels.

Safety and environment

Being a hazardous manufacturing process the company ensured safety consciousness among the employees and periodic review of safety measures have enabled the company once again to maintain safe operations during the year.

Marketing

The company recorded a sale of 274 Mts during 9798 as against the sale of 361 Mts during the pervious year. This was mainly on account of very sluggish industrial market prevailing in the country. The company exported 2 Mts of PTFE dispersions and PTFE billets realising Rs. 24.18 lakhs earnings in foreign exchange.

The free flow compounded resin which was market seeded overseas has been well received. The company was able to realise true market value of CFM-22 resulting in additional net revenue of Rs. 2.20 lakhs per MT of CFM-22 sales for the year 1997-98.

Strategic marketing alliance with M/s Diakin of Japan for PTFE coatings has widened HFL's market reach in fluoropolymers business of the country.

Finance

During the year the company was able to completely repay term loan instalment of State Bank of Hyderabad out of its own generated internal resources. With excellent cash management the company operated within the limited cash credit sanctioned by State Bank of Hyderabad and saved interest to the tune of Rs. 19.01 lakhs for the year.

Future utlook

Taking an Optimistic view that the Indian industry is expected to take off in 1998-99, the company has drawn up plans for 100% capacity utilisation and diversification into areas of value addition, upgradation of the existing technology of PTFE and manufacture of other fluoropolymers. To overcome the vagaries of Indian industry, the company is already active in the international markets.

Hindustan Insecticides Limited

Hindustan Insecticides Limited (HIL) was incorporated in 1954 and set up its factory in Delhi for manufacturing of 700 MT of Technical DDT and its Formulation into 50% wdp to meet the demand of National Malaria Eradication Programme (NMEP) launched by the Govt. of India. This plant came as a gift from WHO and went into production in April, 1995. The production capacity of this unit was doubled in the year 1958-59 and thereafter to reduce the import of DDT, the capacity of the plant was further increased to 2744 MT per annum of Technical DDT and 5488 MT per annum of Formulation DDT in 1969. In 1957, the company set up their second factory at Udyogamandal near Cochin for the manufacture of 1344

MT per annum of Technical DDT and 2688 MT per annum of Formulation DDT. In 1971, a plant was put up for the manufacture of Benzenehexachloride (BHC) having capacity of 3000 MT per annum to meet the requirement of agriculture and public health.

The company had set up in 1977 a plant at Rasayani in Maharashtra for the manufacture of 1800 MT per annum of Technical Malathion and 3200 MT per annum of Malathion (Formulation) an insecticide for public health. Further, another DDT Technical Plant with an annual capacity of 5000 MT and its Formulation with a capacity of 10,000 MT per annum had also been set up at Rasayani in 1983.

HIL, under diversification programme had established manufacturing facilities for Endosulfan Technical 1600 MT and Endosulfan Formulation 1900 KL at Udyogamandal. Production facilities for Butachlor Technical 1000 MT per annum, Butachlor Formulation 905 KL and Monocrotophos Technical 300 MT and Monocrotophos Formulation 255 KL during 1990-91 were also made at Rasayani.

In the year 1995-96, one stream of Butachlor Technical Plant was converted into Phosphamidon Technical Plant of 20OTPA with the technology developed in the company's R&D Complex, Gurgaon. The company has also taken up conversion of Butachlor Plant into Carboxin Plant of 50 TPA capacity . The production of Technical DDVP was started at Rasayani Unit in February' 97 with technology developed in house.

A new project for manufacture of 150 MT per annum of Dicofol Technical at Udyogamandal Unit has been commissioned on 1st July, 1996. In the first year of its commercial operation, the plant has achieved a production of 84% of its installed capacity. New projects like Mancozeb Technical with 1000 TPA and Carboxin with 50 TPA are under erection.

The company has already entered into the field of eco-friendly Bio-pesticides by introducing Bti, a larvicide for public health purposes and Btk a larvicide for controlling insect/pests of the crops. The company plans to enter new areas of eco-friendly botanical based pesticides and plant/insect growth regulators in coming years.

The Company also has a subsidiary company, viz. the Southern Pesticides Corporation Limited (SPEC) with Headquarter at Hyderabad and factory at Kovvur in Andhra Pradesh. The Company continued its in-house R&D activities to reduce the cost of production and improve the productivity and quality as well as to develop new products for import substitution.

As per order of the Hon'ble Supreme Court, the Delhi Unit of the Company stopped functioning w.e.f. 30.11.1996 and is to be relocated. The Govt. has also imposed a ban on the production of BHC in the country. Hence, the company has stopped the operation of BHC at Alwaye Unit w.e.f. 01.04.1997.

The performance of the company is as under:

(Rs./ lakhs)

Financial Year	Production	Turnover before tax	Net profit
1991-92	26042	7186	(–)626.70
1992-93	26401	8254	(+)44.14
1993-94	26000	10901	(+)200.30
1994-95	191777	10393	(+)226.10
1995-96	24534	135778	(+)602.64
1996-97	18765	12813	(+)644.52
1997-98	19176	12004	(–)1977.21

During 1997-98, HIL has reported sales of Rs. 120.04 crores (Previous Year Rs. 128.13 crores) and a loss of Rs. 1.97 crore (Previous Year Profit Rs. 6.45 crores).

The reduction in sales and profit is mainly due to lower supply of DDT to NMEP and idle wages consequent upon closure of operations at Delhi Unit w.e.f. 30.11.1996 in compliance of the Supreme Court Order. Further, no order for Formulated BHC was placed by NMEP during the year due to ban on the usage of BHC from 01.04.1994. The performance otherwise compares favourably with the growth achieved by the Pesticides Industry in the country.

12

Institues

National Institue of Pharmaceuticals Education and Research

As a part of the economic package for the State of Punjab, the setting up of a national level institute in that State was announced by the Government of India. A registered Society in the name and style of the National Institute of Pharmaceuticals Education and Research (NIPER) was set up on the 27th February, 1991.

The Institute has been set up at Sector 67, SAS Nagar, Mohali near Chandigarh on 130 acres of land, provided free of cost by the State Government of Punjab. The Institute with an approved outlay of Rs. 99 crores is ready with basic infrastructure. The Institute has already enrolled students for Post Graduate courses and Ph.D. programme. The National Institute of Pharmaceuticals Education and Research has been conceived as an institute of excellence and learning in pharmaceutical science and technology and it will be the only institute of its kind in the country.

NIPER has been declared an institute of national importance through NIPER Act, 1998 which has come into force from 8th July, 1998. An institute of national importance can chalk out its own courses and award its own degrees. With its multi-disciplinary approach, the NIPER would set standard for pharmaceutical colleges and for research and development in the field of pharmaceuticals. It is expected that the Institute through its students, its faculty and its research programme will assist the pharmaceutical sector of the industry to make a confident entry into the new era of global competition.

Cenral institute of plastics engineering and technology (CIPET)

The Central Institute of Plastics Engineering and Technology (CIPET) was established in the year 1968 with the following primary objectives :

i) Development of technically trained manpower in the areas of Design, Tooling, Processing & Testing for plastics and its allied industries.

ii) Upgradation of technical knowledge of personnel from the industry through conventional and advanced training programmes.

iii) Providing services in the areas of Design and Fabrication of Moulds and Dies, Processing of Plastics, CAD, Fabrication of Equipments and Machineries, Consultancy and Advisory services in the areas related to plastics.

iv) Testing Quality Control and Standardisation of Plastics Materials and Products.

v) Application development in the area of plastics.

CIPET is functioning as an Autonomous Institute under the administrative control of the Deptt. of Chemicals and Petrochemicals, Ministry of Chemicals and Fertilizers, Govt. of India. This institute has the privilege of being associated with United Nations Development Programme (UNDP) since its inception. Modernisation of CIPET facilities with the assistance of World Bank to the tune of US $ 12 million has been fully implemented successfully. All the equipments / machineries related to Tooling, Processing, Testing and

CAD have been procured and installed. Faculty training in overseas countries were also arranged and completed. As desired by World Bank a Draft Implementation Completion Report (ICR) was submitted in March, 1998.

CIPET is an unique institute of its kind in India, having all the facilities required for plastics industries like tooling, designing, processing and testing of plastics under one roof. The institute has established well-equipped Plastics Testing Centres at all centres with the objective of effecting improvement in standards and better quality control with the ultimate aim of improving the quality of products matching international standards.

With a view to render technical assistance and providing skilled manpower to the plastic industries located in other regions of India, the institute, with the assistance of Central and the respective State Govts. has established Extension Centres at Chennai, Ahmedabad, Bhubaneswar, Bhopal, Hyderabad, Lucknow, Amritsar, Imphal and Mysore.

CIPET has also initiated action to set up Extension Centres in Patna, Bihar and Haldia in West Bengal. It has also been proposed to set up an Extension Centre at Guwahati, Assam. It is expected that the three Extension Centres viz., Haldia (West Bengal), Patna (Bihar) and Guwahati (Assam) will be set up during the Ninth Plan Period. CIPET Corporate based at Chennai is the apex body for formulating policies, directing, co-ordinating and monitoring the activities of Extension Centres established in various parts of the country. The highlights of the important achievements and activities of CIPET during 1997-98 are as indicated below:-

Training activity

(a) The target for the intake of students for long term courses which was fixed as 1895 in 1996-97 has been increased to 2430 for the academic year 1997-98.

(b) The actual intake of students for long term courses has increased to 2483 as against 1944 in 1996-97.

(c) 124 short term courses have also been conducted with 1408 participants, as against the target of 95 courses with 1600 participants. The short fall is due to poor response from the industry in a few States consequent to recession in the general economy of the country.

(d) 21 Tailormade courses were organised in various specific areas at the request of industries in which 205 participants have benefitted.

(e) 282 students from colleges/technical institutions underwent inplant/vocational training during the period.

(f) DPTA Type National Vocational training Qualification (NVQ) courses were organised at CIPET Centres at Chennai, Ahmedabad, Lucknow and Mysore with the participation of 46 candidates.

Project proposals

(a) TIFAC-DST sponsored Mission Mode Project at a total cost of Rs. 35.00 lakhs is under implementation. Five short term courses are organised in the areas of FRP and Composite Technology.

(b) The project proposal funded by DST at a cost of Rs. 22.66 lakhs for "Development of Toughened Engineering Plastics" is progressing well.

(c) CIPET has been approved by the Deptt. of Family Welfare, Ministry of Health and Family Welfare for testing and evaluation of Copper-T component. A CIPET official has been nominated to visit various industries for evaluation and assess the qualitative and quantitative capabilities of contraceptive manufacturers in India.

(d) CIPET has entered into a major consultancy activity with M/s Padma PET Bottles International Pvt. Ltd., Bangalore for establishing a two stage PET Bottle Manufacturing facility at an estimated cost of Rs. 25 crores at Bangalore.

(e) CIPET has undertaken an Indo-US funded project from an US agency on " New Curing Systems for Thermoplastics Toughened Thermoset Epoxites" at a total cost of Rs. 14.30 lakhs.

Joint ventures

(a) CIPET, Chennai Testing Laboratory is in the process of getting UL Certification from M/s Underwriters Inc. USA.

(b) The Joint Venture with M/s ASCAMM, Barcelona, Spain is in the advanced stage of signing an MOU for training of candidates at CIPET Centres from various overseas countries.

(c) The Joint Venture with International Training Australia Pvt. Ltd. (ITA) in the area of providing training and technical services is under consideration.

(d) The Co-operative programme on the project entitled "Development of Polymer Materials for Special Applications" was approved under Integrated Long Term Programme (ILTP) between India and Russia.

Institute of pesticide formulation technology (IPFT)

The Institute of Pesticides Formulation Technology at Gurgaon is a non-profit making organisation registered under the Societies Registration Act on May 31,1991. The objective of the Institute is to promote advancement of Pesticide Formulation Technology in India. The Institute aims to develop and promote safer, efficient, economic and environment friendly pesticide formulations utilising indigenously available raw materials. The Institute is recognised by the Department of Scientific and Industrial Research, Ministry of Science and Technology, Government of India. The Institute has also been assigned the role of Technical Coordinator Unit of the Regional Network on Safe Pesticides Production & Information for Asia and the Pacific (RENPAP), a programme of UNDP/UNIDO on Pesticide Formulation and Quality Control.

The Institute has basic research and development laboratories and training facilities on various aspects of formulations like development, manufacture and quality control safety and packaging of pesticides, and has been recognised as an independent test laboratory by Bureau of Indian Standards (BIS) for analysing/testing of pesticide samples and their formulations.

The Institute provides analytical services, method development, method validation and verification of impurity profile of technical pesticides to the pesticides industry and the BIS. The Institute is headed by a Director and is located on Delhi-Jaipur National Highway No. 8 at Sector 20, Udyog Vihar, Gurgaon, Haryana.

Servicess rendered to the pesticide industry

One of the major objectives of the Institute is to develop and provide the pesticide formulation industry with user and environment friendly pesticide formulations so that the Indian farmers can have access to the user friendly products like their counterparts in the developed countries. The universally acceptable safer formulations are Suspension Concentrates (SC), Micro Emulsion and Controlled Release formulations.

Formulation laboratory

The Institute is well equipped with most of the facilities required for the development of state-of-the art pesticide formulations. The specialised equipment available at the laboratory includes Dynomill (KDL special), Eiger Mill, Fluid Bed Spray Granulator, Spray Drier, Turbula Pan and Disc. Granulators, Extruder, Micro Pulversor, Silverson, Mixer, Climatic Chamber Laser Based Particle Size Analyser, Rheometer, Film, Balance Surface and Interfacial Tensio Meters Viscometers and Research Microscopes.

Analytical laboratory

The analytical laboratory of the Institute is fully equipped with the state-of-the-art analytical Instruments namely, Gas Chromatograph coupled with Mass Spectrometric Detector (GC-MSD), High Performance Liquid Chromatograph (HPLC), Super Critical Fluid Chromatograph (SFC), High Performance Thin-Layer Chromatograph (HP-TLC), etc.

Bio science laboratory

The Bio-Science Laboratory which is fully equipped to undertake evaluation of pesticides and their formulations for bio-efficacy, phyto toxicity, compatibility and insect resistance to insecticides has carried out a number of sponsored projects.

Pilot plant

The Institute has a fully equipped pilot plant for scaling up of new formulations developed in the formulation laboratory upto semi-commercial level. The facility includes Dynomill Fluid Energy Mill, Lodige Mixer, Ribbon Blender and Hammer Mill besides various size reduction Mills.

The pilot plant equipments are being utilised for the in-house and conventional work on technology development. The equipments are being used for live demonstrations during the training programmes.

Human resource

The Institute has a team of highly qualified, trained and competent scientists and technologists and many of them have been trained in world famous laboratories as part of expertise building programme under the UNDP/ UNIDO assistance. Some of the staff members have served as UNIDO consultants in the developing countries.

Regional network on safe pesticides, production and information for asia and the pacific (RENPAP)

It is a network programme funded by the UNDP and executed by the UNIDO in association with FAO/WHO/ ESCAP/CIRAD. There are 15 countries of Asia and Pacific region, viz. Afghanistan, Bangladesh, China, Indonesia, Iran, Malaysia, Myanmar, Nepal, Pakistan, Philippines, Republic of Korea, Sri Lanka, Thailand and Vietnam participating in this programme.

The main thrust of the programme is to replace the hazardous pesticide products and technologies with those which are user and environment friendly through mutual sharing of experience among the member countries of the Network. The Government of India has been providing the Secretarial support facilities to the Regional Coordinating Unit.

13

Crop Productivity and Sustainability

The second International Crop Science Congress, held in New Delhi from November 17 to 24, has displayed the International scientific community's will to solve the mankind's basic problem of hunger and to lay the foundation for a vibrant, yet ecologically sustainable, agriculture to meet future needs. The world's largest assembly of crop scientists, over 1500 from nearly 70 countries, emphasised that the modern biotechnology, coupled with traditional wisdom, can mould future to suit the interest of the human society. Though new challenges will keep cropping up, the science would perhaps not only be able to deal with them but might indeed convert them into opportunities for the good of humanity.

The optimism would, however, hold true only if it is matched by political will to raise farm productivity as also to distribute its gains equitably. New technology accompanied by appropriate marketing policies and international cooperation holds the key to ensuring foods security in the years to come.

Deliberations of the mega scientific event, organised jointly by the National Academy of Agricultural Sciences (NAAS) and the Indian Council of Agricultural research (ICAR), once again confirmed the widely held notion that while the scientists would be able to cope with humanity's needs they may become helpless to cope with its greed. The world renowned agricultural expert, Dr. M.S. Swaminathan, who chaired the Congress, did not mince words in passing on this message. He said: "Whether in agriculture or aquaculture, we must curb the greed revolution and promote an ever-green revolution capable of bringing about continuous advances in terrestrial and aquatic productivity without harm to the environmental capital stocks of land, water forests, biological diversity, oceans and climate upon which such advances depend."

The theme of the Congress, "Crop productivity and sustainability—shaping the future"—was highly appropriate and topical for several reasons. Despite phenomenal growth in food production, nearly one-fifth of the world population is still malnourished and hungry. The impact of the green revolution is waning and concerns of productivity decline in major crop production systems are being expressed globally, diminishing per capita availability of land and water resources, expanding biotic and abiotic stresses and natural resources, including land, forest and environment, are fast degrading. This calls for greater resolve to ensure synergism among productivity, profitability and sustainability of major cropping systems. Moreover, for safeguarding food and nutritional security at the household level, crop intensification and diversification are needed on an ecologically sustainable basis.

In agriculture, an Evergreen Revolution is called for, signifying the sustainable use of natural resources.As the eminent scientist Dr M.S. Swaminathan says the time has come to lay emphasis on knowledge-based inputs rather than on the physical inputs only (such as fertilizers and seeds) to derive the best from the land without depletng its inner strngth. A learning revolution is to be brought about. Fortunatley, icon–based computer technoloy shows that literacy need not be a barrier in bringing about a better awareness of theecofriendly methodsof cultivation. It would beachallenge for the plannersto decentralize the knowledge based on agriculture to cover villages using computers and telecommunication links. Modern ecofriendly practices such as biologicalpest control and post–harvest technologies) should find high priority on the S & T agenda.

It is heartening to note that the Ninth Plan approach has emphasized the importance of biocontrol agents and biogenic fertilizers.

Agricultural implements and machinery

The Governmental programmes have been oriented to promote the farm mechanisation and make the improved and modern agricultural machines available to the farmers throughout the country with a view to increasing the agricultural production and removing socio-economical disparity among the farmers. Farmers have been provided assistance for owning agricultural machinery including tractors.

The infrastructure for human resource development on farm machinery has been expanded with a view to imparting training in the proper selection, operation, repair/maintenance and management of farm machinery. During these training programmes, emphasis has also been given on the energy conservation techniques in the use of agricultural machinery. Besides this, farm machines are tested with a view to evaluating their performance characteristics and upgrading their quality. However, despite a progressive increase in the use of agricultural machines, its sustainable benefits towards agricutural development have not been uniform in-as-much as only the improvement has mostly been in the northern states and in a few pockets/areas where irrigation facilities have been developed.

Although animal and human power continue to be the main power sources in agriculture, yet the power driven machines, namely tractors, power-tillers and combine harvestors continue to be in the frontline of farm machanisation. Fuel efficient tractors and better quality farm machines are now available in the country. Tractors are mostly sold in Haryana, Punjab, Uttar Pradesh and Madhya Pradesh and power tillers in Assam, West Bengal, Karnataka, Tamil Nadu, Kerala and Maharashtra.

During the Eighth Plan, thrust has been given to popularise the improved animal/power driven implements and small tractors with the objectives of promotion of mechanisation and to reduce the drudgrey associated with the farm operations. Water management has also been given specific attention and the water saving devices viz., sprinkler and drip irrigation system have been promoted through oilseeds, pulses and horticulture development programmes. Industrial designs, prototypes, jigs and fixtures have also been developed * . These schemes would give a fillip to the promotion of agricultural mechanisation in the country.

Farm Machinery Training and Testing Institutes set up a Budni (Madhya Pradesh), Hissar (Haryana), Garladinne (Andhra Pradesh) and Biswanath Chariali (Assam) impart on-the-job training in selection, operation, maintenance and management of farm machinery. These institutes also undertake testing of farm machinery to ascertain their performance characteristics and suggest improvement in their quality. So far over 43,000 personnel were trained and 1,160 test reports on farm machinery released. Two more institutes are likely to be set up in Rajasthan and Tamil Nadu. To suplement the efforts of these institutes five state agricultural universities have been identified for undertaking training on farm machinery and two agricultural universities for testing activities.

The Government of India and state government jointly established 17 state agro-industries corporations with the objective of streamlining input distribution and extending other agro-services to the farmers. These have significantly contributed to agricultral development, improvement of agro engineering services and promotion of agro-based industries during last two decades. Corporations in Gujarat, Haryana, Kerala, Maharashtra, Punjab and Madhya Pradesh earned estimated profits totalling Rs. 1,192.61 lakh during 1993-94. The National Productivity Performance Award for 1991-92 in the agro-industries sector was won by Punjab Agro-Industries Corporation Limited and Certificate of Merit for sustained productivity efforts was won by the Gujarat Agro-Industries Corporation Limited.

The Dangerous Machines (Regulation) Act, 1983 provides for the regulation of trade and commerce in production, supply, distribution and use of the products of any industry producing dangerous machines with a view to securing the welfare of labourers operating such machines, and for payment of compersation for the death or bodily injury suffered by any farmer/labourer while operating any such machines. The scope of the Act extends to the 'Dangerous Machines' intended to be used in agriculture and rural sectors. However, presently, only power thresher used in the agricultural production process has been brought under the purview of the Act.

The Government of India has adopted Integrated Pest Management (IPM) as a major thrust area and main plan of crop protection programme during Eighth plan. IPM approach is eco-friendly which aims at minimal use of hazardous chemical pesticides by employing all available alternate pest control methods and techniques such as cultural, mechanical and biological and bio-pesticides.

The Government of India has set up IPM Farmers Field Schools (FFS) for rice, cotton, sugarcane, vegetables, oilseeds and pulses etc., to impart training to farmers and extension workers. During, 1994-95, 844 farmers field schools were organised wherein 3,934 extension officers and 25,161 farmers have been trained. Besided 585 agricultural extension officers have been trained through season long training programme organised in rice, cotton and vegetables in various states.

The surveillance for pests and diseases on economically important crops was carried out by sample roving survey on an area of 5.55 lakh hectare and about 1,464 million parasites and predators were released for controlling identified pests on important crops during 1994. All the strategic areas in Thar desert were kept under continuous watch from April to October 1994 by conducting regular surveys and a few small concentration of locust hopper/adults of two grasshoppers species were detected and controlled over a total area of 327 hectare in Jaisalmer, Barmer and Jodhpur areas. As a result of timely operation swarm formation of locust has been effectively checked. To upgrade the skills of farmers and locust staff, two field training on locust control, one each at Bikaner and Palanpur were organised during November 1994.

The current legislation governing the plant quarantine rules entitled, 'The Plants, Fruits and Seeds (Regulation of Import into India) Order, 1989 (PFS Order 1989) came into force replacing the PFS Order 1984 in the wake of New Policy on Seed Development (NPSD) effective from 1 October 1988. The inspection procedure has been simplified in order to boost the export of floriculture and other agricultural commodities under NPSD.

The National Plant Protection Training Institute, Hyderabad continued to organise training programmes on various aspects of plant protection with special emphasis on IPM. It organised 30 training courses for master trainers in which 375 persons were trained. Beside special training course has been organised for technical personnel of fertilizer industry in Integrated Pest Management technology.

The Registration Committee constituted under the Section (5) of the Insecticides Act, 1968 received a total of 3,206 applications out of which 2193 registration certificates have been granted under various sections/ subsections of the Act. With a view to promote safer and non-chemical pesticides in IPM, biocides and plant origin pesticides like Bacillus thuringiensis and Bacillus sphaericus and need based pesticides have been provisionally registered and allowed commercialisation.

Apropos the sectors allied to agriculture, the strategies are as follows:

— Attention is to be paid towards proper blending of technology, credit, scientific management, post—harvest infrastructure and marketing for higher growth. Steps will be taken to increase productivity of perennial fruits and spices, reduce losses at different stages of storage, grading, packing, etc (which amount to 20%—40%) by developing a sound post—harvest infrastructure.

— Steps will be taken to increase productivity, accelerate replanting activities, expand this sector in non—traditional areas, improve packaging and enhance quality standards.

— R & D activities for production of quality fish seeds and feed are to be intensified. to increase fish production and productivity, indiscriminate growth of brackish water farms is to be checked, overexploitation of coastal fisheries will be prevented, and the marketing infrastructure is to be developed.

— This subsector will get greater attention in the Ninth Plan, for it has substantial employment generating avenues, particularly in the rainfed and drought—prone areas. Effective control of animal diseases, declaration of disease—free zones, scientific management of genetic stock resources, extension services, increasing production, productivity and profitability of livestock enterprises, etc will be areas of concern in this Plan. Priority will be given to improvement of breeding services, upgradation of health care services, fooder and feed activities, strengthening of training and research facilities, provision of adequate credit and marketing support, extension of processing facilities and measures for involving entrepreneurs, co–operative institutions and voluntary agencies.

Agro—exports are soght to be given fillip, in recognition of the valuable foreign exchange they bring, besides opening up new employment avenues. The strategies in this sphere are: development of markets and products, branch names and dissemination of information among exporters, improvement in quality and packaging, encouragement to export—oriented units and enhancing backward linkages with growers.

The role of co—operatives is to be enhanced—they are to be made more efficient, viable and competritive, through greater professionalism, diversification of activities, evolving effective recovery systems, technology upgradation, quality improvement, human resource development, etc.

Timber and forests :

India has a total geographical area of 3287263 sq. km. The officially recorded forest area is 765210 sq. km., which constitutes 23.8% of the total geographical area. Over 45000 species of plants occur in the country and several thousand species of them are endemic to India. Their range of distribution is confined only to this country and not reported from any other part of the world. India is equally rich in fauna. The country has about 350 species of birds and qmqore than 20,000 species of insects.

Various sources give different figures of the land use pattern in the country. However, the task of reconciliation of these figures has been assigned to National Remote Sensing Agency (NRSA) and in all probability it would be completely reconciled in the beginning of Ninth Plan, which is to begin from April 1997. Presently, the land use pattern have been quoted from the report published by Directorate of Economics and Statistics (1996), a nodal agency in the country to compile the data related to various departments in the country.

The total area recorded as forest in 1950-51 was 404800 sq. km. Over the years recorded forest area continuously rose and touched the figures of 765210 sq. km. This was on account of unoccupied government lands being declared as the Forest area by state/UT governments. Most of these lands were non-productive and came under the category of wastelands. A unique situation exists in the North-Eastern states of the country. These forest lands are unclassed i.e. without any legal status. In India the total unclassed forest is 125385 sq. km. which constitutes 3.8% and 16.38% of the geoographical area and recorded forest area of the country respectively.

The transfer of forest land to non-forest uses is also one of the important factors which has depleted India's natural forest ecosystem. In between 1951 to 1980, 4.328 million ha. of forest land were officially diverted for non-forestry uses. It would be proper to mention here that the transferred forest lands were highly productive lands and would have contributed much towards enrichment of forest ecosystem, if retained.

While analysing the state-wise forest cover of India it is revealed that owing to specific problems the country may be broadly divided into two regions namely, North Eastern region and rest of the country.

North Eastern region consists of seven states. There has been a decrease in the dense forest and open forest cover in almost every state and there is an alarming proportion of forest degradation in this region.

The loss of forest cover in N-E region because of the practice of shifting cultivation accounts for 1526 sq. km. and for other reasons the loss is 377 sq. km.

In most of the states as mentioned in preceding para, the dense forest cover has shown a deslining trend thereby setting in a chain reaction in the degradation of ecosystem.

In 1995 assessment (fifth cycle) the State wise and above forest category wise detail are not given but it has shown that in totality there has been an increase in the dense forest and Mangrove but open forest has shown a declining trend. Presently, the Forest ecosystem is under tremendous pressure on account of excessive removal of biomass in all forms including diversion of forest lands to non forest uses.

Forestry is one of the cheapest option to bring about a change in rural economy of the country. Forests not only give fuelwood, small timber, timber, and fooder to the people but it also conserves water and soil moisture for the agro-eco system. Development and conservation of forest area will help rural people to improve their level of loving.

The forest wasteland has immense potential in this respect. Degradation of forest has been going on because of various pressure groups on the forest eco-system. Today, various agencies give different figures for the extent of waste land avaliable in the country. Forest Survey of India has given 31 million hectares of degraded forest in the country, though the actual figure may be higher. The Ministry of Environment and Forest considers and extent of forest wasteland around 35 million hectares. The problem of increasing wasteland becomes more complex if the non-forest wasteland is also taken into consideration. The National Commission on Agriculture (1976) has given a figure of 176 million hectares of wasteland available in the country while Society for Promotion for Wasteland Development has given 129 million hectares as wasteland in the country. To arrive at the actual figure the job for assessing wasteland in the country has been assigned to National Remote Sensing Agency (NRSA) and it is believed that a conclusive figure would be provided in the beginning of Ninth Five Year Plan (1997-98).

Regardless of the extent of wasteland available in the country, it becomes all the more important to develop them on priority basis so that the basis requirement of the local populaltion is fully met. The total annual availability of fuelwood and small timber from the forest is 26290 thousand cum. and 8 million cum. respectively whereas the total requirement of fuelwood, fooder and small timber of the country has been estimated and found to be much higher than their annual availability.

All eco-systems develop a set of specialised and integrated structural and functional properties which are in delicate balance. In a stable ecosystem, all the system variables may return to the initial equilibrium, if the disturbance is moinor. The stability of a system, however, may be exclusively or collectively determined by the extent of its resistance and/or resilience. Exploitation of natural resources beyond the threshold limits imposed by the resistance and resilience of the ecosystem warrants immediate attention. Any further mismanagement can lead to damages beyond repair. For example, tropical moist forests, rich in genetic resources, are continuously under biotic pressure resulting in soil erosion, floods,l loss of species, loss of biomass and many others. Therefore, the management of each ecosystem should be site and problem specific if the forests have to be conserved an developed on the principle of sustainability. This has also been seen after a very careful review of the various schemes in the Forestry sector that this sector has not been dealt with adequate attention from planning point of view. For example, the scheme titled "control of forest fire" covers only five states in the country though it is a menace which not only disturbs the existing ecosystem but also leads to extinction of many flora and fauna. Likewise, control of poaching, rhino conservation, forest protection, natural regeneration are many areas where regular efforts or schemes are needed to strengtrhen the infrastructure in general and capacity building in particular.

FAO estimates that in 1994, the world produced 3,419.9 mcum of round wood, out of which India's share was only 293.9 mcum (8.59%). Firewood and charcoal accounted for as much as 91.5% (269.2 mcum) of the Indian Production (FAO, 1994). Although only less than 10% of the total wood production in the country is used for industrial purpopses, industrial demand has been rising sharply. Projected demands for forest products show a 22 to 183% increase from 1990 to 2000. By a long—term trend analysis of forest products in India, Rao (1992) showed that production of almost all products except pulpwood and particles and veneer sheets registered an increase in the 1980s.

The decade from 1975–76 to 1985–86, saw Indian production of wood and wood products recording an increase of 22 to 135%. However, statistics on timber production is less revealing, perhaps as incomplete as its demand itself. Timber is normally obtained from government forests, community and private forests and farm lands. While the timber extracted from the national forests is reported in the official statistics, the timber harvested from the other sources goes unreported in the official statistics. Therefore, the epithet 'recorded production', a gross underestimate of total production is fashionable among foresters.

According to FSI, consumption of firewood exceeded recorded production by a staggering 195 mcum in 1987. All existing projections show that there is a big gap between demand and supply of industrial timber too. Total sustained yield increment of existing forests is stated to be 35 million m^3 With an additional 4–5 million m^3 from private sources, it sums up to a grand total of 40 million m^3 (Campbell, 1987). To meet the industrial needs alone (64.4 mcum in 2000 AD, according to NCA, 1976), an additional sustained yield increment of 24 mcum will be needed. Furthermore, all indicators suggest that this gap is going to grow. Presumably this wide gap between demand and sup[ply is being met from unrecorded sources like farm lands and agroforestry and other privately owned sources.

Given this huge deficit in industrial timber availability in the country, we may probably have two options. The first, is to enhance the area under plantation forests and to improve their productivity. However, given a conservative average productivity of 0.3 cum/ha for long rotation timber and roundwood species, and 3–5 cum/ha for short rotation pulp wood, this would then mean at least 30 million ha of new plantations for timber species and two million ha for pulpwood–a total for 32 million ha for industrial needs alone (Campbell, 1987). Considering the poor productivity of forest plantations and the general inhability to expand area under plantation forestry, it is impossible to achieve such gargantuan targets through the plantation forestry route.

Agroforestry and private forestry (industrial and non–industrial) constitute the second option in this regard. There exists a vast potential for using agriculturtal lands as sources of timber and for meeting the wood requirements of the society. Agricultural lands (net area sown) make up as much as 43.5% of the total geopraphical area of the country, while forests (including degraded) occupy only about 20%. Moreover, many of our traditional land use practices are examples of integrated, intensive farming systems/practices that blend trees with various other life forms. Trees including perennial horticultural crops have traditionally formed an integral component of our agricultural landscape. Growing trees of various kinds is part of the tradition in India. Most people also perceive the economic, social and cultural benefits of trees as a source of fruits, fuelwood, fooder and timber. The Kerala homegardens form a spectacular example in this regard. Homegardens create a forest-like multi–storey canopy structure and is also a source of tremndous agrobiodiversity.

Plantation agriculture, is another important land use activity in many parts of the country. Examples include palms, rubber and many fruit trees. Other salient traditonal agroforestry systems include, growing multipurpose trees (trees that yield fruits, vegetables, fooder, fuelwood, timber etc.) either on the farm boundaries or as scattered trees on the farm fields, growing commercial crops (tea, coffee, pepper etc.) under planted shade trees and/or trained on to them, growing commercial crops (nutmeg, clove, cacao etc.) under the shade of planted commerical tree crops (coconut, arecanut etc.) growing commerical crops (cardamom) under the shade of trees in natural forests, commercial woodlots, live fences, silvopastoralism, grazing in natural forests and shelterbelts.

A wide spectrum of trees and shrubs is often encountered in all these land use systems. The floristic elements, however, vary from region to region and depending on size of holdings, socio—economic factors and the socio-cultural background of farmers. Wood productivity in agroforestry is also correspondingly diverse. Predise macro-level data are, however, not available concerning availability and/or standing stock of wood from agricultural lands. Available microlevel studies, although limited, indicate that standing stock of commercial timber from the Kerala homesteads, is between 6.6 and 50.8 m^3 ha^{-1} (Kumar et al 1994). In another study Krishnankutty (1990)assessed the wood harvested from rubber plantatons of Kerala in 1987 at 0.999 mcum. To enhance timber productivity from the traditional land use systems, therefore, concerted efforts are necessary with respect to selection of better genotypes/provenances/clones of multipurpose trees, making available quality planting stock and evolving appropriate technological packages on tree management.

Private industrial forestry, nevertheless, is a recent phenomenon. It involves growing high value timber species such as teak and other fast growing tree species (e.g. teak, eucalyptus, popular, mangium and many soft wood species) under short rotation intensive cultural systems (SRIC) on private lands. Nonetheless, such practices are in vogue in many developed and less developed nation-states including China New Zealand etc. In the Indian context also, there are many examples where the farmers' initiative has been effectively harnessed by the wood based industries for raw material production.

Examples include tree planting programmes sponsored by industrial houses such as South India Viscose Ltd., ITC Bhadrachalam Paper Boards Ltd. and WIMCO. Such industrial establishments in general supply planting stock and technology packages to the farmers besides, reaching 'buy back' agreements with them on purchase of produce. Private forestry assumes significance in view of the shrinking forest resource base and its ability to ese pressure on shrinking forest resource base. Perhaps with little over 2% of the total geographical area of the world and about 15% of its human and livestock population, India already expereinces a critical imbalance in its natural resource base. The National FOrest Policy 1988 also highlights the importance of the wood based industries producing their own raw materials.

There are, however, institutional, technological and socio—economic factors acting either separately or in unison, which constrain or obstruct the spread and diffusion on tree farming in India. Restrictions on tree felling, non–availability of quality planting stock, lack of appropriate technology packages especially for polycultural systems and the absence of public policy support hamper adoption of tree farming by private entrepreneurs. For fear of interspecific competition, many small farmers are also reluctant to grow timber and fuel wood species in association with woody perennial plantation agricultural species. Furthermore, as agroforestry extension and communication networks are choked, credit and other facilities are limited.

Agroforestry has tremendous potential to convert India into the 'wood basket' of world. Implicit in agroforestry and tree farming are two fundamental themes: ecological security and generation of income and employment. Quite apart the indirect ecological benefits, tree farming is an economically viable land use option.

Demand for timber land other forest products is expanding at a very rapid rate. Incokrporation of tree growing as part of the farm system technology can make significant contribution to the supply of wood based products. However, a paradigm shift in our planning and development thinking is imperative to make it operational. Evolving appropriate technology packages for tree farming (SRIC systems) and provision of inputs are central to this.

Lack of an apropriate public policy support and absence of technological packages too are critical constraints in this regard. Agroforestry extension is particularly weak. At present, enither the Forest Department nor the Agriculture Department considers integrated land use systems such as agroforestry important. Presumably they act as water-tight compartments, although agroforestry is a mixture of agriculture and forestry. Suitable corrective mechanisms are indispensable in this regard. This includes amendment to the restrictive provisions of laws, providing public policy and credit support to the tree farming enterprises, evolving improved post harvest processing techniques, removal of hidden subsidies to the wood based industries, strengthening agroforestry extension and encouraging farmers' initiative in rural afforestation and raw material production for wood based industries.

The meaning attached to the term "Cottage Industries" has undergone changes with the progress in technology and its definition no longer restricts it to industries using manual labour and simple tools only. The use of power and machines has been admitted in the definition of the term. The basic implications which differentiate the cottage industries from large scale and heavy industries are: (1) the small scale of production, and (2) usually the worker works on his own, although the employment of wage-paid labour is not ruled out. Attempts to define the term very precisely have not been quite successful. With technological progress the concept behind cottage industries has been undergoing modifications. However, the sense in which the term is employed is commonly well understood. (Some of the definitions are given in an Appendix to this chapter).

Cottage industries may be divided into four broad classes, viz., handicrafts, home industries, small-scale industries and village industries. The dexterity of human hands and mainly their use in making the final product are the characteristics of handicrafts. Handicrafts, as the name indicates, always represent the best type of art for the art produced by hand can hardly be excelled.

In home industries, hand or power driven machinery may be used. But the chief characteristics of home industries is that raw materials are procurable locally and labour consists normally of family members. If there are any outsiders they are employed only as apprentices. The industry thus gets the most careful attention of the master.

Small industries are distinguishable by the place of work, the amount of capital invested and equipment used. They are carried on either in the house of the artisan or in a small workshop run by the entrepreneur. The capital invested may be theoretically large as is the case with ivory carving. But generally the capital is limited and this places restrictions on the employment of labour, the use of machinery, etc.

Hired labour may be employed both in the small-scale and village industries; but the village industries have necessarily to be located in the villages, while the small industries may even be located in the urban or semi-urban areas. The number or employees in the small industries should also not be large and may not exceed nine persons.

The importance of village and cottage industries is emphasised by the fact that India, in spite of considerable progress towards urbanisation in the recent past, still lives in villages and her national economy is predominantly agricultural. Her agriculture, even when the required degree of intensity of cultivation is achieved through the development of irrigation, use of fertilizers and above all with the assistance of an all-pervading extension service, by its very seasonal nature and overcrowding in it, would not be able to free itself from the disguised unemployment and underemployment.

The industrial development, with its concentration in towns, is no solution to the problem of unemployment in villages. The small enterprises employed about 20 million workers as against about five million workers in the factory establishments in 1966. There has been a great rise in building and other construction activities and people have found new employment opportunities in them. But this is so only during the transitional stage of economic development and the tempo of construction programmes may slow down. Therefore a more stable source of employment has to be looked for. Rural industries provide great promise in this respect.

The greatest advantage of small and cottage industries is that employment is provided in the natural setting of the workers' own place with numerous physical, moral and other benefits that go with such employment. It helps them to develop inherent talents and aptitudes in occupations congenial to them. Another important reason for employment to be found in the villages and not outside is that agriculture may not provide full employment, yet a larger labour force has to remain in villages at certain periods to provide the needed labour for cultivation, weeding, harvesting and other operations. Mechanised agriculture, to any appreciable extent, does not seem to be a practical proposition for many years to come. The introduction and encouragement of well-chosen village industries in each region of India, on grounds of availability of raw material, local talent, the ability of the industry to fit in with and adjust within a limit with the peak labour demand in agriculture, should add to rural welfare in many ways.

— It will reduce considerably unemployment and underemployment in many regions.

— It will provide useful outlet for many of the raw materials and waste material of agriculture, the transport of which, for reasons of their bulk and low value, is not economical over long distances. Such raw material will be converted into national wealth.

— The farmer and his family members will get an additional source of income which is so needed to raise their standard of living and help them tide over difficulties caused by the failure of crops.

— The country is facing an extreme shortage of foreign exchange. The restrictions on imports does not help very much to ease the problem. An all-out effort required to encourage exports. The produce of cottage industries hae fairly reasonable prospects of commanding foreign markets where there is great demand for them. The opening of cottage industries emporia in some of the European countries has already brought to light the potentialities of these products as earners of foreign exchange.

— Phulkaris of Punjab, shawls, wood work and art pieces of Kashmir, are but a few items, which are much in demand in other countries and promise to fetch prices commensurate with the labour put in the production of these commodities.

— The products of small industries which employ local raw materials and talent do not call for any heavy capital investment. This suits our austere economy.

— There need not be any clash between the large and small industries. If properly organised, small industries will provide employment opportunities to enable India to achieve her cherished goal of full employment, but also act as feeders to large industries.

— A developing economy depending upon deficit financing has to face a time lag between the commencement and completion of big projects particularly when the country lacks technical know-how and equipment. During this period, the available consumption goods cannot keep pace with the rise in the purchasing power. Products of cottage and small-scale industries would come in very handy under these circumstances. In addition to making available a variety of consumer goods, they will to a great extent be free from the distribution problem. Transportation over long distances would not be necessary and a major portion of the products would be consumed near the producing centres. These readily available goods will help to mop up the newly released purchasing power and fill the necessary gap, till the investment on capital good strats producing consumer goods.

— India is wedded to a democratic form of government and is committed to a socialistic pattern of society. Like peasant farming in agriculture, cottage and small industries in the industrial sector strengthen the foundation of democracy and socialist structure of society. For this reason also, cottage and small industries have to get a place in the national economy to usher in economic democracy and the desired social order.

In view of the benefits conferred on the national economy and increase in rural welfare, cottage and small scale industries have a very strong case for rehabilitation and development. The power projects completed and nearing completion under the Five Year Plans are adding to the supply of total electricity in the country at reasonable costs. The Government have already taken up the programmes of rural electrification. This should give further impetus to development of small industries in villages. This favourable development in the availability of cheap power in rural areas can greatly help to remove the stigma attached to cottage industries of being sweated ones with low returns. As technological progress in the form of the steam engine gave a staggering blow to the small scale production in the 19th century, the change from steam power to electric power, particularly in countries where the electric power can be produced cheaply, can help in reversing the process from large scale to small scale production in the case of a number of products on economic grounds, considerations of rural welfare and decentraliisation of economy in the interest of a democratic socialistic set up. It is just not a theoretical deducation but is in actual practice in countries like Japan and Switzerland. The various forms of help needed by the small scale industries are described below:

— An organised extension service of technical guidance to the cottage workers in designing, use of tools and machines and production of quality goods or goods according to demand.

— The extension service has to be supported with appropriate research institutions at central, regional and state levels.

— Development of industrial cooperatives for supplies, services, finance, and marketing of products and in some instances even for production. If farming can be run on cooperative lines, there appears no reason why it cannot be done in the production of goods in certain cottage or village industries as well. For an understanding of the causes of failure of cooperative societies in the past, the findings of Sri Vishwanathan Vekumalla who surveyed some of the representative industrial cooperatives in Andhra would be of interest. These are:

— Societies do not have enough capital either to give full time work to members or to enable them to manage until the products are sold. Consequently the members are obliged to produce for the local market or for the local sahukar.

— The limited benefits conferred by the societies make the members disloyal. The artisans distrust one another.

— Some influential members as office beares utilise the societies' funds to further their own personal ends.

— The consumer, majority of whom have low incomes, care more for cheap goods rather than for quality. The member artisans face keen competition from non-members who under-sell by producing inferior stuff for the market.

— Instead of obtaining the cooperation of the supervising officials, the office bearers of some societies actually betray their own cause by hoodwinking them.

With cooperative education, proper training and supervision, these difficulties can be overcome but it must be clearly realised that efforts on a cooperative basis in all possible directions are necessary for the development of handicrafts and cottage industries. It is only through cooperation that these industries can reduce their costs of production and marketing.

— There should be adequate and institutional credit made available to the cottage workers for meeting the financial needs of their business.

— The State should help develop home and foreign markets for cottage goods.

— A system of quality control must be imposed on the cottage products.

— Government should give preference to cottage products in buying their requirements.

Agroforestry

Agroforestry connotes land use systems where woody perennials (trees and shrubs) are deliberately grown with field crops and/or livestock, either simultaneously or sequentially, on the same land management unit. It implies a combination of agriculture and forestry aiming at diversified and sustainable production. Agroforestry practices frequently include tree/pasture systems, tree/speciality crop systems, alley cropping, windbreaks, living fences, etc. riparian buffers, stream band bioengineering, wildlife habitat and some other vegetation management systems also have been lately included under it. Such diverse land use systems encompassed by the generic concept of 'agroforestry', broadly falls under agrisilviculture, silvopasture, agrisilvipasture and other (miscellaneous) systems.

The basic philosophy of all agroforestry, however, is two-fold: (1) to optimise the combined production of woody perennials and agricultural crops and (2) to conserve and improve the site. Agroforestry, thus aims at ecological security, increased productivity and above all, sustainability. It is a prominent example of the traditional ecotechnological aproaches adapted by tropical farmers ('Ecotechnology' denotes technology rooted in the principles of ecology, economics and equity).

Multiplicity of goods and services is a unique feature of agroforestry. Agroforestry systems in general, are capable of producing timber, fuel, fooder and green leaf manure besides, performing various ecological functions such as reducing wind speed, checking soil erosion and causing microclimatic modifications. Production of wood, however, is a dominant function of agroforestry. This is further exemplified by the fact that homesteads, a prominent agroforestry system in Kerala, contribute as much as 74.4 to 83.6% of its effective wood demand (14.645 mcum in 1987-88) and about 67.2–75% of its firewood requirement (Krishanankutty, 1990).

Estimates on timber requirements vary widely in the Indian context. Different agencies voice digressing figures. Statistics on wood requirements and availability, therefore, presents a hazy picture. Precise studies have not been conducted to assess the timber requirement in our country. Furthermore, demand for timber in the unorganised sector has been grossly ignored. The 1988 National Forest Policy also laments about the poor data environment in this regard. It states succinctly, "inadequacy of data regarding forest resources is a matter of great concern...."

Regarding India's industrial timber requirement at the turn of the century, the oft cited National Commission on Agriculture Report (NCA, 1976) indicates a ranges of 47.1 to 64.4 million cubic metres (mcum), depending on production, growth and economic development. Wood requirement of any society, is presumably a function of the size of populaltion, level of development, availability, price ad the like. The higher estimate of NCA pre–supposes a high growth rate and consumption. Of the 64.4 mcum of wood required by India in the year 2000 AD, approximately 30 million for pulp and paper and 13 million for round wood (NCA, 1976).

Inventories made by Forest Survey (FSI, 1987) on demand for woood (other than firewood), however, puts India's total industrial wood requirement at 27.58 mcum and supply at 12 mcum. The Interministerial Group on Wood Substitution, estimate it as 24.88 million m (Singh, 1992). Demand projections of industrial round wood by Rai et al (1983) using a compound growth rate equation and transcendental production function had given figures such as 30 mcum and 11 mcum respectively for the year 1995. In another study, Kalla (1988), estimated that demand for industrial roundwood in Indian in 1990 would be 24.07 mcum.

Nobody quite knows who first propounded the thesis that India could stamp out poverty by setting up agro-industries in a big way. The term came into vogue no more than a decade ago. But since then it has become highly fashionable. Almost everything ranging from a giant nuclear power reactor to cellophane packing is now sought to be justified on the ground that it is necessary to promote agro-industries. Most of the big business houses have already diversified into the field and others want to do so.

For the new entrepreneurs it is not merely a matter of keeping up with the established industrial Joneses. The opportunities are vast and highly attractive, considering the governmental incentives on offer. The authorities in their anxiety to industrialise the countryside have decided to extend the benefits to a large number of industries whose link agriculture is remote if at all one exists. The 155-point list of "agro-industries" issued by the Commissioner of Small-Scale Industries, for instance, includes refrigeration plants for milk and factories for the canning of fish.

The Planning Commission goes even further. It says that any enterprise which processes farm produce, supplies chemical inputs to agriculture (fertilizers, insecticides, etc.), manufactures improved agricultural equipment (hoes, bullock cart tyres, tractors, etc.), or helps raise farm output is an agro-industry. This means that the term not only covers the nation's biggest industry—cotton textiles—but also the whole range of plantations like tea, coffee and cashewnut and of course, jute.

Going only by statistics the result is somewhat ironical. They show that a much bigger segment of the Indian industry was agro-based at the time of Independence than has been the case in recent years. In 1951 agro-industries accounted for 75 per cent of the total productive capital employed and 78 per cent of all value added by manufacturing in the organised sector. By 1963, however, these percentage had fallen respectively to 34 and 53. The steep decline in these figures does not mean that agro-industries are on their way out. But it does indicate that their growth has been slow in comparison with the phenomenal expansion of other industries like steel, oil refining or electronics.

The word "agro-industries" broadly means industries manufacturing "input" for agriculture, or processing agricultural "output." Agencies supporting agriculture by designing and manufacturing inputs are termed as "agro-industrials" and those supported by agricultural products are classed as "agro-based industries."

Generally most of the industries use agricultural output as basic raw material. But the concept of agro-based industries leave out of account "industrial product". It is confined to those industries that are engaged in processing the agricultural produce either for consumption or for the use of industry. They include wheat milling, rice milling, dal-making, oil crushing, cotton ginning, khandsari, fruit beverages, and so on. Thus, the agro-industries serve at both the ends of farming.

In the first instance agro-industrials provide the essential input and in the second phase agro-based industries function as an outlet for agricultural output. The purpose of helping these industries is to make farming a profitable and commercially viable proposition; since agro-industrials directly influence the cost structure of farming and agro-based industries, they have their impact on the receipts of the farmer. Agro-industries also serve as a means for providing better employment opportunities to the labour during off season.

The concept of agro-industrial is not new. Formerly the village smith, the carpenter and cobbler used to prepare and repair the various traditional types of agricultural tools and implements. These industries were, and in some regions still are, the part and parcel of rural life. The agricultural implements are exchanged for a share in the harvest.

Likewise in its refined form modern agro-industrial manufacture, process and supply agriculture inputs either on cash basis or realise the value in instalments. The distribution of fertilizers and seeds has been taken over by the cooperatives for quite a long time now. The various agro-industrial corporations in the states seek to supply agriculture machinery on cash, credit and hire-purchase system.

The idea of "in—kind" assistance has been mooted from the simple fact that outright cash grant to the farmer for production is often misused and misdirected in consumption. Even those genuinely interested in buying implements and machinery, have faced numerous problems in purchasing them at reasonable prices. The farmer who is detached from urban life takes time in locating the supplier and picking up the operating technique. Because of "scarcity" of modern machinery, is said that a "black market" has also grown in agricultural inputs.

The purpose of establishing the agro-industrial corporations, therefore, is not only to equip the farmer with modern implements but also to train him in the operation of machines—so essential at the early stages of mechanisation, ensure proper use of funds and protect the farmer from the difficulties involved in purchasing right type of machinery and implements suitable for cultivation in his region. In India, the soil and climate conditions so sharply differ from one region to another that only regional corporations could take a better view and mould the tools according to regional requirements.

Although there has been an impressive development of large-scale industries during the two decades of planned development, India still remains predominantly a country of villages and small industries. About two crore persons are engaged in these industries, of whom nearly 90 lakhs work in the handloom industries, i.e., more than the total number of persons employed in the organised industries and mining put together.

The small-scale and village industries sector covers a wide range of traditional and modern small-scale industries including handloom, khadi, powerloom, sericulture, coir, handicrafts, village industries and mechanised small-scale industries.

This sector consists broadly of (i) traditional cottage and household industries (viz., handloom, khadi & village industries, handicrafts, sericulture and coir industry), and (ii) modern small scale industries (defined as those having investment of up to Rs. 10 lakhs in plant and machinery and Rs. 15 lakhs in the case of ancillary industries). As distinguished from modern small scale industries, the traditional cottage and household industries are located mostly in rural and semi-urban areas. A large number of these traditional industries do not use power-operated appliances and equipment. These also involve relatively lower levels of investment and technology and provide largely part-time employment. A very large number of the persons dependent on traditional industries belong to the poorer sections of the society and live below the poverty line. However, a number of these industries produce certain essential articles required by the masses and also some other items which are exported. The number of persons employed in principal traditional industries is estimated at 140 lakhs, including about 57 lakhs in the handloom industry and about 36 lakhs in sericulture. Much of this employment is neither full-time nor well remunerative. Modern small scale industries are estimated to provide full-time employment to about 28 lakh persons.

It is estimated that 175 mha of India's land is degraded. This includes 85 mha under agriculture and 35 mha of forest land. Among the various reasons for the land losing its productivity are the over-application of chemical fertilizers in agriculture, waterlogging as a result of over-irrigaiton, canal seepage, poor drainage, overgrazing of common grazing lands and deforestation. The seriousness of deforestation has been dramatically brought out through the use of modern monitoring and mapping thechnologies.

Land, water and biological resources are intricately linked to one another. With excessive pressure on the biomass, the vegetative cover starts to disappear. As a consequence, the runoff of water during the rains increases and groundwater recharge is diminished. Without vegetation, the topsoil that has taken centuries to form is washed away and the land gets eroded. In hilly areas, the process starts an almost irreversible cycle of degradation.

Two of the main pressures on the vegetative cover are the need for fuelwood and fodder. In India almost 87 per cent of energy for cooking is obtained from firewood, agricultural wastes and cow-dung, and only 13 per cent cooking energy is from commercial sources. Firewood alone provides 50 per cent of the cooking energy in cities and 70 per cent in villages. This dependence on firewood has put a great pressure on forest, and in fact on all vegetative matter. The demand, estimated at 157 million tonnes in 1986-87, is far in excess of the supply. With the consequent disappearance of trees and other vegetation, women, who are the principal collectors of fuelwood, have to spend a much greater amount of time on collection thereby putting up the 'cost' of fuelwood.

The other pressure is the need for fodder. With the world's largest cattle popultion of over 400 million animals, fodder availability in India is grossly inadequate. Pasture land only constitutes 3.9 per cent of the land and as a result is degraded. The pressure on forests is once again heavy. The cattle which are undernourished produce low quantities of milk. In degraded environments people find it easier to keep goats, and the increase in te goat population has been much more rapid than that of cattle, buffaloes and sheep. But goats in fragile ecosystems are as much a problem as a solution and, unless properly managed, can further degrade the environment.

Realizing the urgent need to increase biomass production, social foresty programmes were started in the late 1970s. These included raising rural fuelwood plantations and village wood lots, starting tree nurseries, distribution of tree spalings, encouragement to plantations around agricultural fields, as well as promotion of farm forestry and strip plantation on roadsides and canel banks. But while there were many successes, this programme was not able to arrest the increasing degradation of land caused by over-exploitation.

By 1985 about half of India's land was estimated to be wasteland—land which had hardly any vegetation left on it. Rajiv Gandhi, who was then Prime Minister, announced the development of wastelands as a major thrust area. The social forestry experience had shown that such programmes were more effective if carried out with the participation of the local communities at every stage. Without this it would not be possible to protect the plantations. The National Wastelands Development Board was set up to encourage wastelands development and, working with a number of voluntary agencies, to involve people in this process.

While these programmes were being initiated several experiments were underway, including the one at Arabari in West Bengal, in which people were being involved in managing forest areas along with the Forest Department. The cumulative experience of such efforts led to a Government circular in 1990, asking all state forest departments to try the Joint Forest Management model. It will be some time before such a concept can be fully implemented, but the circular itself represents a significant recognition regarding the management of forests.

When the forest regulations, and indeed the Forest Department, were established during the colonial period, they were seen as agencies for the controlled exploitation of forests for wood and revenue. The growing pressure on forests has seen the gradual transformation of the Department into a conservation agency. The recent circular speaks not of protecting forests from the people, but rather of conserving forests for the people, with the help of the people. While there is a long way to go in strengthening this partnership, the new initiative marks the beginning of a new era in the management of forests India's largest publicly held biological resource.

The initiatives for conserving biological resources have not come from Government alone. The Bishnoi example and movements like Chipko have been based on local communities protecting these resources and taking up afforestation programmes. people are involved in selecting the species most relevant to them, and take the responsibility for their protection which leads to high survival rates of the saplings.

While greater generation of biomass is one way of dealing with the pressure on this resource, its more efficient use is another. Several initiatives have been taken in this direction by both NGOs and the Government. But changing practices is a slow process. New technologies need to be explored while certain old practices need to be reaffirmed. There are practices that were once beneficial but are no longer sustainable. An example is that of shifting cultivation, practised in north-east India, parts of Andhra Pradesh etc. This used to operate under cycles of 20-30 years or more, but with increased population and reduced availability of land the cycle has been shortened, making the practice unviable today.

New improved chulhas (wood-fuelled stoves) can, if used properly, reduce the requirement of firewood by as much as 40 per cent. New experiments such as those under the Programme of Integrated Energy Systems for Villages of the Department of Non-Conventional Energy Sources go even beyond this. their aim is not only to make the village self-sufficient in cooking energy but also to fulfil its energy requirements for agriculture, pumping, lighting and heating. Experiments such as those by the Gujarat Energy Development Agency (GEDA) have made villages like Methan and Kalyanpura self sufficient in energy. The strategy is based on growing biomass on village fallow land and using a wood gasifier to generate motive power. This is combined with direct solar-thermal power for heating water. The gasifier uses the biomass five times as efficiently as conventional methods. The key to this success story, as in the case of forest management, is a self-managed system controlled by the local community.

Biogas is a low-cost appropriate energy technology with major potential in rural areas. The National Biogas Development Programme has, as its main objectives, the maximisation of recycling of organic wastes in order to provide gas for cooking, and small decentralized power generation systems for operating water pumps, flour mills and other rural industries. At present 1.4 million family-size biogas plants generate energy for cooking in village households across the country. The progress with community biogas plants has been less encouraging, with only around 300 such plants operating in the country today.

The shortage of fodder would similarly have to be dealt with through a combination of more production and better utilization. The current estimate of availability of green and dry fodder in the country is 250 million tonnes and 440 million tonnes respectively, while the requirement is about 932 million tonnes and 780 million tonnes respectively. About 100 million head or 25 per cent of the cattle population is estimated to be grazing on forest land. To close the gap between demand and supply and to reduce pressure on grazing land, practices like stall feeding of cattle need to be promoted.

The problem is, however, that with a large number of unproductive cattle, stall feeding is not always viable. The livestock issue is complex because of the very intricate relationship cattle have with life in rural India. The cow-dung is used for manure or as fuel. Bullocks are used as drought animals. The social status of a family is often linked to the number of animals owned by it. Cows are not slaughtered for meat. The unproductive animals graze on public lands, and are maintained at virtually no cost to the owner. But the price is paid in terms of the pressures on the local environment. Excessive grazing leads to land deterioration, soil erosion and the suppression of the regeneration of useful species.

Just as excessive pressure on bio-resources leads to land denudation and decline in groundwater recharge, the excessive demand for water leads to a decrease in land and agricultural productivity due to waterlogging and salinity. In addition, the large projects to supply such quantities of water can lead to several environmental problems.

Harnessing the water resources of India was identified as a major task at the time of Independence. Large dams were seen as a solution. But India's first Prime Minister Jawaharlal Nehru in 1957 cautioned. "We have many large scale river valley projects which are carefully worked out by engineers. I wonder, however, how much thought is given before the project is launched to having an ecological survey of the area and to find out what the effect would be to the drainage system or to the flora and fauna of the area. It would be desirable to have such an ecological survey of these areas before the project is launched and thus avoid an imbalance of nature.

Nehru's apprehensions have today become major environmental issues. They are central to the debate over large dams. Issues of resettlement of affected persons and rights of tribal communities, the impact on biodiversity and fragile ecological systems, the correctness of assessment of parameters like siltation rates, drainage and waterlogging are at the centre of the debate. The imbalance perceived as to who pays the cost and who benefits has led to arguments on equity. The whole issue of scale, of small irrigation projects compared to large projects, is a major environmental debate in India.

Sustainable utilization of groundwater resources necessitates a shift from extraction-focused development to conservation and creation of management systems. To date, most development efforts have concentrated on ways to increase groundwater extraction. Nationwide the number of diesel and electric pump sets have grown from 87,000 in 1950 to 12,581 million in 1990. Over 20 per cent of the electricity generated in India is currently used for pumping. Groundwater accounts for 42 per cent of India's irrigation potential and for nearly 48 per cent of the net area actually irrigated. Over exploitation of groundwater is causing the water table to drop in most hard-rock and aridzones, and saline intrusion is occurring in extensive areas along the coasts.

The official planners have been very brave, indeed foolhardy, to scale up from 3.5 per cent to 4.5 per cent, reportedly under political pressure, the agricultural growth rate target for the Ninth Plan. This may please the powerful lobby of rich farmers and pander to their high growth ambitions. But it casts grave doubts on the veracity and credibility of the planning exercise, especially so when the sharp set-back to agricultural production in 1995-96, a good monsoon year, should have made the planners doubly cautious in their approach to the ticklish problems and uncertain prospects of Indian agriculture.

Disturbing trends

The disturbing indications that really must hot be ignored cavalierly are that the Green Revolution in irrigated areas based on viable farmers and subsidized inputs especially chemical fertilizers, may have touched the plateau. Also to reckon with is the shrinking social base of farming, with small and marginal farmers being squeezed out and the big gentlemen farmers with large land holdings and access to modern inputs and technologies furiously developing a nexus with urban business corporations, including multinational corporations. The agricultural growth target of 4.5 per cent for the Ninth Five Year Plan may, in this context, make some sense only if it is projected not for the total production or food security for the people of India, especially half the population suffering from poverty, hunger and malnutrition, but for marketable surpluses to meet effective demand, that is demand backed by purchasing power for agricultural products, including food grains, in the domestic and the global markets.

The performance of Indian agriculture after gaining political independence has been impressive and should not be derided as has been done by the votaries of the market-oriented growth of industry as well as agriculture. Food production quadrupled between 1951 and 1991. There was also significant growth of what are known as case crops to augment supplies for a wide variety of processing industries. This success was achieved with positive intervention of the Indian State, including large public investment in irrigation, research and development and, supplies of subsidized inputs like quality seeds, fertilizers and power. This was combined with judicious support prices for agricultural produce, especially food grains. Since the launching of the so-called economic reform policies in 1991 to bring about what is loftily claimed to be the structural adjustment of the Indian economy, the position of Indian agriculture has changed ominously. The fluctuations in agriculture production have become sharper. There is shift away from food grains to cash crops. Within the food crops, production of rice and wheat has been given generous price and other incentives. The production of coarse cereals, pulses and grains has tended to decline. With the per capita availability of cereals declining, the poor have been hit hard by their rising prices. The nature and content of agricultural growth has not even been properly comprehended, let alone tackled in the approach paper on the Ninth Plan.

New strategy

A marked feature of agricultural policy or what is known as the new agricultural strategy launched in the mid-sixties was a decisive shift of emphasis from institutional reform to technological improvement. This found expression in the organization of modern inputs for viable farming. Expansion of irrigation, especially on private account, and supply of chemical fertilizers, pesticide and quality seeds registerd a relatively big advance and helped to enhance production and productivity of farmers with addess to these facilities. Since the farmers with marketable surpluses were at the same time assured of rising levels of incentive-procurement prices, the govenment was able, side to mop up adequate qualities of agricultural produce, especially of food grains, for current consumption well as building up of the buffer stocks.

The problem of feeding the urban population and the growing non-agricultural force was acute in the fifties and the sixties. This was indeed the biggest stumbling block in the way of overall economic stability and growth. Reliance on aided imports of food grains necessarily imposed sever strains, economic and political. It may well be claimed that Indian agriculture has by now developed to a point where it is in a position to meet effective demand for food grains in the Indian market. In this sense, the agrarian crisis as it manifested itself till the mid-seventies can be said to have been resolved. But the question now to be faced is the further growth of agriculture, its content and direction.

It is not without significance either that land reforms are no longer projected in official policy as an essential prerequisite for overcoming bottlenecks to higher production and productivity in agriculture. They are at best treated as desirable purely from the social justice angle. The talk of land reforms which the political leaders indulge in from time to time is, is therefore more of a populist gesture that carries little conviction in the political power system.

Crop production

Agricultural crop production in 1996—97 is expected to show good recovery from the slower growth in 1995—96. Growth is projected at 3 per cent after a fall of 0.4 per cent in 1995—96. The sharp decline in foodgrains production by 3.4 per cent, which was responsible for the slow growth in 1995—96, is expected to be reversed by an increased of 3.3 per cent in 1996—97. Foodgrains production is expected to recovery is primarily due to coarse cereals, as well as an anticipated rise in wheat production which suffered a sharp setback in 1995—96.

As the agricultureal year runs from July to June, the estimates for 1995—96 were only firmed up after the end of the financial year. A large downward revision (of 3 million tonnes) was made in the estimate of wheat production for 1995—96. The revision was unexpected and unexplained, because average rainfall in 1995—96 was quite normal. The revision, late in calendar year 1996, also created severe problems for the management of the food economy.

Commercial crop production has done extremely well in 1996—97 with oilseeds and cotton expected to reach record levels of 24.1 million tonnes and 14.3 million tonnes, respectively. Jute and mesta have also shown a growth of 3.4 per cent this year. Sugarcane output is, however, unlikely to maintain the record level of 283 million tonnes attained in 1995—96.

Industrial production (as measured by the index of industrial production–IIP), grew by 9.8 per cent in the first seven months of 1996—97, 1.9 percentage points slower than the 11.7 per cent growth in the in the corresponding period of 1995—96. The good performance of industrial production in 1996—97 is due entirely to the manufacturing sector, which has maintained its high growth.

The slowing of industrial production is clearly attributable to the dramatic fall in the rate of growth of electricity production and a slowing of growth in the mining sector mainly because of the 10 per cent decline in crude oil production. During the first seven months of 1996—97, electricity production (as measured by the index) has grown by only 3.4 per cent compared to the 10.1 per cent growth in the corresponding period of 1995—96. It is somewhat surprising that manufacturing sector growth has been barely affected by the slow growth in electricity production. One possibility is that captive electricity generation, which is increasingly used as a back—up to public supply, has substituted for the lack of generation by electricity boards. The high growth of diesel imports, about 22 per cent by volume in the first seven months of 1996—97 (with total refinery throughput growing in the normal range of around 4 per cent), is consistent with this hypothesis. At present, electricity statistics incorporate little or no data on captive power generation.

Another noteworthy aspect of industrial growth this year is the acceleration in the rate of growth of capital goods production to 16.6 per cent in the first seven months of this year from 15 per cent in the first seven months of last year. This has off—set the decline in the rate of growth of consumer goods and basic goos. In contrast, capital goods imports have declined by 6 per cent in the first seven months of 1996—97. This shows the increased competitiveness of the domestic capital goods industry.

The overall performance of the core and infrastructure sectors during the first 8 months of 1996—97 (April—November) has been poor. Six industries namely, electricity generation, coal, steel, crude oil, petroleum products and cement, with a combined weight of 28.8 per cent in the Index of Industrial Production (IIP), averaged a growth of 4.1 per cent in April—November, 1996, less than half the 8.9 per cent, in April—November, 1995. The deceleration in the growth rate of these infrastructure industries is mainly due to a decline in crude oil production and power generation. Hydro power generation declined by 7.7 per cent, and thermal power generation grew by only 6.4 per cent in the April—November, 1996 as compared to 14.6 per cent in the April—March, 1995—96. Coal, cement and refineries' throughput have grown faster in April—November, 1996—97 compared to the corresponding period of 1995—96. Growth of sectors such as railways, ports and telecommunications, which do not appear in the IIP, also slowed. The rate of growth of railways' revenue earning goods traffic decelerated marginally from 7 per cent during 1995—96 to 6.3 per cent for April–November 1996. Growth of cargo handled at major ports and new telephone connections provided decelerated more sharply to 4.7 per cent in April—November, 1996 (from 9.1 per cent in 1995—96) and 8.3 per cent in April—November, 1996 (from 23.3 per cent in 1995–96), respectively.

The slower growth in cargo handled by ports in probably the result of a deceleration in the growth of external trade. The telecomunications slowdown, however, suggests that the pace of implementation of telecommunications reform needs to be accelerated and its scope widened to include Department of Telecommunications as a service provider. Given the parlous financial state of many public utilities, particularly the State Electricity Boards, the possibility of crises worsens with each passing year. The new government has repeatedly stressed its firm determination to reform the infrastructure and energy sectors. In line with this commitment, a number of policy decisions have been taken and new initiatives launched.

The rate of agricultural growth of the order of around 3.2 per cent per annum during the fifties was derived from acreage increases to the extent of 70 per cent. In the sixties, the rate of growth which was only 2.1 per cent in this sector and did not neutralize even the rate of increase of population in that decade, could be derived from acreage increase to the extent of 30 per cent only. The scope for any further increase in acreage for increasing agricultural peoduction has exhausted in the seventies and the entire increase in farm production had to come from improvement in per acre productivity. This has required high level of capital–intensive effort in the development of the agricultural sector.

According to a competent study, the capital output ratio in Indian agriculture has already touched the figure of four and is close to the same scale as is required in industry. For the same reason, the fact has to be reckoned with that absorption of labour in agriculture through a significant rise in yields on land has tended to be a comparatively limited and expensive process and this process alone cannot be relied upon to solve the growing unemployment problem. The running controversy on priorities as between agriculture and industry, in particular heavy industry, is thus futile and misleading in the context of the realities of Indian economic situation and its growth prospects. The idea that India enjoys a comparative advantage in agricultural output inIndia is now crucially dependent on growth of inputs from industry. The need is thus not to fforeclose available resources in the economy for the so called development needs of the agricultural sector but to mop up a substained part of the surpluses and incremental incomes generating in the agricultural sector to meet the investment requirements of infrastructural development, including heavy and intermediate goods industries,to inputs for agriculture at a rapid and accelerating pace.

If much credit is taken for achieving self—sufficiency in food grains relative to effective domestic demand, there is now much brave talk of making India one of the few "grain powers" in the world even while large number of Indian people still do not have access to adequate food. Agriculture in India will have to go a long way yet before it can feed the Indian people. It is too early to talk of India becoming a "grain power." But the official policy has already veered to the postion that the government would not come in the way of the farmers exporting their produce and these exports would not be banned "merely" for bringing supplies and prices down for the domestic consumers. The upshot has been that while good grains have been exported, two million tonnes of wheat are being imported in the current year, 1996—97 to meet even the effective demand in the domestic market. The danger inherent in this position is not imaginary.

The widening disparities in incomes and levels of living combined with growing concentration of land and the swelling ranks of landless rural labourers are manifest. It is not amiss either to consider the pricing of agricultural produce, more especially food grains—the primary wage goods—and examine its influence on the general price trend and structure of relative prices in the Indian economy. The Agricultural Prices Commission, to start with, recommended a particular set of prices based on its studies of the cost of production, fair return to the farmer and fair prices for the consumer. It has been a practice, by and large, to improve upon the prices recommended by the APC in order to provide additional incentives to the surplus farmers to increase production for the market. After the launching of the so—called economic reforms in 1991, however, the baalance between the claims of the surplus farmer and the consumer has been tilting sharply in favour of the former and the inflationary impact of "incentive prices" for good grains and other agricultural produce has been ignored. Subsidised farming by way of what are called "incentive prices" for farm produce and subsidised inputs for agriculture like chemical fertilizers, private irrigation facilities like tubewells and pumpsets, power andcomparative soft—term credit, was conceived in the wake of the disastrous drought years of 1964-65 as the means of stimulating agricultural production for the market and securing control over a substantial part of the marketable surpluses so produced. There were probably compelling reasons under the given ownership pattern in cultivable land for adopting this strategy when shortages of agricultural commodities, especially of food grains, ad emerged as an endemic problem of the economy—its stability and further growth. But the concomitant of this development has been the growing commercialization of agriculture and emergence within it to prominence of that segment of farmers with their commercial interests which produce and control agricultural surpluses. In the course of time, however, as shortage in cereals or other crops are overcome relative, of course, to effective market demand at the present low-level of purchasing power in the economy, the system of subsidised production and marketing in agriculture has become in essence a mechanism to ensure to the surplus producer a monopoly to all the gains arising from incrreases in production and productivity.

Among the vast numbers of Indian farmers, only a small fraction, and more than 10 per cent of the total, commanding the best cultivable land produces for the market on any scale. They also monopolise the subsidised supply of inputs and credit and benefits of infrastructural facilities such as irrigation and power created by public investment.

Food production

The Ninth Five Year (1997–2002) envisages targeted food production of 230 million tonnes as against 190 million tonnes during 19945—96. Food production and its availability to at least those 39 per cent of the population living below the poverty line and around more than half (53%) of all children under the age of four, who are underweight or stunted is most essential in the context of the present socio—economic—politico environment in India.

Despite the fact that the yield of wheat and rice per hectare has appreciably increased during the post—Green Revolution period, our yields are comparatively very low. Wheat yield in India is 2,420 kg per hecatare as against 8,771 kg in the Netherlands with 2,501 kg being the Asian average. Similarly, rice yield is 2,800 kg as compared to 8,000 kg in Greece and 3,731 kg in Asia. It is also a matter of concern that India ranks 96th and 61st in the productivity of wheat and rice respectively. Irrigated land of 48 million hectares produces about 2,500 kg of food grains per hectare and rainfed area of 92 million hectares produces only about one tonne per hectare.

Apart from this, wheat productivity in Punjab with 96 per cent area under irrigation is above four tonnes per hectare while it is only 2,400 kg in Uttar Pradesh with 90 per cent of irrigated wheat and only, 1,700 kg in Bihar with 86 per cent area under irrigated wheat.

In respect of rice, the annual compounded growth rat of rice yield declined considerably from 4 per cent during 1982—93 to 1.73 per cent during 1991—95 in northern zone, from 3.80 per cent to 2.62 per cent in southern zone and from 5.60 per cent to 2.08 pe cent in eastern zone as against a phenomental rise from 1.80 per cent to 5.36 per cent in western zone. Even after the advent of high yield technology, a sizeable area falls under the category oflow productivity. About 60 per cent of low productivity area are in Bihar, Orissa, Assam, West Bengal and Uttar Pradesh. It is a matter of serious concern that 32 per cent of the irrigated area are of low productivity. Studies reveal that about 30 per cent to 40 per cent of the potential yield are yet to be harvested in the available high yielding varieties in the high productivity irrigated area itself.

Fisheries play an important role in the economy of India. It helps in augmenting food supply, generating employment, raising nutritional level and earning foreign exchange. The main objectives of fisheries development programmes are: (i) enhancing production and productivity of fishermen, fish farmers and fishing industry; (ii) augmenting export of marine products thourgh production support and thereby increasing foreign exchange earnings; (iii) generating employment folr the coastal and rural poor; and (iv) improving welfare of fishermen and their socio-economic conditions. In persuance of these objectives, the Fisheries Division of the Department of Agriculture and Cooperation has been undertaking directly and through state governments various production-oriented, input supply and infrastructure development programmes and welfare-oriented schemes besides formulating/initiating appropriate policies to increase production and productivity in the fisheries sector.

In recognition of the important role of inland fisheries in overall production of fish, Government has been implementing an important programme in inland sector since Fifth Plan viz., Development of Fresh Water Aquaculture through Fish Farmers Development Agencies (FFDAs). A network of 414 FFDAs is functioning now. Water area brought under intensive fish culture through the efforts of these FFDAs is 3.96 lakh hectare upto 1993-94. On fish seed production front, marked improvement occurred as it has more than doubled from 400 crore fry in 1983-84 to 1,451 crore fry in 1993-94. The production was estimated to be about 1,480 crore fry in 1994-95.

Apart from four major fishing harbours, viz., Cochin, Madras, Visakhapatnam and Roychowk, 26 minor fishing harbours and 99 fish landing centres have been constructed to provide landing and berthing facilities to fishing craft. The construction of two major fishing harbours at Sassoon Dock in Bombay and at Paradip is nearing completion. Government is providing subsidy to poor fishermen for motorising their traditional craft which increases area and frequency.* About 13,500 traditional craft were motorised upto 1993-94. Improved beach landing craft made of fibre glass and other light materials are also being supplied to groups of fishermen. The Government has also been operating a scheme of re-imbursing the Central excise duty on HSD oil used by fishing vessels below 20 m length to off-set the opertational cost, incurred by small mechanised fishing boat operators. Objective of this scheme is to utilise country's vast brackish-water for fish prawn culture. So far, projects covering an area of 15,000 hectare have been sanctioned. A pilot project for the construction of five pilot prawn farms and five prawn-hatcheries taken up during the Seventh Plan with UNDP assistance was completed. Thrity eight Brackish-Water Fish Farmers' Development Agencies (BFDA) are functioning in the coastal areas of the country at present. These a provide a package of technical, financial and extension support to shrimp farmers.

There are three important programmes for the welfare of traditional fishermen, namely: (i) group accident insurance scheme for active fishermen; (ii) development of model fishermen villages; and (iii) savings-cum-relief for fishermen in maritime states. Fishermen are insured for Rs. 25,000 in case of death or permanent disability and Rs. 12,500 in case of partial disability. Annual premium of Rs. 11.25 is shared between Centre and states. Number of fishermen in 1993-94 was about eight lakh. The programme of savings-cum-relief for marine fishermen are induced to save a modest amount of Rs. 45 per month for a period of eight fishing months aggregating to Rs. 360. Equal contributions are provided by the Central and state governments and the sum of Rs. 1,080, thus accrued, is distributed to the fishermen during the four lean fishing months at the rate of Rs. 270 per month. About two lakh fishermen were targeted to be benefitted under the scheme during 1994-95.

The Central Institute of Fisheries Nautical and Engineering Training (CIFNET), Cochin, aims at making available sufficient number of operators for deep-sea fishing vessels and technicians for shore establishments. It has a unit each at Madras and Visakhapatnam. The Institute has an intake capacity of about 400 trainees in a year. Integrated Fisheries Project, Cochin, envisages processing, popularising and marketing of unconventional varieties of fish.

The Central Institute of Coastal Engineering for Fisheries, Bangalore is engaged in techno-economic feasibility study for location of fishing harbour sites and brackish-water fish farms.

There has been a spectacular increase in export of marine products. It went up from Rs. 597.85 crore during 1988-89 to Rs. 3,273 crore in 1994-95. During the Eighth Plan, marine products have been identified as a major thrust area for exports.

Animal husbandry plays a vital role in supplementing family income and generating additional gainful employment for the weaker sections of the society, particularly the small/marginal farmers and agricultural labourers. According to the National Sample Survey Organisation, the annual growth rate in employment in livestock sector in rural areas during 1972-88 was about 4.15 per cent as against 1.1 in agriculture sector. This sector provides more self-employment opportunities to the socially and economically disadvantaged sections of the society including rural women, unemployed youth etc., than any other sector of rural economy. Special programmes of animal husbandry like Special Livestock Breeding Programme (SLBP) and the scheme of dairying, have tremendously helped the beneficiaries of Integrated Rural Development Programme to cross the poverty line.

As a result of concerted efforts by the Centre and state governments, the milk production which was almost stagnant between 1947 and 1970 with annual growth rate of merely one per cent has since then registered a vigorous growth at an average rate of 4.5 per cent per annum during the Seventh Plan. It continued to further increase during the Eighth Plan and is expected to reach the level of 63.5 million tonnes during 1994-95.

Livestock also provides for industrial use of raw materials such as hides and skins and by-products like blood, bone, fat and casings. Farm manure is a useful and income-generating product in this sector. Animal power for transportation and agricultural operations, particularly in the rural areas, also makes a significant contribution. According to the provisional estimates of the Central Statistical Organisation (CSO), the gross value of output from livestock sector alone at current prices was about Rs. 642 billion in 1993-94, which is about 26 per cent of the value of total agricultural output. This excludes the contribution of animal drought power.

According to the provisional results of livestock census of 1987, the country has about 195.87 million cattle, 76.77 million buffaloes, 44.84 million sheep, 99.41 million goats, 10.76 million pigs, 2.9 million pack animals and 258.34 million poultry birds. Special emphasis is laid on enhancing the production of various species of livestock genetic improvement and effective health cover.

India possesses 26 good breeds of tropical cattle and six breeds of buffaloes. India's cattle are well-known in the world for their quality of hardness, endurance and resistance to tropical animal disease, especially tick-born and protozon infections. Recognising the importance of cattle in rural economy and their contribution to the national income, both Central and state governments are devoting considerable attention for their development. Important state sector schemes aimed at all-round development of cattle initiated are key village blocks (KVBs) and intensive cattle development projects (ICOPs). Under these and other schemes more than 35,000 artificial insemination (AI) centres, have been set up to provide input and extension support in rural areas. The number of artificial insemination centres with exotic bull semen increased from 153 lakh during 1991-92 to 180 lakh during 1992.-93.

Seven Central Cattle Breeding Farms at Suratgarh (Rajasthan), Dhamrod (Gujarat) Alamadhi(Tamil Nadu), Chiplima, Similiguda (Orissa), Andeshnagar (Uttar Pradesh) and Hessarghatta (Karnataka) are engaged in scientific cattle breeding programme and progeny testing of selected breeds of indigenous as well as exotic cattle and buffaloes. During the Seventh Plan period, 2,237 artificial insemination centres, 17* were established in various states with Central assistance. A Central sector scheme for production of proven bulls by progency testing under field conditions was in operation in Andhra Pradesh, Assam, Kerala, Maharashtra and Orissa and 301 bulls were testmated.

Poultry is one of the important components of the farmers' economy as it provides additional income and job opportunities to a large number of rural population in the shortest possible time. As a result of government's efforts, strains of birds with high egg productivity and meat type birds have been developed in the country and dependence on imported grand parent stock has been minimised. During the Seventh Plan period, egg and broiler production registered a compound growth rate of 7.3 per cent and 18 per cent respectively. The egg production is estimated to be about 26.1 billion in 1994-95.

Central poultry breeding farms at Bombay, Bhubaneswar, Hessarghatta and Chandigarh engaged in scientific poultry breeding programme developed high egg producing hybrid and fast growing broiler strains and are supplying parent-stock chicks. Central duck breeding farm at Hessarghatta, is catering to requirements of high egg producing khaki campbell breeding stock ducklings to various states/union territories. Four random sample poultry performance testing centres at Bangalore, Bombay, Bhubaneswar and

Gurgaon conduct egg laying and broiler tests and provide useful information to poultry farmers, hatcheries and breeding organisations about performance of various participating layer and broiler stocks in the country (both from public/private sector organisations). Central Poultry Training Institute at Hessarghatta is imparting short term practical courses in different disciplines of poultry to officials of state governments/union territory administrations, agricultural universities, research institutions and private sector organisations. Regional feed analytical laboratories at Chandigarh, Bombay and Bhubaneswar provide feed analysis facilities to farmers, public and private sector organisations.

India stands sixth in sheep population amongst the countries in the world. The sheep population in the country has been 448 lakh as per livestock census 1987. It has been estimated that the average wool yield of sheep is less than one kg per year. Total wool production in the country during 1994-95 is estimated to reach a level of about 436 lakh kg. Total requirement of wool in the country is above 800 lakh kg per annum. To bridge the gap between demand and supply, about 30 lakh kg of fine wool is imported every year. Total availability of wool for carpet manufacture is estimated at around 200 lakh kg which is insufficient to meet present requirement of the carpet industry.

Principal objective of sheep development is to make the country self-sufficient in wool production vis-a-vis meat production through scientific breeding and raise the status of sheep breedes/wool growers. Strategy for sheep and wool development encompasses production both for meeting requirement of apparel wool and carpet wool for export purposes. Breeding policy envisages selective breeding of important carpet wool breed and cross-breeding involving suitable exotic breeds with coarse carpet type. India is importing large number of exotic fine wool breed sheep from USA and Australia in a phased manner.

A Central Sheep Breeding Farm with exotic breed of sheep has been established at Hissar. At present, it is having a breeding programme with pure exotic breed as well as cross breeding for production of superior rams. It has distributed over 12,000 exotic/cross breed rams to different states since its establishment. The farm also trains officers and shepherds from different states in modern sheep management. National ram/buck production programme and programme for rabit development as Centrally-sponsored *scheme-in-aid to large sheep breeding farms for production and supply of superior genetic make of rams, (ii) market intervention operation (MIO) for strengthening of state wool boards/ corporations/federations *(goat development) for improving the productivity of goats; and (iv) programme for rabbit development.

There are at present about 4,000 recognised slaughter houses in the country. It is the local body's obligation to provide for meat inspection in order to safeguard public health. To provide safe and wholesome meat and prevent environmental pollution, it is necessary to modernise the existing slaughter houses/abattoirs in the country and Government has made efforts in this direction in spite of various socio-economic constraints. A Centrally-sponsored scheme 'assistance to states for improvement/modernisation of abattoirs/establishment of carcass utilisation centres and primary flaying units' is being implemented in the Eighth Plan period. The scheme aims to improve/upgrade the existing slaughter houses and to establish carcass utilisation centres and primary flaying units by providing grants-in-aid to the state governments. Project proposals for establishment of sheep and goat slaughter house at Gwalior and improvement of large animals slaughter house and sheep and goat slaughter house at Shrirampur have been sanctioned and Rs. 5.18 million grant has been provided. Slaughter house improvement proposals from Aurangabad and Kalyani and new slaughter houses at Ahmednagar, Shimla, Tripunithura and Thiruvananthapuram are likely to be finalised soon.

Meat and meat products worth Rs. 430 crore (estimated) was exported during 1994-95. Other animal by-products like casings etc., are also being exported. By-products like horn-meal, hoof-meal, bone-meal, crushed bone, steamed bone-gelatine glue, brush etc., have also been exported. Emphasis is being given for establishment of integrated meat production and processing complexes for export of meat at higher unit value.

There are more than 100 lakh pigs in the country, of which approximately 10 per cent are of graded and exotic variety. Pig farming has a great significance as it can play an important role in improving the socio-economic status of sizeable section of the weaker rural communities especially in north eastern states where nearly everly family in the village rears pigs for meat. At present, there are about 100 pig farm units in the country run by the state governments/union terriories maintaining approximately 29,000 livestock (pigs). These farms breed pigs and supply boards and sows to the farmers for cross breeding and improvement of desi stock.

A Centrally-sponsored scheme 'Assistance to States for Integrated Piggery Development' is being implemented for strengthening the pig breeding farms in the states. During 1994-95, an amount of Rs. 9.31 million, was released providing assistance to 13 pig breeding farms.

For improvement of our vast livestock resources through proper scientific methods, availability of nutritious feed and fodder is essential. To make available scientific fodder production technology, seven regional stations have been established in different agro-climatic zones, i.e., at Hissar (Haryana) Kalyani (West Bengal), Gandhinagar (Gujarat), Alamadi (Tamil Nadu) Hyderabad (Andhra Pradesh), Suratgarh (Rajasthan) and Shehama (Jammu and Kashmir). These are also engaged in producing and propagation of certified quality fodder seeds. During 1993-94, these stations produced 241 tonnes of fodder seeds and conducted 1,092 field demonstrations. During 1994-95 they produced 166.60 tonnes of fodder seeds against the target of 240 tonnes and conducted 1,036 field demonstrations against the target of 2000 upto October 1994.

Many sites are used for demonstration and training of farmers from nearby villages. A Central Fodder Seed production Farm is in operation at Hessarghatta, Karnataka since 1980. During the Seventh Plan period, the Farm had producted 1,557 tonnes of seeds of different varieties of fodder crops and grasses/legumes. During 1994-95 (upto October 1994) the Farm has produced 73.4 tonnes of fodder seeds. A Central project of fodder minikit demonstration is under implementation for popularising high yielding fodder varieties on a large scale. Over 1.3 lakh kits are distributed annually. A Centrally-sponsored scheme, viz., Assistance to States for Food and Fodder Development is in progress. During Eighth Five Year Plan, there is provision to provide assistance to states for strengthening of state fodder seed farms, establishment of fodder banks, seed production through registered growers, enrichment of straw and cellulosic waste, establishment of silvipasture system, grassland development and survey for area, production and requirements in fodder crops.

While the quality of livestock has improved with the launching of extensive cross breeding programmes, their susceptibility to various diseases including exotic diseases has increased simultaneously. In order to reduce morbidity and mortality, efforts are being made to provide better health care through polyclinics/veterinary hospitals/dispensaries/first-aid centres including mobile dispensaries. A network of 19,791 polyclinics/hospitals/ dispensaries and 20,302 veterinary aid centres (including Stockmen centres)/mobile dispensaries was functioning/ established in 1992-93. These field institutions are fully supported by about 250 disease diagnostic laboratories functioning in the states and UTs for quick and proper diagnosis of diseases. Further, for control of major livestock and poultry diseases by way of prophylactic vaccination, the required quantity of vaccines are produced in the country at 26 veterinary vaccine production units. Of these, 19 are in the public sector and seven in private sector. Import of vaccines by private agencies are also permitted when required. Through a Centrally-sponsored scheme 'Assistance to States for Control of Animal Diseases', the Government of India is providing grants-in-aid to states/UTs for control of livestock diseases.

The importance of dairying extends well beyond the mere production of milk and milk products. It has provided numerous small/marginal farmers and agricultural labourers with supplemental employment and a regular source of income. The significant role played by cooperatives in stimulating dairying has also proved to be an important source of progress. Operation Flood programme, which is an integrated dairy development programme has made considerable progress in achieving its outlined objectives. By September 1994, about 68,900 dairy cooperative societies were organised in 170 milksheds involving over 8.8 million farmer members. The average milk procurement during April-September 1994 was 94.5 lakh kg of milk per day. The programme has made a sound impact on rural masses and has encouraged them to take up dairying as a subsidiary occupation. It has offered a reliable and regular source of income as more than 62 per cent of milk procurement in the Operation Flood areas comes from the marginal, small and landless farmers. The programme is presently in its third phase, the first and second phase having ended in 1981 and 1985 respectively.

Milk production which was almost stagnant between 1947 and 1970 with an annual growth rate of merely one per cent, has since then registered a vigorous growth at an average rate of 4.5 per cent during the Seventh Plan. It continued to further increase during the Eighth Plan and is expected to reach the level of 63.5 million tonnes during 1994-95. The per capita availability of milk is expected to increase to 192 gm/day during 1994-95 compared to the level of 107 gm/day during 1969-70. The per capita availability of milk is targeted at 204 gm/day by thd end of the Eighth Plan as against the recommended nutritional requirement of 220 gm/day.

Technology Mission on Dairy Development (TMDD) was launched by the Government of India in August 1988. At the national, level, the Mission is supported by an Empowered Committee, at the state level by the State Level Co-ordination Committees (SLCCs) and at the district level by the district Level Co-ordination Committees (DLCCs). While the Empowered Committee is responsible for reviewing the existing statutes and policies related to dairying development, the state level and the district level coordination committees are expected to remove difficulties in implementing the dairy development programmes and ensure dovetailing of all the ongoing programmes of animal husbandry and dairy development to avoid duplication and wastage of resources. The Mission has so far identified 28 need-based research programmes and these have been assigned to various national research institutes, agricultural universitites and National Dairy Development Board (NDDB) to carry out on a time bound basis. While some of the projects have been completed, others are progressing satisfactorily.

The gross value of output from livestock sector (at current prices) is estimated to account for 26 per cent of the total value of output from Agriculture sector. This excludes the contribution of animal draught power. Animal husbandary is an important source of self employment and subsidiary occupation in rural and semi-urban areas and more so for people living in the drought prone, hilly, tribal and other poorly developed areas, where crop production on its own may not sustain them fully. As revealed by NSS, 1987-88 was 4.15 per cent as against 1.1 per cent for the agriculture sectore as a whole. The recent Land and Livestock Holding Survey (NSS, forth-eitghth round) further reveals that during eighties there was a substantial growth of dairy farming in the country. The ratio of in-milk bovine stock to 100 households rose from 37 in 1981-82 to 46 in 1991-92. It also highlighted that the rise in ratio during eighties was most pronounced in the states with relvatively high average in milk stock, like Punjab, Haryana and Fajasthan. On the other hand, there was little improvement in the ratio in Kerala, Orissa and Tamil Nadu. The marginal and small holdings constitute the core of the milk production sector accounting for about 66 per cent of the in-milk bovine stock (1991-92 estimate).

In 1995-96, the country produced 66 million tonnes of milk. This represents an average annual growth of 4.5 per cent since 1990-91.

Poultry Farming has become an important activity providing additional income to the weaker sections of the population in rural and semi-urban areas. Poultry farming has made good progess due to research and developmental efforts of the Government and the organised private sector. Egg production is expected to have increased to about 27 billion during 1995-96. Land and Livestock Holding Survey (NSS, forty eighth round, October, 1996) point out that there has been a rapid growth in poultry farming during 1970s and 1980s. The poultry stock per hundred households rose steadily from 107 in 1971-72 to 195 in 1991-92. In 1991-92, the marginal category of farm households (constituting 48 per cent of the households) alone accounted for 55 per cent of poultry stock.

Under the cattle insurance policy, cover is provided for the sum insured or the market value of the animal at the time of death, whichever is less. Animals are normally insured upto 100 per cent of their market value. General Insurance Corporation (GIC) implements various cattle insurance programmes through its four companies under their "Market Agreement on Cattle Insurance". Buffaloes, calves/heifers, stud bulls, bullocks etc. of specified age groups are insured against death due to accidents inclusive of natural causes like fire, lighting, floods, storm, earthquakes, famine diseases, surgical operation, riot, strike and civil commotion and risk of breeding an calving. Insurance policy can also be extended to cover permanent total disability on payment of extra premium. Cattle purchase under poverty allevation programmes are insured under Master Policy. The animals are insured at concessional rate and part of the premium is subsidised by the Government. Under the Cattle Insurance Scheme, at present, about 10 per cent of the total cattle population is covered. The projected target for insuring cattle during 1996-97 was 88 lakhs out of which 48 lakhs was for 'scheme' animals and 40 likhs for 'non-scheme' animals. The position regarding number of cattel covered, premium collected and claims paid during the past 5 years. After taking into account management expenses and incentives, the scheme is presently operating on no-profit-no-loss basis. The scheme is thus operated by the Insurance Companies on their own risk.

India is the seventh largest producer of fish in the world and, perhaps, second in Inland fish production. Fishery sector plays a vital role in sustaining a fairly large proportion of population along the long 8129 kms. coast line. The contribution of fisheries to the net domestic product has increased from Rs. 1479 crore in 1984-85 to Rs. 9826 crore in 1994-95 at current in 1994-95 at current prices showing about six and a half times increase in ten years. The trend of fish production and exports. The target for fish production in 1996-97 is 51.40 lakh tonnes comprising 28.57 lakh tonnes from marine and 22.83 lakh tonnes from Inland waters. An area of 3.86 lakh hactares has been brought under scientific fish culture and 5.04 lakh farmers have been trained in improved practices upto 1995-96 through active support provided under Fish Farmers Development Agencies. Development of brackish water aquaculture through Brakish Water Fish Farmers Development Agencies have been established in the coastal states for providing a package of technical, financial and extension support for shrimp farming. A shrimp and fish culture project is under implementation with the World Bank assistance in 5 states.

Against the per capita net availability of 501.9 gms of cereals the estimated consumption of cereals was of the order of 394 gms i.e. 78.6 per cent of the net availability. similarly in the case of pulses, per capita consumption was 28.05 gms. i.e. 75.8 per cent of net availability. Inequality in the consumption of foods among different income groups gets masked in the overall consumption estimates. Among the poor, nearly

80 per cent of consumption expenditure goes for food items. Recent surveys indicate:

- — Percapita cereal consumption has declined over the years resulting in the aggregate energy intake of 1859 k.cal per capita as against 2200 k.cal recommended.
- — 47.7 per cent of households have calorie inadequacy and 19.8 per cent of households have protein inadequacy. 19.5 per cent of households have both calorie and protein inadequacy.
- — The exetent of moderate and severe growth retardation in preschool children varied from 34 per cent in Kerala to 72 per cent in Gujarat.
- — 47 per cent of adults have body mass index value below 18.5 indicating large scale prevalance of chronic energy deficiency in the community.
- — Haemoglobin levels among pregnant mothers reveal that as many as 87.5 per cent of mothers were anaemic.
- — About 30 per cent of infants born had low birth weight.
- — 167 million people are considered to be at risk for iodine deficiency disorders and 54 million have goitre.
- — Preventable blindness due to Vitamin A deficiency still large.

Looking back the distance travelled and counting on various milestones towards food security, the country can be proud of some of the achievements so far. Yet the final milestone looks to be a long march. Shrinking arable land resources, soil degradation and depletion of nutrients from the soil, poor water management and unsustainable use of ground water, loss of momentum in the growth of food output, inefficient biological utilisation of the nutrients consumed due to poor environment and growing population are some of the problems the country faces in the march towards the final milestone of a hunger-free nation. The over-exploitation of the aquifer is also leading to the leaching of high levels of arsenic from natural underground sources into thousands of village wells in West Bengal. As estimated 200,000 people already have arsenic-induced skin lesions.

It is estimated that there are about 20 million species of poants, out of which 50,000 are edible. However, we are not using more than 200 plants as food, 80 per cent of our food supply however comes only from about eight species. We are today laying much emphgasis on developing new varieties of these few plants. We should enlarge the food basket by including the excluded. Many nutritious grains fall under the classification "coarse grains". It is time we start referring to them as "nutritious grains". They are rich in micronutrients like Fe and Ca.

Poverty line and food security

In 1993-94, the Planning Commission stated that only 18.96 per cent of the Indian people were below the poverty line. Now we are told that it is 40 per cent. A couple of shocking statistics, recently released by the National Council of Applied Economic Research (NCAER) provide a horrifying picture of where we are. The first figure is that 39 per cent of India's population of nearly one billion remain under the poverty line, a number that has not changed in a decade. In real terms, this means a very large number of Indians have an earning capacity of a couple of chapatis. According to another survey by the NCAER, 37 per cent lof the country's rural population are landless and therefore unable to grow their own crop to put off hunger.

The second figure, less publicised but avilable from international agencies, is that food grains production is 1991 million tonnes in 1994-95 to 185 million tonnes in 1995-96 and in the case of wheat from 65.5 million tonnes to 62.6 million tonnes in same period. Unsurprisingly the worst shortfalls are in the politically volatile States of Uttar Pradesh and Bihar and yet the naked face of hunger continues to be maskedby the hypocrisy that India is a food grain exporter.

Apart from the rising poulation, agro-economists put forward a number of reasons for fall in food grain production, among them soil exhaustion and the larger number of landless that are concentrated in the States of UP, Bihar and eastern India. What they don't spell out is the endemic political instability and coruption these States, and the interminable cycle of fodder scams and caste wars, that are pushing the poor deeper into the poverty trap.

Economic reports do not point out that the agricultural ministry for many years has been managed by ministers, who only represent the narrow interests of wealthy landed farmers like themselves, and have no truck with the poor landless peasants.

The Ninth Plan will be an heir to the same hypocrisy despite agriculture being put on the top by all then nine objectives of the Plan.

J. Gaur, a retired officer of Rajasthan government has a telling story about his visit to one of the villages of Dungarpur district. He was shocked to know from one of the poor schoolboys that he was served the family had ten members. This speaks volumes about our rural development and family planning programmes. The population clock outside the Capital's (Delhi) All-India Institute of Medical Sciences is galloping ahead but, for India's shoddy family planning programme, time has stood still. The latest census data is proof, if any were needed, that we are sitting on a population time bomb. By 2040, India will be the world's most populous nation. In a situation where over 18 million—or six Singapores—are being added to the population every year, it can be of little comfort to learn that curde birth rates have declined from 34.7 per cent in 1991 or indeed that fertility levels have shown a negligible decrease of two per cent in that period. If the population has to stabilize at even a staggering 100 crore by 2001-2005, the average birth rate has to be reduced to two cnildren per woman. But so far, only Kerala and Tamil Nadu have achieved this with Madhya Pradesh stated to do so only after 2060, Rajasthan by 2048, Bihar by 2039 and Uttar Pradesh by 2100. The government has confined itself to making tall claims about running a family planning campaign which is so "people oriented" that all targets have been removed. The truth is that it is Central run and almost totally dependent on female sterilisation ignoring the variety of options which are available.

The desired goal of population as mentioned as one of the objectives of the Ninth Plan could be achieved only through the willing co-operation of the population and specially of the rural people. The magic words are 'literacy' and 'healthcare'.

There is no "political will" as is evident from the fact that no political party has cared to emphasize the need for some concrete steps to restrict population growth in their election manifestoes. There is no mention of family planning even in the Common Minimum Programme of the United Front government.

It should be a matter of deep concern for every thinking Indian that after 45 years of the so-called planning, the country does not have a comprehensive education policy. This is despite the constitutional objective to provite universal primary education and eradication of funding, enormous sums have been wasted on subsidies and populist schemes from which money is easily diverted into the pockets of corrupt politicians and officials. Even in education, priorities have been misplaced. While primary and vocational education, which would improve the skills of the work force, have been neglected, money has been spent on creating an army of inadequately unemployable at various levels. The crying need of the hour is not elaborate plans but the 'political will' to act and innovate.

Development—real criteria : The late S.K. Dey, a Minister of State in Nehru's Cabinet once visited Tamil Nadu. He met the late Kumarappa at Gandhi Niketan and with some pride of achievenment he claimed that the Community Development Programe was a grand success. Kumarappa was sharp to retort : "What is your scale for measuring the success of your projects? S.K. Dey answered by giving elaborate statistics of the miles of roads constructed, number of wells dug, school-buildings built, dispensaries opened, fertilizers distributed, improved seeds introduced, the manure pits constructed, and all the usual figures. Kumarappa looked doubtfully at S.K. Dey and said in a derisive voice, "this is your scale" and laughed. Pricked by Kumarappa's remarks, Dey asked, "what then is your scale of success?" Kumarappa in a very emphatic tone said: "Mr Dey, before I cover an area with the Community Development Programme, I would select some six poor persons, count their ribs and if after three years (or five years) of implementing the C.D. Programme, there is some flesh to cover these ribs, thn I will call it a success". Dey was dismayed and implicitly accepted that his approach was defective. Kumarappa continued to say thay S.K. Dey was "trying to throw a silk shirt on a hungry person". The essentials of development are brought out in this one sentence.

Kalia a poor villager at the time of India's Independence thought, he was poor. He was told he was not poor but needy. Then as to be called needy was self-defeating, he was addressed as deprived which was again changed to underprivileged. This term was also later changed to disadvantaged. Kalia said : "I have no dime or rupee yet but a rich vocabulary". He further said : "I have no idea of Five Year Plan". He was about 20 years of age at the time of India's Independence. Now he is about 70 years of age. In the last two-and -a-half decades, he was not able to eat chapatis with pulses. His earnings are so meagre that he is unable to afford prices to buy pulses for his family consisting of six members.

Industry

Attainment of industrialisation over the last 48 years has been striking feature of Indian economic development process which was launched as a conscious and deliberate policy in the early fifties. In pursuance of this policy, large investment has been made in building up capacity over a wide spectrum of industries. Industrial production has made rapid strides in terms of variety, quality and quantity. There has been a substantial diversification of industrial base during this period with the consequent ability to produce a very broad range of industrial goods. Self-reliance has been achieved in basic and capital good. Indigenous capabilities have now been established to the point of virtual self-sufficiency so that further expansion in various sectors such as mining, irrigation, power chemicals, transport and communication can be based primarily on indigenous equipment. Process of industrialisation has also fostered entrepreneurship and development of a wide variety of technical, managerial and operative skills. Today, the country is in a position to provide consultancy services as well as managers, technicians and skilled workers for setting up industrial projects aborad.

The Industrial Policy Resolution of 1948 marked the beginning of the evolution of Indian Industrial Policy. The resolution not only defined the broad contours of the policy, it delineated the role of the State in the industrial development both as an entrepreneur and as an authority.

Successive policy resolutions also reiterated this basic tilt in favour of the public sector. The Industrial Policy Resolution of 1956 gave the public sector a strategic role in the economy. It categorised industries which would be the exclusive responsibility of state or would progressively come under state control and others. Earmarking the pre-eminent position to the public sector, it envisaged private sector co-existing with the State and thus attempted to give the policy framework flexibility.

The Industrial Policy initiatives undertaken by Government since July 1991 have been designed to build on the past industrial achievements and to accelerate the process of making Indian industry internatinally competitive. It recognises the strength and maturity of the industry and attempts to provide the competitive stimulus for higher growth. The thrust of these initiatives has been to increase domestic and external competition through extensive application of market mechanism and facilitating forging of dynamic relationships with foreign investors and suppliers of technology. The process of reform has been continuous.

As on 31 March 1993 there were 245 central public sector undertakings, comprising of eight in the construction sector, 72 in services and remaining 165 in the manufacturing. The number of CPSUs as indicated above exclude nine companies, six insurance companies and three financial institutions with Central Government investment but without direct responsibility of management.

The total capital employed in the 245 CPSUs increased from Rs. 1,179.91 billion in 1991-92 to Rs. 1,399.33 billion in 1992-93. The overall rate of return on capital employed in the PSUs also increased from 2.0 per cent in 1991-92 to 2.43 per cent in 1992-93.

The number of small scale units as at the end of 31 March 1994 were 2.38 million comprising of 1.77 million registered units and 0.61 un-registered. The overall production in the small scale sector during 1993-94 has been estimated to have reached Rs. 2,416.5 billion. The total value of exports of these units has been Rs. 177.85 billion in 1992-93.

Industrial production grew by 9.7 per cent in the first seven months of 1996—97, 1.9 percentage points slower than the 11.7 per cent growth in the first seven months of the previous year, which was the highest in 25 years. The growth of 9.5 to 10.5 per cent would still be the second highest growth rate in 25 years. It says, "the good performance of industrial production in 1996—97 is due entirely to the manufacturing sector, which has maintained its high growth." During the first seven months of the year the rate of growth of the manufacturing sector was 12.1 per cent, virtually the same as 12.3 per cent in 1995—96.

The Survey attributes the slowing of industrial production to the dramatic fall in the rate of growth of electricity production and a slowing down of growth in the mining sector, mainly because of the 10 per cent decline in crude oil production. During the first seven months of the year, electricity production has grown only by 3.4 per cent compared to 10.1 per cent in the corresponding period of 1995—96. If despite slowdown of electricity generation, manufacturing has recorded good growth, one possible reason could be captive generation, which is increasingly being used as a backup to public supply, the Survey adds. This hypothesis is supported by the growth of about 22 per cent in the volume of diesel imports.

Another noteworthy aspect of industrial production in 1996—97 has been acceleration in the rate of growth of capital goods production to 16.5 per cent from 15 per cent in the first seven months of the previous year. In contrast capital goods inports have declined by six per cent in the first seven months of the year. This according to the Survey, shows the increased competitiveness of the domestic capital goods industry.

The Survey also refers to the deceleration in the growth rate in the production of consumer durables, such as cars, to 9.8 per cent in the first seven months of 1996—97, compared to 30.2 per cent in the first seven months of the previous year. The delisensing of investment in consumer durable and decontrol of imports of parts of these goods, contributed to boom in investment and production in the sector. The decline in growth during 1996—97 suggests that the pent—up demand in the domestic economy has been met. Further growth will depend on increased cost competitiveness, which requires fuller exploitation of the comparative advantage that India has in the production of labour—intensive parts. Some analysts, however, seen in the sudden saturation of the demand a falacy in the general belief of the size of the middle class with good purchasing power, estimated at 200 million.

The Survey rates as poor the overall performance of the core and infrastructure sectors during the first 8 months of 1996—97 (April—November). Six industries, namely electricity generation, coal, steel, crude oil, petroleum products and cement, with a combined weight of 28.8 per cent in the Index of Industrial Production (IIP), averaged a growth of 4.1 poer cent in April—November, 1995. It says the previous Surveys had emphasised the need to accelerate, widen and deepen reforms of th non—tradable infrastructure and energy sectors, to avert an impending mismatch between economic growth and provision of these services. The new government, it says has repeatedly stressed its firm determination to reform the infrastructure and energy sectors and has take a number of policy decisions and new initiatives.

The Survey says continuing restraint on money supply growth is among the factors that have kept the prices in check. Despite the recent rising trend inthe growth of WPI, the average inflation for 1996—97 is expected to be at least one percentage point less than the average inflation in the previous year. There was complete change in the sectoral pattern of price changes du;ring 1996—97. The annual rate of inflation accelerated sharply in the "fuel, power, light and lubricants" and primary articles, while decelerating in the "manufactures" group. The annual rate of price increase in the fuel—power group went up to 17.4 per cent in January 1997 from 1.1 per cent a year ago because of administered price increase, while that of primary articles to 11.7 per cent from 2.6 per cent. The rate of growth in prices of manufactured goods declined to 3.6 poer cent from 6.9 per cent in the previous year. The rise in prices of primary goods has largely been due to rise in prices of cereals and fruits and vegetables.

Money supply growth has been higher in 1996—97 than in 1995—96, the Survey says, adding "Upto the fornight ended January 17, 1997, broad money (M3) grew by 10.6 per cent as against 8.2 per cent growth in the corresponding period of 1995—96. The average call money rate declined from a high of 13.75 per cent at the beginning of the currently financial year to a range of 5 to 11 per cent in September 1996 and ruled between 10 and 11 per cent in December 1996, before falling to low single digits in January 1997. The reversal of the 1997—96 excess demand for funds for investment in 1996–97 has led to a general softening of interest rates during the year. The cut—off yields on 91—day treasury bills has come down from 12.4 per cent in the first week of July to around 7.5 per cent at the end of January 1997.

Control over fiscal deficit was identified by the Update to the Economic Survey, presented by the United Front Government last year as one of the three challenges for economicpolicy. The Budget for 1996—97 envisaged a reduction of the fiscal dificit by 0.8 per cent of GDP to 5 per cent from 5.8 per cent in 1995—96 (RE). The primary deficit is also budgeted to fall from 1.1 poer cent of GDP to 0.2 per cent, while the revenue deficit to 2.5 per cent of GDP from 3 per cent in 1995—96.

The reduction in fiscal deficit has been attempted through an increase in revenues coupled with a reduction in expenditure. Revenue receipts (net) are budgeted to increase by 18.3 per cent during 1996—97 (BE). Despite a larger outgo on account of interest payments, subsidies and provision for revision of salaries and pension, total revenue expenditure is budgeted to grow at a lower rate of 12.7 per cent compared to 17.5 per cent in the previously year (RE). This deceleration in the growth of revenue expenditure has led to a decline in revenue expenditure to GDP ratio from 13.1 per cent in 1995—96 to 12.9 per cent in 1996—97 (BE). This favourable outcome, the Survey claims, is largely on account of containment of non—interest, non—plan expenditure growth at 9.3 per cent during 1996—97, about half the growth of 18.6 per cent in 1995—96 (RE). Consequently, non–interest revenue expenditure as a proportion of GDP is budgeted to fall to 8.1 per cent from 8.3 per cent in 1996—97 (RE). The revenue deficit is budgeted to fall by 0.5 per cent point of GDP. One may, however, note that the comparison of Budget estimates (BE) with Revenue Estimates (RE) is not very realistic.

According to index of industrial production the industrial sector recorded a growth of 5.1 per cent during 1993-94 as against a marginal growth of 2.3 per cent in 1992-93. Mining and quarring sector showed an increase of 3.2 per cent, manufacturing sector 4.9 per cent and electricity generation 7.5 per cent during 1993-94.

Detailed industry-group-wise figures showed that in manufacturing sector 13 out of 17 industry groups have recorded positive rate of growth during 1993-94. Notable among them are beverage, tobacco and tobacco product (21.3 per cent), basic metal and alloy industry (20.9 per cent), jute, hemp and mesta textile (18.6 per cent), chemical and chemical products (7.6 per cent), leather and fur products (7.4 per cent), paper and products (6.6 per cent), cotton textiles (6.6 per cent) and transport equipment (5.2 per cent).

Technical advice and assistance to small scale manufacturers is provided by the Small Industries Development Organisation through its network of 16 service institutes, 16 branch institutes, 58 extension, production and training centres. The organisation also provides common service and tool room facilities in workshops attached to small industries, service institutes and extension centres. It conducts courses in management and technical disciplines. During 1974-75, it provided technical assistance to 1,02,684 entrepreneurs and visited 70,965 factories for spot guidance.

Two new centres namely the Central Insititute of Tool Design, Hyderabad, and The Institute for Design of Electrical Measuring Instruments, Bombay, have started providing technical guidance and training for entrepreneurs.

The National Small Industries Corporation, which was set up in 1955, operates the scheme of procuring machinery for small-scale manufacturers on a hire-purchase basis on concessional terms. The value of machines delivered under this scheme during the period April-October 1974 was Rs. 5.69 crores as against Rs. 3.25 crores during the corresponding period of the previous year. It also assists the small-scale sector in processing orders from government departments and agencies. The value of stores purchased by the Directorate General of Supply and Disposals from April to November 1974 was about Rs. 37 crores. The Prototype Development and Training Centres set up with American, West German and Japanese assistance at Rajkot, Okhla (Delhi) and Howrah impart training to persons engaged in small-scale industries.

Hitherto the emphasis was minly on agro-based industries. The growth of these industries was no doubt important for providing a ready market to the agricultural outputs, to create employment opportunities in view of seasonal nature of agriculture and to stabilise the farmer's income. Several specialised agencies such as the State Finance Corporations, Small Scale Reserve Bank, and the various technical guidance and assistance schemes of the Central Government, State Governments, Reserve Bank and State Bank of India were directed mainly to sustain the growth of small scale and cottage industries.

It was, however, realised at a later stage that the institutional at the "output" end is only one part of the game. Indian agriculture does not face any serious problem from the demand side. It is with the improvement in the technique of production that the cost of farming can be reduced and the productivity of the land can be improved in order to meet ever growing demand of agricultural outpout from direct consumers as well as from industries. The institutional set-up was, therefore, geared up to discover means for improving the technique of agricultural production and also to manufacture agriculture machinery.

At the highest level various agricultural research centres, headed by Indian Council of Agriculture Research, are performing important functions in the development and distribution of scientific knowledge of agriculture. There is also the Indian Society of Agriculture Engineers which provides a wealth of information for the application of science and technology to farming. At the village level cooperative societies are propagating and, where possible, implementing, the programmes of the research centres.

Cooperative societies and various official organisations have performed important functions but because of their limitations, these agencies could not meet the requirements of mechanised agriculture which has recetly gained importance for improving agricultural productivity.

Thus with a view to meeting the rapidly growing demand of farmers for standard agricultural machinery equipment, e.g., tractors, power tillers, power threshers, seed-cum-fertilisers, drills, power sprayers and dusters, diesel and electric pump-sets, on cash or hire-purchase basis, the State Agro-Industrial Corporations have been established by the Government.

These corporation have been established in almost all the states. They are performing multifarious activities connected with not only the supply of agricultural machinery but also providing credit for the purpose. Some of them have ambitious programmes of designing and assembling tractors and manufacturing various tools and implements. But in fairness to the Corporations it must be recorded that none of them is more than three years old. What is more, some of them have the right ideas. In Gujarat, for instance, the AIC has decided to accord priority to the setting up of new cold storage plants in Banaskantha and Balsar, Onion dehydration plants at Jamnagar and Bhavnagar and hydrogenated oil unit in the Saurashtra region. In West Bengal, the AIC will supply diesel pumping sets to poor farmers owning two to five acres of land on payment of Rs. 70 cash down, the balance of the price–Rs. 3,500–being recoverable in easy instanlments. In Tamil Nadu the AIC is not only going into the processing and marketing of farm produce but will also set up factories for the servicing and repair of the 1,000 new tractors which are sold in the state every year.

It is evidnt that the growth of agro-industries cannot reverse the process of urbanisation. Most of the plants for processing farm products or "waste" materials released by the existing agro-based industries like textiles must be established near the consuming centres if they are to pave their way. All that can be done in the circumstances is to establish new industrial units, both big and small, in district towns and away from the major cities. Any effort to confine the new agro-industries to the rural or semi-urban areas is bound to hinder their growth and will in the end be self-defeating.

Since there are quite a number of common problems which these institutions are likely to face, it might be worthwhile to establish a Central Agro-Industrial Corporation of India to coordinate the work of these state institutions. Besides coordinating the working of the state corporations, the central organisation can be entrusted with research and development of technology. Centralisation of research will eliminate waste and duplication. The State Corporations will, however, continue to collect data rom their regional offices to make them available to the central organisation. It will also be the task of the cental agency to arrange the production of different components of machinery and implements in different areas according to the local facilities available on the "comparative cost" basis. The proposed corporation can also serve as an effective agency in arranging the colllection of technical knowledge from abroad and distribution of imported machinery.

The massive expenditure that the Government has incurred on agricultural development has in one way or another gone to prop up a new rich class by passing millions of small farmers and landless labourers. There are growing indications of discontent among those who have found the cost of acquiring modern equipment and agricultural inputs soaring, on the one hand, and official and somehow getting channelled away from them, on the other.

The Government's decision to establish 500 pilot agro-service centres in the country is a step in the right direction. The programme is being jointly sponsored by the Ministry of Agriculture and the Ministry of Industrial Development and is designed to provide a wide range of services from custom-hiring of tractors and other farm equiptment and repair and maintenance of agricultural machinery to soil testing, crop spraying, water anaylsis and land and field services such as levelling and contour surveying. The scheme is intended to provide employment in the rural area as well as to accelerate the process of modernisation in the villages. It is particularly aimed at providing help to the small farmers and the weaker sections of the rural community in the relatively backward areas. The rapid increase in the use of tractors, pumps, mechanical threshers and other machines, not to speak of community radios, transistors and other personal gadgetry, has created a demand for easily available repair and maintenance facilities on a wide scale.

Then agro-service centres can perform a valuable function provided they are suitably staffed and have the requisite managerial competence. The Government has negotiated World Bank assistance for tractor-cum-groundwater development projects in Punjab, Haryana and Tamil Nadu. Agro-service centres could be established alongside these programmes for a start.

As far as mechanical equipment like tractors and pumps are concerned, it would be most' desirable for the country to standardise on a few broad categories (not necessarily makes) so that problems of maintenance and the stocking of parts and components are not needlessly complicated by type differences. Little thought appears to have been given to this matter so far. But it is obviously something that calls for an early policy consideration.

The momentum of growth witnessed in 1995—96 with a GDP growth of over 7 per cent, has been maintained in 1996—97, thus providing increasing evidence that the growth potential has improved as a result of the reforms initiated in 1991. With the growing participation of virtually the entire spectrum of political opinion inthe reform process, there is a good prospect that a higher growth rate would become a permanent feature of the economy.

The initial spurt of reforms from 1991—92 to 1993—94 was very successful by all accounts, resulting in a jump in economic growth to 7.2 per cent in 1994—95 (in terms of GDP at factor cost). Since 1994—95, however, there was a marked slow down in the pace of reforms. Nevertheless, GDP grew by 7.1 per cent in 1995—96. The slackening of reforms preceding and during the election period may have been responsible for some loss of momentum, but this has been revived with a series of measures in recent months.

Economic growth in 1996—97 is estimated by CSO to be around 6.8 per cent (GDP at factor cost). Thus, the Eighth Plan is likely to end with an average growth of 6.5 per cent per annum, 0.9 per cent point higher than the target rate of 5.6 per cent, and 0.5 per cent point higher than the actual achievement of the Seventh Plan. More important for the future is the fact that the average growth during the latest three years is 7 per cent, probably placing India among the top ten performers in the world during this period.

As the final year of the Eighth Plan draws to a close, a comparison of some salient dimensions of some salilent dimensions of economic performance between the Eighth Plan period and its predecessor reveals the following:

— Overall economic growth has been faster;

— The manufacturing sector has grown almost 2 per cent points faster per year in the Eighth Plan period;

— Agriculture and allied sectors have grown at about 3.5 per cent per annum in both periods;

— Both exports and imports have grown significantly faster in the Eighth Plan period;

— The balance of payments has strengthened considerably, with trade and current account deficits declining as ratios of GDP, while exports and imports have grown rapidly both in value terms as well as in proportion to GDP.

— The Central Government's fiscal deficit as a proportion of GDP has declined significantly;

— The average rate of gross domestic savings has risen substantially from 20.6 per cent of GDP in the Seventh Plan period to 23.9 per cent in the first four years of the Eighth Plan;

— With the exception of telecommunications, the rate of growth of net output (value added) of infrastructure sectors has slowed;

— The average rate of inflation has risen somewhat, though remaining below double digits.

Total gross domestic saving reached a new peak of 25.6 per cent of GDP in 1995—96, exceeding its previous peak of 24.9 per cent of GDP in 1994–95. This seems to vindicate the reform strategy of encouraging savings by expanding saving and investment opportunities, rather than giving special incentives.

Gross domestic investment (adjusted), as a proportion of GDP at current prices, rose even faster than gross domestic saving in 1995—96 to a high of 27.4 per cent from 26 per cent in the previous year. Gross domestic investment in real terms, as a proportion of GDP at constant prices, reached a new peak of 27.1 per cent, exceeding the previous peak of 25.9 per cent in 1990—91. Gross fixed capital formation which is even more important for productivity and growth, reached a new peak of 24.1 per cent of GDP in 1995—96. Private sector investment appears to have responded vigorously to the policy of promoting competition, removing policy distortions and hurdles, and improving access to factors of production (e.g. technology, capital).

Estimates of savings and investment in 1996—97 are not yet available. Indicators are mixed. On the one hand, domestic capital goods production is buoyent and disbursement of financial institutions are significantly higher, on the other hand, capital goods imports have declined, non—oil imports are lower in the first nine months of the year, corporate demand for credit appears slack, and sanctions of financial institutions are substantially lower.

The economy in 1996—97 so far presents a mixed picture in other dimensions as well. Although overall economic growth remains high at 6.8 per cent, and agriculture has rebounded, the growth of manufacturing value added has slowed and the performance of key infrastructure sectors, especially power and crude oil, is weak. The annual rate of inflation (point to point) has risen back to average long—term levels and export growth has decelerated markedly in recent months. Despite the slowdown in exports, a combination of sluggish imports and reasonably buoyant inflows of invisibles and capital flows have led to a build—up of foreign exchange reserves by over $ 2.5 billion.

Challenges

As said, formidable challenges lay before the Ninth Plan. In the first instance, it may be interpreted as the challenge of a seven per cent rate of GDP growth, which would be a break with the historical rate of growth of Indian planning of some 3.5 per cent to 6 per cent, depending on the moods of rain gods and the gods have been exceptionally kind to us consecutively for the last eight years, and let us hope and pray that they would be in the Ninth Plan also. It may seem an amazing assertion to say that the seven per cent growth rate is the least of the challenges of the Plan.

Without exaggeration and bravado 8-10 per cent rate of growth is within the reach of the economy. What is seven per cent after all for a plan of nearly Rs. 1 m crore investment to which the plan investment should be rounded off. If a seven per cent rate of growth is not within the grasp of the economy, then what is all this liberalization, globalization, opening of the economy, etc. for? With improved management and evaluation and monitoring, an eight per cent rate of growth would be within easy reach.

That is, by all reckoning the seven per cent rate of growth appears to be a pessimistic rate of growth which in all likelihood would end up in an eight per cent rate of growth. That is the experience of the VIII Plan and there is no reason to believe that it won't repeat itself in the Ninth Plan with the economic fundamentals of inflation, forex, FDI, etc. more in place. Like the export pessimism of the yester-years, the economy appears to be afflicted with growth pessimism bordering on defeatism and self-deprecation. This is evident in the panic reaction of the national industrial houses against MNCs and their threat of take-over. It is sorrowful if the Indian industry had not yet come of age. When would it? Never?

The whole planning debate is being expended on the rate of growth, the rate of saving (26.2%), the rate of investment (29.6%), ICOR (4.2%) and so, in a great exercise of not seeing the wood for the trees. There can be no doubt concerning the attainability and validity of these figures, which are the minor points of the plan. The economy in these respects appears to suffer from underestimates. The savings potential and rate of the Indian economy should not be underestimated, so also the size of the economy. There is a labyrinthine part of the economy which is quite formidable. There is no proper planning, strategy and foresight to utilized the economy's potential. In addition, there is an estimated 20 m Indian community abroad who still have their roots in the country. Their savings are estimated anywhere between $ 100 billion to $ 300 billion.

Triggering off rural economic revolution: The real challenges of the Ninth Plan are in the areas of rural development. The real planning and economic action must be planned in that vast rural sector. The strength as well as weakness of the economy is in the rural sector. Agriculture needs not just a 4.5 per cent rate of growth, which is most likely to be unattainable. There is no second Green Revolution in sight, even after nearly three decades of the first one. Economic revolution of the country, yet to take place, has to come about from the countryside or rural areas. One looks forward hopefully to an Indian economic miracle like the Japanese ad the South Korean ones. When is it likely to be? Not even after nearly 50 years of planning and planned economic development? Where are the millions of jobs to be created except in rural areas for quite some time? If urbanization of the 80s of less than five per cent is any indication, a lot of economic action ought to take place in the countryside from HRD to social economic infrastructure to environmental planning.

We have had enough of Malthusianism. It, without enough of rural development, is aggravating land wars. Only increased agricultural productivity, still a long way behind the world standards by about 60 per cent even in the 'developed' agricultural State, could considerably bring down the agrarian tensions. In other words, the Indian economic revolutions to be set from the countryside and it would be an indigenous revolution with all economic reforms and foreign capital participation confined to industry, services and urban areas. It must be the task of the Ninth Plan to trigger off the rural economic revolution and bring forth a second Green Revolution countrywide.

The economy, first, is suffering from improper house keeping and management on account of which it is caught in thick cobwebs. The first task of the Plan would be to clear the economy of these cobwebs, which are of social and economic overheads, infrastructural and improper and uneconomical plan and economy management. The economy on the eve of the 21st century and the Ninth Plan is in need of stock-taking, spring cleaning, proper housekeeping and management, having grown without proper management and housekeeping over the last so many years. This is the first task and challenge of the Ninth Plan. Later on, it has challenges of proper housekeeping and management resources development.

Formidable tasks and challenges lay at the doorsteps of the Ninth Plan. The great task of rural development, fighting poverty employment generation, food security, HRD, population control, etc. The said thankless and profitless jobs would be the responsibility and challenges of the Plan, so also public enterprises profitability and viability.

Not that one is making too much of the Ninth Plan and trying to entrust with formidable tasks and challenges. They are very much there.

At the time of India's Independence, our priority was the provision of the basic human needs of food, fuel, shelter, health, employment, etc., to our vast population. As such the focus of our Five Year Plans was on agriculture, health, family welfare etc. In the Fourth Five Year Plan, problems related to environment received direct attention and a Committee was set up in 1972 to look into these problems and suggest a solution in consulation with experts and concerned minstries/ departments of the government. Another Committee was set up in January 1980, for reviewing the existing legislative measures and administrative machinery for ensuring environmental protection and for recommending ways to strengthen them.

On the recommendation of this high-powered Committee, the Department of Environment was set up in 1980. Consequently in 1985, it was upgraded to a full-fledged Ministry of Environment and Forests to serve as the focal point in the administrative structure for the planning, promotion and coordination of environmental and forestry programmes.

Environmental problem in India can be classified into two broad categories: (a) those arising as negative effects of the very process of development and (b) those arising from conditions of poverty and under-development. The first category has to do with the impact of efforts to achieve rapid economic growth and development. Poorly planned developmental projects are usually environmentally destructive. The second category has to do with the impact on the health and integrity of our natural resources such as land, soil, water, forests, wildlife, space, etc., as a result of proverty.

There are about 30 major enactments related to protection of environment now being administered by the Central and state governments. Prominent among these are: Wildlife (Protection) Act, 1972; The Forest (Conservation) Act, 1980; The Water (Prevention and Control of Pollution) Act, 1974; The Air (Prevention and Control of Pollution) Act, 1981; The Water (Prevention and Control of Pollution) Cess Act, 1977; The Environment (Protection) Act, 1986; The Public Liability Insurance Act; 1991; The Motor Vehicle Act, 1938 as amended in 1988; The Factories Act and the Insecticides Act. These are implemented through several organisations like Central and state pollution control boards, chief inspectors of factories and insecticides inspectors of agriculture departments, etc.

The Environment (Protection) Act, 1986, brought into force from 19 November 1986 is a landmark legislation as it is an umbrella Act for the protection of environment and aims at plugging the loopholes in the other related Acts. The salient features of this Act are as follows: (a) conferring powers on the Central

Government to; (i) take all necessary measures for protecting quality of environment; (ii) coordinate activities of states, officers and other authorities under the Act or under any other law related to the objects of this Act; (iii) Plan and execute a nationwide programme for prevention, control and abatement of environmental pollution; (iv) lay down standards for discharge of environmental pollutant; (v) empower any person to enter, inspect, take samples and test; (vi) establish or recognise environmental laboratories; (vii) appoint or recognise analysts; (viii) lay down standards for quality of environment; (ix) restrict areas in which industries, operations or process may not be carried out or shall be carried out subject to certain safeguards; (x) lay down safeguards for prevention of accidents and take remedial measures in case of such accidents; (xi) lay down procedures and safeguards for handling hazardous substances; (xii) constitute an authority or authorities for exercising powers; (xiii) issue directions to any person, officer or authority including the power direct closure, prohibition or regulation of any industry, operation or process or stoppage or regulations of supply of electricity, water or any other services; (xiv) require any person, officer, state government or authority to furnish any prescribed information; and (xv) delegate powers to any of a state or authority; (b) it confers powers on persons to complain to courts regarding any violation of the provisions of the Act, after a notice of 60 days to prescribed authorities; (c) the Act makes it obligatory for the person incharge of a place to inform the prescribed authorities regarding any accidental discharge or apprehended discharge of any pollutant in excess of prescribed standards. Authorities on receipt of such information or otherwise shall take remedial measures are recoverable with inerest from the pollute; (d) it prescribes penalties for violation of the provisions of the

Act. No distinction is shown between government department and other companies; and (e) jurisdiction of civil courts is barred under the Act.

Government has taken several steps to provide adequate legal and institutional basis for implementation of the Act. These include issue of rules, notification of standards, action regarding environmental laboratories, strengthening of state departments of environment and pollution control boards, delegation of powers, identification of agencies for carrying out various activities for hazardous chemical management and setting up of environemtn protection councils in the states. The Water (Prevention and Control of Pollution) Act, 1974 and the Air (Prevention and Control of Pollution) Act, 1981, have been made more stringent. Steps have been taken to: (i) prevent pollution at source; (ii) encourage, develop and apply the best available practicable and technical solutions; (iii) ensure that the polluter pays for the pollution and control arrangements; (iv) focus protection on heavily polluted areas and river stretches; and (v) involve the public in decision-making.

Environment and Development: A Perspective

One in every seven persons on this planet lives in India. With 16 per cent of the world's population and only 2.4 per cent of its land area, there is obviously a great demand on the natural resources including land.

This is so in spite of the fact that an average Indian consumes a much lower quantum of resources than a person in the developed world. If an average person in the South were to consume as much as an average person in a developed country, the environmental crisis would be unimaginable. While, to a large extent, the lcwer per capita consumption is due to poverty, an important reason is also that a majority of the population in India follows a sustainable lifestyle which is based on environmentally sound practices evolved over thousands of years.

The environmental problem today is being precipitated partly because practices which were appropriate earlier, like shifting cultivation and unrestricted cattle grazing, are not so anymore. For instance, as a result of increasing population and decreasing availability of land, crop-fallow cycles in shifting cultivation have been reduced to a mere five years from a more sustainable 20-40 years in the past.

But just as there were learnings and difficulties with regard to traditional practices, so was the case with newly introduced technologies. Many measures, at one time seen as solutions, are today extracting an unanticipated price. The Green Revolution of the 1960s met India's growing demand for food. While it helped India to dramatically increase foodgrain production, what was not fully appreciated then was that the Green Revolution would on the one hand affect the country's natural resource capital, and on the other, create dependencies on inputs such as chemical fertilizers and pesticides. There are indications of soil health problems such as deficiency of micronutrients and organic matter, incidence of soil salinity and damage to the physical structure of the soil, apart from increasing dependence on chemical inputs, many of which are imported.

Today there is widespread realization that there can be no readymade solutions, that technology alone cannot solve problems, that we have to use all our ingenuity to find solutions which combine the best of the old practices with the benefits that modern science and technology can offer. The challenges are staggering in number, scale and complexity. We need to develop and to modernize in less wasteful ways than is the current paradigm, but not lose our sound traditional values and practices. India will have to leap-frog over wasteful and polluting technologies and go for technologies which are the most environmentally sound, and are based on maximizing recycling and efficient use of resources practices which are inherent in India's traditions. It is when such development comes about that the population pressures will ease, as development brings down demographic growth rates.

The task is stupendous. For while the challenge of development might seem to be 'how to get there' the real challenges is 'how not to get there'. Urbanization, industrial growth, transportation systems, agriculture, housing... all have to stop imitating practices that are already being phased out in the developed world. With the North becoming more conscious about the condition of their own environment, 'dirty' factories are moving South. To cite only one example, the production of harmful and toxic dyestuff intermediates such as H-acid, K-acid, gamma acid and metanilic acid taken up in the 60s stands at over 41,000 tonnes in the country today, with an estimated Rs. 6 billion worth for export to the developed countries.

The forces which are taking India, and much of the developing world, on the conventional and largely imitative and unimaginative development path are many. But this path is not sustainable—for India or for the world. As Mahatma Gandhi remarked over 60 years ago. "God forbid that India should ever take to industrialism after the manner of the West. The economic imperialism of a single, tiny... kingdom is today keeping the world in chains. If an entire nation of 300 million took to similar economic exploitation, it would strip the world bare like locusts. When the West developed, it did so perhaps in ignorance of the environmental impact of its activities.

Today we know that such a path is neither practicable nor desirable for countries which are raising their standards of living. We, along with other developing countries, have to find alternative paths to an alternative goal. A goal which ultimately is the true goal of development—an environmentaly sound and sustainable quality of life, which is socially just and equitable. A goal that must be common to all citizens of the planet. A goal that is perhaps as distant from the developing world as it is from the over-consuming, wasteful societies of what is currently referred to as the 'developed' world.

It is this goal of development that we seek together as people, as organizations and as governments at the United Nations Conference on Environment and Development. It is this intermeshing of environmental and developmental concerns that must form the goal of humankind.

The world is rapidly realizing that environmental issues such as global warming and ozone depletion, acid rain, marine pollution and the threat to biodiversity are global and not merely national issues. But in a world where per capita GNP varies from US $ 80 in Mozambique to US $ 29,880 in Switzerland; where life expectancy at birth varies from 42 years in Sierra Leone to 79 years in Japan; and where literacy rates vary from about 12 per cent in Somalia to over 95 per cent in the United States, what is not as explicitly understood is that development too is a global issue. And perhaps even less understood is the fact that a sustainable and viable planet requires that development be global. As Mrs. Indira Gandhi, then Prime Minister of India and the only visiting head of government to attend the UN Conference on the Human Environment in Stockholm in 1972, said, the removal of poverty is an integral part of the goal of an environmental strategy for the world.

It is towards this goal that several efforts are under way in India. These are environmental initiatives—not merely of government at various levels, but of people and organizations outside the government. They are efforts which may not all succeed, but they represent initiatives that are continuously under review and change. They represent the broad base of concern and the vibrancy of environmental efforts in India. These initiatives need to be shared in an effort to find the alternative paths that will lead all nations towards the true goal of development without environmental and social damage.

India is a land of physical, ecological, social, cultural and linguistic diversity. Bounded by the Himalayan mountain ranges in the north and the Indian Ocean in the south, it has a multitude of climates, soil types and geographical areas—and consequently of habitats and wildlife. But it is not only the physical and biological diversity that is enormous. The census reports 1,652 languages as mother tongues. Of these, 33 are spoken by over a 100,000 people each. India is also home to many religious communities and its ancient tradition of secularism is manifested in its Constitution.

Each of these languages and religions contributes to the vibrancy and variety of Indian life, and to the mosaic of India's social, cultural and economic life. 'Unity in Diversity' has been the maxim of cultural pluralism in India. But at times of resource shortages and allocation, it is not always easy to keep regional or sectorial aspirations subservient to national ones. To maintain the unity of India with all its diversity remains a challenge—but the binding forces evolved over centuries help meet this challenge.

India's population of 844 million is today growing at 2.11 per cent every year. This is expected to stabilize only in the second half of the next century, when India will be the most populous country in the world. Adding over 17 million people each year puts considerable pressure on the country's natural resources and reduces the gains of development.

The challenge underlying limiting population growth was brought out by Prime Minister P.V. Narasimha Rao who stressed recently the need for the country to "take upon itself the challenge to deal with population-related issues whish are inextricably linked to the total development of our nation." The `link' is usually misunderstood. It is not that population control will lead to development, but that development leads to a decrease in population growth rates.

High population growth rate is usually an indicator of poverty, and not the cause of it. This is perhaps best seen in the case of women's development. Taking just one indicator—female literacy—some trends become clear. States such as Kerala and Tamil Nadu which have among the highest female literacy rates in India (86.93 per cent and 52.29 per cent, respectively) are also among the states with the lowest decennial population growth rates (13.98 per cent and 14.94 per cent). This is just one development factor out of the many which act together to affect population.

Based on ideals long cherished by its people, the Constitution of India defines India as a 'Sovereign, Socialist, Secular, Democratic Republic'. the system of government is parliamentary with a federal structure, power and responsibility being shared between the Central and State Governments, and in turn with many local and district level authorities. The cooperation between various levels of government is crucial to development. A challenge before a large country like India is to find the right blend between centralized and decentralized decision-making and between micro-level planning and macro-level planning. Decision-making that involves people at various levels brings in different perceptions and enriches the process. The importance of involving local people in decision-making, to bring in a better perspective of their requirements and in finding implementable solutions, is also being recognized. Starting from colonial times, several policies, laws and procedures have tended to alienate people from their natural resources. Evolving methods for the participation of local people in the management of common property resources is a major challenge for natural resource management.

The floodplains of the great rivers are India's food bowls. So far, food production has kept abreast of population increase. But the Green Revolution, which was largely responsible for this, has raised some questions of environmental costs. High-yielding varieties, making crops more vulnerable to disease. Soil health problems such as deficiency of micro-nutrients and organic matter, incidence of soil salinity, and damage to the physical structure of soil have arisen in the intensively cultivated areas. The need for higher inputs has resulted in chemical inputs going up from about 1.9 kg per ha of gross cropped area in 1960 to over 72 kg per ha by 1990-91. The challenge is not only to sustain and increase agricultural growth, but to do so without damaging the environment.

Of the total 329 million hectares (mha) of land, it is estimated that only 266 mha possess any potential for production. Of this, 143 mha is agricultural land and it is estimated that 85 mha suffers from varying degrees of soil degradation. Of the remaining 123 mha, 40 are completely unproductive. The balance 83 mha are classified as forest lands, of which over half are denuded to various degrees.

India has the world's largest cattle population. The 406 million head of livestock have to be supported on 13 mha, or less than 4 per cent of the land which is classified as pasture lands, most of which is overgrazed. Thus, out of 266 mha, about 175 mha or 66 per cent is degraded to varying degrees. Water and wind erosion account for the degradation of almost 150 mha of this. The challenge of prevention of erosion, and indeed of restoration of India's land resources, is intricately related to strategies for the management of land, water and vegetative cover.

Forests in India have been shrinking for several centuries owing to pressures of agriculture, commercial and industrial use, urbanization and other uses. The process continued after Independence. Vast areas that were once green are today wastelands. Bringing these back under vegetative cover is a major challenge.

Like indigenous people all over the world, the tribal communities that live in forests respect the trees, and the birds and animals that give them sustenance. Strategies are being developed for a greater degree of people's participation in forest management. The role of forest-dwelling communities in restoring and conserving forests is now being increasingly recognized. The challenge is to attempt to integrate the modern knowledge and skills of the Forest Department with the traditional knowledge and experience of the local communities, and to evolve strategies for the joint management of forests.

As in most places in the world, the forests and the agricultural plains have an intimate relationship. Forests usually act as catchments for rivers. With the increasing demand for water, plans were made to harness the mighty rivers through large irrigation projects. Typically, these would submerge forests, displace local communities and benefit agriculture in the plains. Today some of these, like the dam on the river Narmada and the Tehri dam, have become areas of debate. This is an issue which poses very difficult questions regarding the relationship between environment and development, and resolving these is a challenge the country faces.

If the world's rainfall were averaged over its landmass, it is seen that India receives more than one-and-a-half times the rain that other parts of the world get. But this rainfall has a large spatial and temporal variation and is highly seasonal. Eighty per cent of the country gets 80 per cent or more of the annual rainfall during the four months of the monsoon.

Managing water so that it is available when and where it is required is a major issue. Of the total 400 million hectare metres (mham) annual precipitation that India receives, approximately 150 mham percolates into the soil, 180 mham joins the surface flow and 70 mham evaporates. Of the 150 mham which enters the soil, about 110 mham constitutes soil moisture while 40 mham percolates into groundwater aquifers. Of the 180 mham run-off, major and minor irrigation projects have so far succeeded in trapping 17 mham in their reservoirs. Another 4 or 5 mham are stored in tanks and small reservoirs. Thus only about 16 per cent of the annual rainfall is available for irrigation.

Large dams which replaced traditional water-harvesting techniques in modern India were initially seen as the solution. But today the problems of displacement, submergence and drainage are subjects of serious debate. Increasing demands and new technologies are leading to the over-exploitation of groundwater, leading to an alarming drop in water tables in certain areas. This has even led to the problem of extreme salinity in some parts of the country. Rationalizing the use of groundwater is another important issue.

Community wastes, industrial effluents and excessive use of chemical fertilizers and pesticides are polluting surface water and affecting the quality of groundwater. The implications of this on human health and aquatic life are obvious. Finding optimal strategies for the conservation of water, provision of safe drinking water and keeping warer bodies clean are difficult challenges.

India is very rich in biodiversity. Preserving this heritage is a major challenge, as also utilizing this for development. With the considerably large financial resources and research capabilities available with the North, the benefits emanating from this biodiversity are being exploited more rapidly by the North than by the countries of its origin.

Although India is largely rural and agricultural, the 27 per cent Indians who live in urban areas constitute a large number in absolute terms. A very large number of these are the urban poor who live in highly degraded slums. Urbanization and industrialization pose a host of environmental problems that need urgent attention. Over 30 per cent of urban Indians live in slums. Out of India's 3,245 towns and cities, only 21 have partial or full sewerage and sewage treatment facilities. Coping with rapid urbanization is a major challenge facing the country today.

Several of India's cities started out as trading towns centred in agricultural area. As these grew, urban land requirements ate into some of the best agricultural lands. Location policies for urban and industrial growth from this point of view are other challenges to planning in India.

While on the one hand India has some of the most sophisticated industrial plants, there are many more using outdated, polluting technologies and makeshift facilities, with negligible provision for treating their wastes. As a result, there are many cities and industrial ares that would perhaps be classified among the worst in terms of their air and water pollution. Major initiatives are however being taken. The Environment Protection Act (1986), the Water (Prevention and Control of Pollution) Act, 1974, and the Air (Prevention and Control of Pollution) Act, 1981, have set standards that certain industries must fulfill. Much pollution control equipment is now available in the country. The Central Pollution Control Board and State Pollution Control Boards have their own machinery to monitor emission and pollution levels.

The choices, however, are difficult. Substantial resources, technical expertise, political and social will, awareness among the people and their support are required to implement these rules. Industries may need to be relocated, and new equipment added to treat the wastes. New, clean technologies need to replace older ones. In some cases plants may even need to be scrapped. These measures may involve loss of jobs in the short run and have an immediate consequence on the cost of products. These are difficult choices, especially in a developing country.

The Challenges of meeting India's growing energy requirements are many. presently, commercial and non-commercial sources contribute almost equally to fulfilling these needs. The current use of bio-resources for meeting energy requirements is far in excess of their regenerative capacities. Each source of commercial energy-hydel, thermal or nuclear—has major environmental consequences and the challenge is to utilize these resources with the least environmental damage. This involves determining the optimal technology, scale and location of such projects.

There is considerable scope for energy saving. For instance, the inefficiencies of the system can be seen from the fact that 100 tonnes of coal mined for the purpose of power generation provide only the energy equivalent of 5 tonnes of coal in the form of actual irrigation when we use electric pumping in the agricultural sector. A full 95 tonnes of coal is lost in energy euqivalent terms in the process of power generation, transmission and distribution, inefficiencies in the pump set itself and the irrigation system which finally reaches water to the farmer's field. Major investment would be required in the area of technology upgradation for increasing efficiency of generation, transmission and utilization of commercial energy. There are also technology constraints in using existing sources. Huge quantities of natural gas estimated to be worth about Rs. 50 million a day are today flared, rather than utilized for power generation, domestic fuel or feedstock for the production of fertilizer.

Another challenge is that of reorienting to today's conditions and needs, institutions, attitudes and infrastructures essentially built up during the colonial times. This change must take into account India's traditions of resource use, management, education etc. The change needs to come about in education, in attitudes, in administrative procedures and in institutions, for it affects the way people view technology, resources, and indeed development itself.

Poverty, however, remains the central issue and the biggest challenge. While the annual per capita income has been slowly rising over time, about 40 per cent of the people are below what is considered the poverty line. The challenge is therefore not only to find development paths and models which are environmentally sustainable but that are also socially just and culturally acceptable. For a very large number of the poor who depend on the resources of their immediate environment, poverty has been compounded by environmental degradation. Not only does the natural resource base of the immediate environment provide their basic requirements, it is also the basis of their livelihood and security. The challenge of poverty and the challenge of environment are therefore not two different challenges but two facets of the same challenge.

The problems are complex and the choices difficult. Each issue needs its own resolution, not a borrowed solution. A large number of areas need research and constant monitoring. Citizens and decision-makers need to become more aware of their environment and the intricate relationship it bears to development. Today in India we see the seeds of this effort. A national Ministry of Environment and Forest was set up in 1985. Most states have set up Departments of Environment and associated agencies. Several hundred institutions and several thousand NGOs are today, in one way or another, working towards coping with the challenges of environment and development. But the most hopeful sing perhaps is an increasing number of people who, individually and through their communities, are taking action—action that leads to a better environment and a better life. It is these efforts that need to be shared widely. The efforts of the people, NGOs and the Government.

The rapid increase in industrialisation and urbanisation has exerted extra pressure on the infrastructural facilities of human settlements manifesting in environment problems like increased incidence of air, water and noise pollution. The ambient aire quality major towns and cities in the country is being monitored under the National Ambient Air Quality Monitoring (NAAQM) programme. The monitoring results indicate that Sulphur Dioxide and Nitrogen dioxide levels are mostly within the permissible limits whereas Suspended Particulate

Matter (SPM) values are higher than the prescribed limits at some places due to vehicular and air pollution, burning of fossil fuel and natural dusty conditions. The pollution caused by vehicles contributes significantly towards air pollution. The problem of suspended particulate matter is more acute during the summer due to local dusty conditions. During the winter months, lower ambient temperatures, lower mixing depth temperature inversion, higher traffic density, higher consumption of domestic fuels, aggravate the pollution problems.

The data on ambient water quality of rivers indicates that levels of coliform count and Biological Oxygen Demand (BOD) are generally high resulting in deterioration of water quality. This is primarily due to inadequate sanitation facilities and discharge of waste water into the surfa ce water bodies without proper treatment.

Urban noise levels in major cities also indicate and incresing trend due to rise in human population, automobiles and industrial activities. Specific studies reveal that noise levels in industrial areas are generally within the prescribed limits but exceed the standards in respect of commercial, residential and silence zones during certain hours. The problem is more conspicuous near the traffic intersections and commercial centres.

The on-going initiatives of Government to improve environment include preventive as well as promotive measures. Fiscal incentives are provided by the Government to encourage the installation of appropriate pollution abatement equipment in the form of custom waive off and soft loans. While the industries are encouraged and the fiscal incentives are provided for installing equipment for control of pollution, punitive measures including legal action is taken against the defaulting units.

To achieve the goal pollution abatement, emission and effluent standards for air, water and noise have been notified. Regular monitoring is carried out and the enforcement efforts have been intensified. At present, a majority of identified units have already installed the requisite pollution control equipment. According to the data collected by the Central Pollution Control Board (CPCB) on September 30, 1996, out of 1,551 units belonging to 17 categories of highly polluting industries, 1,259 units had facilities to comply with the environmental standards, 112 were closed and 180 were not having adequate facilities. Show cause notices under Section 5 of the Environment (Protection) Act 1986 have been issued to all the defaulting units.

Apart from notifications of effluent and emission standards for the major categories of polluting industries, national ambient air quality standards including ambient noise standards have been notified. Industries have been directed to instal necessary pollution control equipment within a stipulated time frame. More stringent norms for vehicular emissions have been notified under the Central Motor Vehicles Rules which have come into effect from April, 1996. Supply of unleaded petrol in four metropolitan cities of Mumbai, Calcutta, Delhi and Chennal has been introduced with effect from April 1, 1995 for use in four wheel vehicles fitted with catalytic converters. The use of unleaded petrol will be gradually expanded to other cities in the country.

Twenty-four critically polluted areas in the country have been identified and action plans have been drawn up to improve the quality of environment in these areas. Adoption of clean technologies of production and formation of Waste Minimisation Circles is being encouraged to minimise environmental pollution. Under the World Bank aided Industrial Pollution Control Project, technical and financial assistance is provided for setting up Common Effluent Treatment Plants (CETPs) in clusters of small scale industrial units. An "Eco-Mark" scheme has been launched to certify various products of the industries which fulfil the prescribed pollution control standards to achieve the objective of environment-friendly production, packaging and waste disposal. To increase public awareness and participation, several public awareness campaigns on effects of pollution and measures to control it have been launched.

The Polity Statement for Abatement of Pollution indicates adoption of best available clean and practicable technologies, rather than end-of-the-pipe treatment, as the key elements for pollution prevention. As a part of this thrust, the Ministry of Environment & Forests has set up a Clean Technologies Division for identifying cleaner technologies that can be introduced in different development sectors. Techniques like coal beneficiation are being promoted. The programme envisages setting up a National Clearing House for cleaner technologies as the overall co-ordinating agency and sectoral centres in different areas of development to focus on their activities. Another initiative taken to motivate environmentally oriented technologies and practices is mandatory submission of Annual Environmental Statements which would be subsequently evolved into environmental audit.

Prior environmental clearance of development projects based on impact assessment is being increasingly emphasised. Such clearance has been made mandatory for 29 specified categories of development projects through a statutory notification issued in January, 1994. This has been done with a view to mitigating the adverse environmental effects of these projects and in integrating the environmental concerns into development. This mechanism is also of help in catalysing the process of inducing cleaner environment-friendly technologies into the developmental process.

The success of the Ganga Action Plan has encouraged its replication for water pollution abatement in tributaries of the Ganga (Yamuna, Gomati and Damodar) under Ganga Action Plan Phase-II. A wider scheme called the National River conservation Plan covering pollution abatement works for grossly polluted stretches in 18 major rivers in 10 States of the country has also been initiated. Further, a programme for conservation of selected lakes has also been formulated by the Ministry.

The National Environmental Tribunal Act, providing relief, compensation and restitution to victims of accidents while handling hazardous substances, and for environmental damages, came into force from 17 June, 1995. The Act provides (i) strict liabilitiy for damages arising out of any accident occurring while handling any hazardous substances and (ii) Establishment of National Environmental Tribunal for effective and expenditious disposals of cases arising from such accidents with a view to give relief and compensation for damage to persons, property and the environment and (iii) matters connected therewith or incidental thereto.

The National Environment Appellate Authority (NEAA) has been set up by the Government in January 1997. Public hearings have now been built into the environment impact assessment. The machinary for hearing appeals against environment pollution impact assessment is also being set up. The measures are to ensure greater transparency and faster decision-making in matters concerning the environmental impact of industrial projects.

Prevention and control of pollution

As per the Policy Statement of Abatement of Pollution announced in February 1992, the key elements for pollution prevention are adoption of the best available clean and praticable technologies rather than end of the pipe treatment. The focus is on source reduction and substitution of chemicals, with safe alternatives. The thrust has, therefore, been made for considering process changes which involve significant improvements in energy and water conservation. To follow up on the various issues covered in the Policy Statement for Abatement of Pollution, the National Conservation Strategy and the Forest Policy Statement, several new programmes and studies have been initiated and commissioned. An Environment Action Programme has been formulated covering a wide ambit of subjects such as clean and low-waste technologies, improvement of water quality, institutional and human resources development, forestry and natural resources accouning.

To integrate natural resource accounting into the national accounting process, collection and analysis of environmental data has been initiated. It is proposed to produce a computerised map of the critically polluted areas through digitisation, on a format based on Geographic Information System. Base thematic maps on 1.6 M scale have been prepared for the country on the following themes: (i) major river basins and drainage network; (ii) administrative divisions; (iii) designated best use classification of streams; (iv) location of water and air pollution monitoring stations; (v) location of critically polluted areas; and (vi) major cities of India (above one lakh population).

The gazette notification on environmental audit issued in 1992 has been amended and now applies to all units seeking environmental clearance, and such units are required to submit environmental statements for the period ending 31 March on or before 30 September every year beginning from 1993 To facilitate industries in preparing environmental statements, model environmental statement reports for six categories of industries have been prepared. A booklet titled "Environmental Statement as part of environmental audit" has also been prepared by the Ministry. A software package 'Paryavaran' along with a user manual, has been prepared for analysis of information submitted in these environmental statements and is being distributed to all the SPCBs.

An 'Eco-Mark' label has been introduced to label consumer products that are environment friendly. Sixteen products have been identified for labelling and standards for toilet soaps and detergents, paper, paints, architectural paints and laundry soaps have been notified for awarding this label. The procedure for granting consent to small scale industries has been simplified. A new format for the consent application and for authorisation required under the Environment (Protection) Act, 1986 has been developed and notified. Under the scheme "Adoption of clean technology in the small scale industries and to extend necessary technical support", training and awareness programmes for personnel in small Industry Development Organisation and entrepreneurs are being organised. A manual "From Waste to Profits" giving guidelines for waste minimisation has been prepared.

The Central Pollution Control Board (CPCB) is the national apex body for assessment, monitoring and control of water and air pollution. The executive responsibilities for enforcement of the Acts for Prevention and Control of Pollution of Water (1974) and Air (1981) and also of the Water (Cess) Act, 1977 are carried out through are Board. Twenty three states and union territories have already adopted the Act and respective state pollution control boards have been constituted. These states are Andhra Pradesh, Assam, Bihar, Goa, Gujarat, Haryana, Himachal Pradesh, Jammu and Kashmir, Karnataka, Kerala, Madhya Pradesh,

Maharashtra, Meghalaya, Mizoram, Orissa, Punjab, Rajasthan, Sikkim, Tamil Nadu, Tripura, Uttar Pradesh, West Bengal, Delhi and Pondicherry. Arunachal Pradesh has adopted the Act, but is yet to constitute the board. Enactment of the Enviornment (Protection) Act, 1986 has further extended the scope of the activities of the Board. Under the Environment (Protection) Act, 1986, effluent and emission standards in respect of 6[illegible] categories of industries have been notified. So far, 84 laboratories have been recognised as environmental laboratories. Minimum National Standards (MINAS) for effluents and emissions from specific industries have been formulated and control measures are being implemented in a phased manner. A notification consolidating all the environmental standards including general effluent, emission and noise standards has been issued. It also includes standards for waste water generation in respect of 11 categories of industries. Further mass emission norms which would come into effect from 1 April 1996 have also been issued for petrol and diesel driven vehicles under the Central Motor Vehicles Rules of the Ministry of Surface Transport. Unleaded petrol of Delhi, Bombay, Madras and Calcutta from 1 April 1995. Petrol with a maximum lead content of 0.15 g/l has been introduced at all the retail outlets of these four metro cities since June 1994.

Seventeen categories of heavily polluting industries have been identified namely, cement, thermal powre plants, distilleries, sugar, fertilizer, integrated iron and steel, oil refineries, pulp and paper, petrochemicals, pesticides, tanneries, basic drugs and pharmaceuticals, dye and dye intermediates, caustic soda, zinc smelter, copper smelter and aluminium smelter. Action is taken against the defaulting units in these categories on priority. On the basis of the designated best use of criteria CPCB has identified 13 grossly polluted stretches of Sabarmati, Subernarekha, Godavari, Krishna, Indus (tributaries), Sutlej, Ganga (tributaries), Yamuna, Hindon, Chambal, Damodar, Gomati, and Kali rivers to formulate short-term result oriented programmes. The CPCB, in consultation with SPCBs has identified 22 critically polluted areas in the country which need special attention for control of pollution. These are Vapi (Gujarat), Singrauli (U.P.), Korba, Ratlam, Nagoda (Madhya Pradesh), Digboi (Assam), Talcher (Orissa), Bhadravati (Karnataka), Howrah (West Bengal), Dhanbad (Bihar), Pali and * Pataucheru (Andhra Pradesh), Chembur (Maharashtra), Najafgarh (Delhi), Govindhgarh (Punjab), Udyog Mandal (Kerala) and Parwanoo and Kala Amb (HP). The progress in abatement of pollution in these areas is being reviewed. A Bill has been introduced in the Parliament for establishing a National Environment Tribunal.

Environmental Impact Assessment (EIA)

The objective of all development is to add to the economic well-being of the people so that their standard of living can be improved. Development projects are, therefore, taken up to convert the natural resources into goods and services. It is imperative to incorporate environmental aspects into the development projects right at the inception stage to prevent the erosion of the resouces base itself. Impact assessment is a handy tool to assess the environmental compatibility of the projects in terms of their location, suitability of technology, efficiency in resource utilisation and recycling etc. Impact assessment was introduced in 1978 and now covers almost all major projects.

At present environmental impact assessment is being done for the following types of project: (a) (i) river valley; (ii) thermal power; (iii) mining; (iv) industries; (v) atomic power; (vi) rail, road, highways, bridges; (vii) ports and harbours; (viii) airport; (iv) new towns and (x) communication projects, (b) projects which require approval of the Public Investment Board/Planning Commission/Central Electricity Authority; (c) projects referred to the Ministry of Environment and Forests by other ministries; (d) projects which are sensitive and located in environmentally degraded areas; (e) public sector undertakings of the Centre where the project cost is more than Rs. 50 crore. A notification has been issued in January 1994 which makes Environmental Impact Assessement statutory for 29 categories of developmental projects under various sectors such as industrial, mining, irrigation, power, transport, tourism, communication, etc. The notification contains details aimed at rationalising and standarding the procedure for environmental clearance. Extensive delegations to the stae governments are also provided in this notification. An amendment to this notification stipulates inter alia that all applications complete in every material aspect have to be examined and decision conveyed to the applicants within 30 days in the case of site clearances and 120 days in the case of environmental clearnce of projects. Once an application has been submitted by project authority the preliminary scrutiny of the project is done by the respective technical divisions and the overall appraisal of the projects is undertaken by specially constituted environmental appraisal committees of experts. In addition, special groups/committees and task forces are constituted as and when needed for expert inputs on major projects. After a detailed scrutiny and assessment, the appraisal committee makes its recommendation for approval or rejection of the projects. Depending on the nature of the project, certain safeguards are recommended. For monitoring and timely implementation of safeguards suggested, six regional centres have been set up by the Ministry at Shillong, Bhubaneswar, Chandigarh, Bangalore, Lucknow and Bhopal.

Under the Forests (Conservation) Act, 1980 diversion of forest land for non-forest purpose requires prior approval from the Central Government. While proposals involving forest land less than 20 hectare can be decided by the state forest departments, proposals involving more than that are appriased by the Advisory Committee of the Ministry, constituted under the Forests (Conservation) Act, 1980 as amended in 1988.

When a project requires both environemental and forest clearance, the proposals are simultaneously processed under the Single Window Celearance Scheme. All cases with complete environmental data and action plans are decided within three months. In the case of diversion of forest land, the decision is taken within six months.

Major environmental impacts of river vally projects which need consideration are: (i) degradation of catchment areas; (ii) command area development; (iii) rehabilitation of those affected; (iv) incresed incidence of water-borne diseases; (v) reservoir induced seismicity; and (vi) deforestation and loss of flora and fauna including gene-pool reserves.

Major environmental impacts of mining operations are: (i) degradation of land; (ii) pollution of surface and ground water resources; (iii) pollution of air; (iv) deforestation including loss of flora and fauna; (v) rehabilitation of affected populationincluding tribals; and (vi) impact on historical monuments and religious places. A major component of the mining operations in India is the opencast mining which severely affects land use pattern. Mining operations have serious adverse impact on the growth of vegetation and general landscape. Minerals extracted interact with surface and ground water thus polluting the water resources. Loss of top-soil due to deforestation also depletes ground water resources and results in drying up of perennial sources like springs and streams especially in hill areas.

Major environmental impacts of thermal power projects include; (a) air pollution; (b) water pollution; (c) deforestation; (d) rehabilitation; and (e) land degradation. Flue gases emerging from stacks containing sulphur dioxide, oxides of nitrogen, carbon monoxide, etc., are detrimental to human beings and vegetation. Water pollution from thermal stations can due to release of slurry which is a mixture of flyash and water. Thermal pollution is due to release of cooling water which can affect acquatic life. Solution to disposal of ash problem is in its recycling by converting it into building blocks and its use in other construction works. Another step which helps in abating pollution cuased by ash is stabilisation of ash dumps through suitable vegetation.

Major environmenal impacts of industrial projects include (i) are pollution; (ii) water pollution; and (iii) disposal and utilisation of solid waste. Impacts of projects in specific areas are examined in great detail and suitable control measures suggested. Linkages of project requirements to utilisation of resources in an optimal way is an essential pre-requisite. Concept of recycling, reuse and adoption of clean technologies is increasingly becoming predominant.

Projects considered under the transport sector include laying of railway lines, roads and bridge construction, airport construction and establishing of ports and harbours. The environmental parameters affected by the transport projects have been classified into (i) natural physical resources; (ii) natural ecological resources; (iii) human/economic development resources; and (iv) quality of life values including aesthetic and cultural values. Adverse impacts on above environmental parameters are to be identified and mitigation measures provided for to offset such impacts.

Under the Environment (Protection) Act, 1986, a notification on Coastal Zone Regulation has been issued declaring coastal stretches of seas, bays, estuaries, creaks, rivers and backwater within 500 meter of High Tide line as Coastal Regulation Zones. Setting up of new industries or expansion of existing industies except those directly related to waterfront, manufacturing, handling, storage or disposal of hazardous substances and setting up and expansion of units/mechanisms for disposal of wastes and effluents etc., are prohibited in these Costal Regulation Zone. All the seven coastal states are required to prepare coastal management plans which would provide protection to ecologically fragile coastal areas rich in biological diversity and provide for land use zoning. The Coastal Regulation Zone notification, 1991, has been amended.

In nuclear power plants, safety from radiation during the operation of the plants and after, and disposal of nuclear wastes are of prime concern. Major environmental impacts of nuclear power projects which need consideration are; (i) radio-active contamination of air, water and soil; (ii) thermal pollution due to discharge of cooling water; (iii) deforestation and loss of flora and fauna; (iv) rehabilitation; and (v) radio-active waste disposal. Exposure to radio-active radiations in excess of the prescribed limits are detrimental to human beings, aquatic life, flora and fauna. The long half life periods for radio-active decay necessitate sealing of the reactor vessel and components for a dormant period of about 30 years after decommissioning of the plant.

Life-support systems

In India, as in most traditional societies, people lived a life that rarely, if ever, threatened their environment. For centuries populations were more or less steady and local resources were sufficient to meet the demands of food, fuel, shelter and other basic requirements of life. Practices specifically suited to each area evolved over hundreds of years. Practices that ensured utilization of natural resources without degrading them.

While these systems were environmentally sound, life was vulnerable to many externaly factors. This was reflected in the low life-expectancy at birth, which was about 30 years at best. Communities were highly vulnerable to disease, epidemics and calamities like floods and drought. It is estimated that about 2.5 million people died during the Bengal famine of 1943. During the decade 1911-1921, the great influenze epidemic took a toll of 12 million lives. In fact, during this period the number of deaths exceeded the number of births, resulting in a population decline.

At the time of independence in 1947, the challenges before the new nation were many. Prime in importance was the task of decreasing human vulnerability to natural calamities. India needed not only to become self-sufficient in food production, but also to build enough reserves to tide over a drought year. Changes were also required in policies laid down during colonial times which dealt with the use and distribution of basic requirements.

With better health services and sanitation, increased food production and better nutrition, life expectancy at birth went up from 32 years at Independence to 64 years in 1991. Death rate decreased rapidly from 22.8 per thousand in 1951 to 10.9 in 1988. Birth rates have also decreased with overall development, but these have been slower in coming down. The net effect was a rapid increase in population from 361 million in 1951 to 844 million in 1991, a 134 per cent increase. To meet the challenge of sustaining this increased population, nes land was brought under the plough. The total cultivated area went up from 118.75 mha in 195-51 to 140.90 mha in 1984-85, levelling off thereafter. Irrigation potential went up from 22.6 mha in the '50s to 74.3 mha by 1989-90. New seeds and higher inputs brought about the Green Revolution, and India's agricultural growth rate went up from a mere 0.3 per cent in pre-Independence years to 3.5 per cent after 1977. Between 1950-51 and 1988-89, the country's foodgrain production rose from 50.8 million tonnes per annum to 170.2 million tonnes per annum, an increase of 235 per cent.

Milk production has gone up from 17,406 thousand tonnes in 1950 to 44,300 thousand tonnes in 1986—an increase of 180 per cent. Largely operating through producers cooperatives, India has a sophisticated dairy industry. However, despite a livestock population of over 400 million—the world's largest—India milk yield per animal is still very low. Bullocks are used for traction in fields and for rural transport, making for a close relationship between cattle and agriculture. Animal dung acts as a source of fertilizer as well as fuel.

India is no longer dependent on import of foodgrains. While gains in food production have taken India towards self-sufficiency, the country still depends on imports of certain agricultural inputs. While floods and drought are a recurrent reality, no longer do they lead to mass starvation deaths. A buffer stock of foodgrains, with rice and wheat amounting to about 15 million tonnes, has been built up.

While achievements have been considerable, the gains in the quality of life have been slow. The increasing population continues to erode the net benefits. Although they spend 85 per cent of their income on food, the poorest 20 per cent of the population are still unable to consume more than 1,500 calories a day, as against the 2,300 considered a necessary minimum by the Planning commission.

Efforts are on to ensure that all 600,000 villages in India, have a safe and protected source of drinking water. The implications of this on health and sanitation, and on the amount of time and energy spent by women on fetching water are enormous. While the challenge of vulnerability has been met, poverty remains an issue central to India's development.

But while the effect of population increase in decreasing the net benefits of development was understood, there was something else, less noticed, which was threatening the gains of development. This was the erosion of the biological and environmental base of the country. Many of the gains of the first few decades had come at the cost of India's biological and environmental 'capital'. Intensive agriculture led to problems like land deterioration, water depletion, pest infestations and loss of genetic diversity of crops. Excessive use of chemical fertilizers and pesticided, and poor drainage have led to pollution in several rural areas.

Land, water and the biological resources which support agriculture and animal husbandry and provide the essential requirements of food, drinking water and fuel are all under severe pressure. Protecting and reclaiming these and managing them more carefully is essential to sustaining India's life-support systems.

Sustainable regional development

Ecologically sustainable economic development has become a policy issue of major significance. conceptualizing and analysing sustainable development is very important at the regional level. This paper investigates sustainable in a practical planning context and seeks to highlight the notions of sustainable resource use. Economics provides some guidelines for planning responsibilities, although ecological considerations should also be taken into account.

A region is a geographical area consisting of a coherent entity from the standpoint of description, analysis, administration, planning, or policy. Among the various types of regions are homogenous and functional regions. Functional environmental regions are often based on the interactions between environmental resources like ground-water, river, and meteorological systems within a particular region. Homogenous environmental regions are based on the existence of common resources in the area concerned. Regions can also be distinguished as natural regions, economic regions, administrative regions, etc.

Regional development is often critically dependent on the regional availability of resources. A region's economic development may be directly dependent on the resources in the region. Usually, in such cases the dependence is on resources that may serve as essential and cheap productive inputs for economic activities. Concomitantly, the environmental capacity to absorb waste materials and pollution can restrict economic activity. Some regions may depend on export of resources as the main source of income. A regional resource sector may have several effects on the activities in a region such as increased demand for public services, utilities, and infrastructure; demand for labour; capital, space and spin-offs to other private sectors. Thus, the development of a resource sector might lead to shifts in sector allocation, income levels, distribution, and exchange rates.

From the standpoint of welfare, regional sustainable development ensures that the regional population attains an acceptable level of welfare both at present and in the future and that this regional development is not only compatible with ecological circumstances in the long run but also tries to accomplish a globally sustainable development.

Consequently, regional sustainable development has to fulfil the following goals:

— It should ensure the regional population a sustained acceptable level of welfare;

— It should not have conflict with sustainable development at a supraregional level;

— It should ensure economic progress and/or developoment of potential of the region concerned;

— It should maintain ecological values and/or relieve constraints of the area concerned; and

— It should ensure the economic and environmental interest of the parties involved.

The economic-ecological interactions arise in general, because concerted socio-economic development requires a compromise between material growth and environmental parameters, including environmental quality and vital natural resources. Although in the short run, the conflict between material growth and environmental quality may be severe, in the long run, a mitigating effect may emerge, because continued economic growth needs a sound resource base and structural protection and upgrading of environmental quality.

Such a coevolutionary development, in both the developed and the developing countries takes for granted that the economy and the ecology ultimately do not conflict with each other. Such coevolution is also based on equitable development options for the present and future generations. It does not necessarily require mutual positive spill-over effects between the economy and the ecology. This idea is echoed in the notion of ecologically sustainable economic development.

This paper, investigates sustainable development in a practical planning context and seeks to highlight the notion of sustainable resource use. An attempt has also been made to provide a practical framework, as renewable stocks of natural resources are key factors of sustainable development.

The National Conservation Strategy and Policy Statement on Environment and Development, adopted by the Government of India in June 1992, lays down strategies and actions for integration of environmental considerations in the development activities of various sectors of the country, thus paving the way for achieving sustainable development. The action points pertaining to individual ministries/departments have been communicated to them to ensure that they take action for re-orienting their policies and programmes in conformity with the strategy.

Biosphere reserves are multi-purpose protected areas to preserve the genetic diversity in representative eco-systems. The major objectives of biosphere reserves are: (i) to conserve diversity and integrity of plants, animals and micro-organisms; (ii) to promote research on ecological conservation and other environmental apsects and (iii) to provide facilities for education, awareness and training. So far, eight biosphere reserves have been set up viz., (i) Nilgiri; (ii) Nanda Devi; (iii) Nokrek; (iv) Great Nicobar; (v) Gulf of Manar; (vi) Manas; (vii) Sunderbans and (viii) Similipal. Comprehensive guidelines have been prepared which emphasize on formulation of eco-development and demonstration projects, development of data base, conservation plans of key species, establishment of research stations and implementation of social welfare activities. Non-government organisations will be involved in the biosphere reserve programme for creation of public awareness.

India has a wealth of wetland eco-systems distributed in different geographical regions raning from cold arid zone of Ladakh to wet humid climate of Imphal; warm arid zone of Rajasthan to tropical monsoonic central India; and wet and humid zone of southern peninsula. Most of the wetlands in India are directly or indirectly linked with major river systems such as Ganga, Brahmaputra, Narmada, Tapti, Godavari, Krishna, Cauveri, etc.

A National Committee on Wetlands, Mangroves and Coral Reefs constituted for advising the government on appropriate policies and measures to be taken for conservation and management of the wetlands has identified 21 wetlands for conservation and management on priority basis. Steering committees have been set up by the concerned state governments in which representatives of state government departments, universities and research institutions are included. Nodal research/academic institutions have been identified for each of the selected wetlands. Management Action Plans have been drawn up for 12 wetlands so far. A directory on wetlands of India has been published which give information on location, area and ecological categorisation of wetlands in different parts of the country. India is a signatory to the Convention on Wetlands of international importance especially as waterfowl habitat and six Indian wetlands have been designated under this convention.

Mangroves are very specialised forest eco-systems of tropical and subtroipical regions of the world bordering the sheltered sea coasts and estuaries. They stabilise the shoreline and act as bulwark against encorachments by the sea. Mangrove forests are dominated by salt tolerant inter-tidal halophytic sea plants of diverse structures. Mangroves occur all along the Indian coastline in sheltered estuary, tidal creeks, backwaters, salt marshes and mudflats coverin a total area of 6,740 sq km which is about seven per cent of the world's total mangrove area. Based on the recommendations of the National Committee on Wetlands, Mangroves and Coral Reefs, 15 mangrove areas have been identified for intensive conservation and management purposes: Northern Andaman and Nicobar (Andaman and Nicobar Islands), Sunderbans (West Bengal), Bhitarkanika (Orissa), Coringa, Godavari Delta and Krishna Estuary (Andhra Pradesh), Mahanadi Delta (Orissa), Pichavaram and Point Calimar (Tamil Nadu), Goa (Goa), Gulf of Kutch (Gujarat), Coondapur (Karnataka), Achra/Ratnagiri (Maharashtra) and Vembanad (Kerala). Management action plans for all the 15 mangrove areas have been sanctioned.

Four cora areas have been identified viz., Gulf of Mannar, Andaman and Nicobar Islands, Lakshadweep Islands and Gulf of Kutch for conservation and management. State level steering committees have been constituted for the formulation and implementation of the management action plans. A Management Action Plan for the coral reefs of Andaman and Nicobar has been approved. Information on all aspects of wetlands, mangroves and coral reefs if given in a publication India's Wetlands, Mangroves and Coral Reefs brought out by the Ministry of Enviorment and Forests.

A programme for the conservation of selected lakes has been prepared under the National Lake Conservation Plan (NLCP). This will concentrate, in the first stage, on urban lakes which have not been covered under the existing programmes of the Ministry.

The Convention on Biological Diversity, signed by India in June 1992, has come into force for India from 19 May 1994. Detailed reports are being prepared for implementing the 50 action points indentified from the

Convention. A National Action Plan on Biodiversity is under preparation. India has signed the International Convention to Combat Desertification; action has, therefore, been initiated to prepare a National Action Programme to combat desertification and to mitigate the effects of drought.

The basic aim of the National Natural Resource Management System is to utilise remote-sensing techniques for scientific management of natural resources. In pursuance of this, several projects have been funded to monitor the environmental changes associated with mining, industrialisation, urbanisation and other developmental activities. The overall approach is to identify critical areas and to help in developing strategies for developmental planning of these areas.

National Wastelands Development Board (NWDB) established in May 1985 has been bifurcated into a new Department of Wastelands Development and a National Afforestation and Eco-Development Board (NAEB). While the NAEB is a part of the Ministry of Environment and Forests, the Department of Wastelands Development has been transferred to the Ministry of Rural Development. The responsibilities of the NAEB include promotion of afforestation, tree plantation, ecological restoration and eco-development activities in the country with special attention to the degraded forest areas and lands adjoining the forest areas, national parks, sanctuaries and other protected areas as well as the ecologically fragile areas like the Western Himalayas, Aravallis, Western Ghats etc. The NAEB seeks to carry out its responsibilities through several schemes such as the integrated wastelands development projects, fuelwood and fodder projects, minor forest produce including medicinal plants scheme, aerial seeding, seed development, technology extension, grants-in-aid to voluntary agencies etc.

Eco-task forcers of ex-servicemen have been deployed in the state of UP, Rajasthan and Jammu and Kashmir for undertaking eco-restoration work through afforestation, pasture development and other water and soil conservation measures in selected highly degraded and inhospitable areas of these states. Several policy advisory groups have been set up to address crucial policy issues relating to fuelwood conservation, wood substitution, grazing and livestock management and draft reports on grazing and livestock management and benefit distribution from common lands have been prepared.

The National Fund for Afforestation and Wastelands Development set up earlier has been redesignated as the National Fund for Afforestation and Eco-development. Donations from individuals as well as coporate/non-corporate bodies are eligible for cent per cent tax deduction under the relevant provisions of the Income Tax Act. The NAEB also functions as a nodal agency for bilateral and multilateral cooperation in the field of forestry development programmes. As such financial assistance is being received from the World Bank, European Economic Community, Swedish Interantional Development Agency, Overseas development Agency, Overseas Economics Cooperation Fund, etc., for implementing forestry projects in various states. A new scheme called "The Rajive Paryavaran Pariyojana" has ben launched for integrated and intensive environmental action and eco-development in 50 selected districts of the country.